Foresight in Organiza

Foresight in Organizations will acquaint the reader with various foresight methods and tools, to show the reader how these methods are used, what the pitfalls are and how the methods relate to each other. This innovative volume offers the reader the ability to carry out a study of the future by him- or herself and apply the results in a decision-making strategy process.

The authors address the following methods: scenarios, trend analysis, the Delphi method, quantitative trend extrapolation, technology assessment, back-casting and roadmapping; the most relevant and popular methods that also cover the range of approaches from predictive, via normative to explorative. Every chapter also contains references to additional literature about the methods being discussed.

This book is essential reading for researchers, academics and students in the areas of community development, sociology of organizations, change management, social entrepreneurship, sustainable development and participative planning.

Patrick van der Duin is Assistant Professor at Delft University of Technology, Faculty of Technology, Policy and Management, the Netherlands, and Associate Professor Futures Research and Trendwatching at Fontys Academy for Creative Industries, the Netherlands.

Routledge Advances in Management and Business Studies

Foresight in Organizations

Methods and Tools

Edited by
Patrick van der Duin

Routledge
Taylor & Francis Group

NEW YORK AND LONDON

First published 2016
by Routledge
711 Third Avenue, New York, NY 10017

and by Routledge
2 Park Square, Milton Park, Abingdon, Oxfordshire OX14 4RN

First issued in paperback 2016

Routledge is an imprint of the Taylor & Francis Group, an informa business

Library of Congress Cataloging in Publication Data
Foresight in organizations : methods and tools / edited by Patrick van der Duin.
    pages cm. – (Routledge advances in management and business studies)
    Includes bibliographical references and index.
    ISBN 978-1-138-84491-9 (hardback) – ISBN 978-1-315-72851-3
    (ebook) 1. Business forecasting. 2. Business planning. I. Duin, Patrick
    van der, editor.
    HD30.27.F68955 2016
    658.4'032–dc23   2015027901

ISBN 13: 978-1-138-69286-2 (pbk)
ISBN 13: 978-1-138-84491-9 (hbk)

Typeset in Bembo
by Wearset Ltd, Boldon, Tyne and Wear

Contents

Figures

Tables

Contributors

Henk-Jan van Alphen has extensive experience in futures studies and has worked as an advisor for organizations in both the public and private sectors. He currently works as a researcher at KWR Watercycle Research Institute where he focuses on the future of water management in Europe. He is trained as a political scientist at the Free University Amsterdam and the University of North Carolina at Chapel Hill.

Nik Baerten is a knowledge engineer by training. For several years he was active as a multidisciplinary researcher at the Digital Culture department of the Maastricht McLuhan Institute (NL), where he blended insights across disciplines such as history, new media, philosophy, intelligent systems, architecture, organic systems, interaction design. In 2004 he co-founded Pantopicon, a studio for foresight and design, based in Antwerp (Belgium), which crafts provocative futures in order to stimulate debate regarding tomorrow's challenges and opportunities. It supports both public and private organizations in exploring the long term, in building visions and strategies, in designing concepts for new products, services and experiences. As such it assists in the understanding and anticipation of systemic change. Besides a frequent keynote speaker/moderator on all things futures, he also lectures in foresight and design, as well as its relation to social innovation, at the LUCA School of Arts and other academic institutions internationally.

Saskia Bol studied Visual Marketing as well as Policy, Communication and Organizational Management. She worked at Futureconsult on various scenario-projects for governments, non-profit organizations and companies. She is specialized in using future scenarios for concept development. She gave lectures on Future Studies at the Design Academy in Eindhoven and she wrote a study booklet on creativity for students in Multimedia Design. At present she teaches Design Thinking at the Design Academy in Eindhoven. She is also developing a learning tool for future thinking in companies.

Bram Castelein followed a pedagogical study for teacher at the Pedagogical Academy Mariahoeve in The Hague, the Netherlands. He also studied organizational sociology at the Erasmus University in Rotterdam. In the period 1980 to 1987 he was a teacher/Deputy Director at the Mgr. Bekkersschool in

Delft. From 1987 until 1998 he worked as a consultant/project manager at Capgemini in the field of information technology. Since 1998 he has worked at the Ministry of Social Affairs and Employment, first as information manager and later as a senior consultant and team leader in the learning and development institute of the Ministry. At the time he launched the Future Centre concept. Today he focuses on achieving business impact through the use of dedicated learning interventions. As a facilitator he has extensive experience in applying the acceleration method.

Tessa Cramer (1985) is lecturer in futures studies, research and sociology at Fontys Academy for Creative Industries. Simultaneously she works on a PhD study at Maastricht University on the professionalization of futures work. She is board member of the Dutch Future Society. Previous work includes research for trend forecasting agencies and contributions for trend magazine *Second Sight*.

Scott W. Cunningham is an Associate Professor of Policy Analysis at the Delft University of Technology. He is currently working on the social, political and economic impacts of Big Data, as part of the BYTE Project, a European Commission funded project. He is the European Associate Editor for the journal *Technological Forecasting and Social Change*, and is the co-author of two books on technological forecasting and tech mining.

Eefje Cuppen is Assistant Professor at the Department of Multi Actor Systems in the Faculty of Technology, Policy and Management of TU Delft. Her research focuses on participatory foresight, public engagement with (energy) technology, responsible innovation and participatory governance. She received her Master's degree in Innovation Sciences from Eindhoven University of Technology (2004). She completed her dissertation at VU University Amsterdam on methodology for stakeholder participation in environmental issues in January 2010.

Patrick van der Duin is Assistant Professor, Foresight and Innovation Management at Delft University of Technology and Associate Professor Futures Research and Trendwatching at Fontys University of Applied Sciences, Academy for Creative Industries. He has published in journals such as *Futures*, *Foresight*, *Technological Forecasting and Social Change* and the *Journal of Futures Studies*. He studied macro-economics at the University of Amsterdam and formerly worked as a futurist at KPN Research.

René Hartman holds a Master's degree in Industrial Design Engineering from Delft University, worked in industry (General Electric Plastics, Ericsson), at the Free University Amsterdam (setting up spin-off companies) and consultancy (Innovation Centres) before he started his own consultancy company in 2004. He is co-founder of Innovatiewerkplaats.nl and trained innovation teams from, e.g., DAF trucks, VGZ insurance company and Microsoft Europe. He recently worked for AB Inbev, Alpro, Arcadis, Bridgestone, CIIC Sydney, City of Amsterdam/Arnhem/Leiden/Rotterdam, DAF Trucks, Essent, Inalfa

Sunroofs, Janssen Pharma, Chambre of Commerce/Inretail, Microsoft, National Police, Eurosonic Festival, Philips, Rabobank, Sanoma Publishers, Schiphol Airport, Studio 100, Umicore and the Universities of Antwerp and Maastricht.

Johan den Hartog is a drama teacher and has extended experience as trainer of social skills, team coach, actor and stage director. He focuses on his work with students, actors and trainees on behavioral dimensions of face to face communication. He has worked with students, starting at about 18 years of age, PhDs, amateur and semi-professional actors. He taught interviewing techniques and conversational skills that are useful to the field of scientific research and has lectured a lot on negotiation skills. During his professional life he has worked as a freelance trainer, stage director and actor, and as lecturer (at Delft University of Technology). He has directed many performances of dramatic plays, ranging from Shakespeare to Pinter to Handke. In 2013 he commenced his fourth career in life, this time as an actor, and in 2015 he started writing his first play for the stage.

Christianne Heselmans studied economic-social history at the Radboud University and graduated on the forming of the welfare state after World War II. After ten years of working in the creative industries she is now lecturer in sustainable futures, concepting and service design thinking at International Lifestyle Studies at the Fontys Academy for Creative Industries. As member of the lectureship Futures Research and Trendwatching her research interest is in combining trend analysis with grand societal challenges and in prototyping the future. She is co-author of *Business in a Changing World* (2008), a textbook for higher education.

Susan van 't Klooster was trained as a cultural scientist at Maastricht University. In 2002 she became a PhD student at the Science, Technology and Society Research Unit at Maastricht University. In her thesis ("Future telling: ambition and practice") she describes and analyzes several pitfalls related to foresight and the production of future knowledge in particular (defended in 2008). After her PhD research, she worked as a researcher at the Institute for Environmental Studies (IVM) at the VU University in Amsterdam. She was involved as a scenario expert and methodologist in several multi-institute projects dealing with foresight methodology, the role of knowledge and expertise in policy processes, and public participation in knowledge production/policy making. Since 2011, she has worked as a freelance advisor at SAVIA (www.savia.nl). She offers research and advice in the field of foresight and strategic decision-making.

Jan H. Kwakkel is an Assistant Professor of Policy Analysis at Delft University of Technology. His current research focuses on the design of adaptive policies and plans for coping with the expected future impacts of climate change. His main interest is in model-based approaches for scenario development and robust decision-making. He has also published multiple papers on text mining and bibliometrics.

Erik van de Linde (Royal Netherlands Academy of Arts and Sciences) studied biophysics at the State Universities of Groningen and Utrecht. He worked as a researcher at the Netherlands Organization for Applied Scientific Research TNO, was attaché for Science and Technology at the Netherlands Royal Embassy in Washington, DC, and was Director at the Netherlands Study Center for Technology Trends STT. He also worked at the international consultancy company RAND Europe, at the Technology Foundation STW (part of the National Science Foundation), and at Leiden University. He is currently head of the Policy Advice Division of the Royal Netherlands Academy of Arts and Sciences.

Vincent Marchau (Radboud University Nijmegen (RU) – Institute for Management Research (IMR)) holds a chair on Uncertainty and Adaptivity of Societal Systems. This chair is supported by the Netherlands Study Centre for Technology Trends (STT). He received a PhD from TU Delft in 2000 for his research on technology assessment in transport policy-making. He is also Managing Director of the Dutch Research School for Transport, Infrastructure and Logistics (TRAIL), with 100 PhD students and 50 staff members across six Dutch universities. His research focuses on long-term planning under uncertainty in transportation, logistics, spatial planning, energy, water and security.

Karel Mulder works at Delft University of Technology. He studied Physics and Philosophy of Science and Technology, and obtained a PhD in Business Administration in 1992. He was president of the Technology and Society Department of the Dutch Royal Institute of Engineers from 1994 to 1999. He has been responsible for setting up education in Technology and Sustainable Development in Delft and was the initiator of the Engineering Education in Sustainable Development (EESD) Conferences. He teaches in the areas of innovation and sustainable development. His current research interests are especially focused upon innovation in urban infrastructures and urban symbiosis. He published two books on sustainable development and technology, and dozens of papers and book chapters.

Jan Nekkers is Founder and CEO of Futureconsult, an Amsterdam-based consultancy company specialized in future scenarios. Futureconsult facilitates organizations, firms and governments to think about their future in a structured and meaningful way. He studied political science at the University of Nijmegen and the University of Amsterdam. He worked as a researcher at Leiden University, as a staff member at the Wiardi Beckman Foundation, as a policy advisor at the Dutch Labour Party and as organizational consultant. He facilitated scenario projects with clients ranging from Dutch companies, multinationals, local and national governments and NGOs. In 2007 his bestselling practical handbook about scenario planning *Wijzer In De Toekomst (Futurewise)* was published. He gives lectures and masterclasses on scenario planning for various audiences. Based on more than 20 years of experience in scenario planning, he is a well-known consultant regarding long-term strategic issues for business and governmental organizations.

Kim van Oorschot is an Associate Professor of Project Management and System Dynamics in the Department of Leadership and Organizational Behaviour at the BI Norwegian Business School. Her current research focuses on decision-making, trade-offs and tipping points in dynamically complex settings, like new product development (NPD) projects. Before working at BI, she was an Assistant Professor at the Eindhoven University of Technology (the Netherlands), in the School of Industrial Engineering. Before that, she was a Post-Doc at Tilburg University at the Information Management Department and a research fellow at INSEAD, France. From 2002 until 2006 (after finishing her PhD project), she was a consultant at Minase Consulting BV, working for large international companies like ASML, DSM, KPN, NXP and Stork Fokker on projects aimed at improving business processes. She has published in such journals as *Academy of Management Journal*, *Journal of Management Studies*, *Production and Operations Management*, *Journal of Product Innovation Management*, *Journal of the Operational Research Society* and *International Journal of Operations and Production Management*.

Jaco Quist is an Assistant Professor on Sustainable Innovation at the Energy and Industry section of the faculty of Technology, Policy, Management, Delft University of Technology. His research and teaching focuses on backcasting and transition management, sustainable innovation, sustainability transitions and technology assessment. He has completed a dissertation on participatory backcasting that was published by Eburon Publishers in 2007 as *Backcasting for a Sustainable Future: The Impact after 10 Years* (see www.eburon.nl or repository.tudelft.nl). This is the first book that has reported on a systematic evaluation of the follow-up and spin-off of backcasting experiments ten years after completion. He (co)edited special issues on "Backcasting for Sustainability" (*Technological Forecasting and Social Change*), "Knowledge Collaboration and Learning for Sustainable Innovation" (*Joournal of Cleaner Production*, 2013) and "Sustainable Innovation and Business Models" (*Journal of Cleaner Production*, 2013).

Ben Römgens has a Master's degree in business economics and in change management. Ben is principal consultant future planning at DNV GL with over 20 years of experience in scenario, roadmap and strategy development for government, industry and nonprofit organizations in Europe. As a trainer and change manager he also implemented scenario and roadmap development in the strategic and business development processes of several companies.

1 Introduction

Patrick van der Duin

Introduction

This book is meant for everyone who is interested in looking at the future. For everyone who thinks the future is important, perhaps even more important than the past. And many people are involved with the future. Whether you are a student, a civil servant at a government ministry or in a small municipality, a politician, a techno-starter or an innovation manager at a large company, for many people the future is an important playing field. This book is meant to familiarize the reader with a number of different methods that can be used to look at the future, and the tools that can be employed in doing so. And although, strictly speaking, this book is not a handbook, we do hope that, after reading this book, the reader is able to carry out a study of the future independently and to apply the results in the decisions being made. And if there are good reasons to outsource the futures study, this book is meant to provide enough information to make it possible to assess the quality and usefulness of the results of such an outsourced study.

In light of the scope of foresight, this book cannot possibly include every single method. And because the future keeps changing, new methods will doubtlessly be developed in years to come. However, we are of the opinion that we provide a good sample of the main methods available. A number of chapters also offer reading tips for those who want to know more about the method in question.

Looking at the future has a long history and, as mentioned above, almost everybody is involved with the future. Having said that, when you introduce yourself as a foresight professional or futurologist, you are often met with a suppressed snigger and a raised eyebrow. It would seem that people see looking at the future as a precarious undertaking that is reserved for present-day Don Quixotes. How can anyone take that seriously? But the raised eyebrow has to be taken seriously, because it is often followed by claims that "the future does not exist" and "it is impossible to predict the future." Many foresight professionals agree with the former statement. *The* future does indeed not exist, because each person imagines and interprets the future differently. What may fill some people with hopeful optimism, may be a deeply depressing prospect to others. While some people focus on technological developments, others look at demographic shifts. Incidentally, the claim that the future does not exist as an entity is incorrect (Van der

Duin, 2014). What that means is that the future may not exist as a "physical entity" (in the way that a car does), it does exist as a "social construct." The mere fact that people think about the future and, in doing so, give direction to their decisions and actions in the present, makes the future real and relevant. And even if the prediction of the future is incorrect (which is often the case with predictions), it can still affect the actual future situation. To some extent, this is comparable to when people used to believe that the Earth was flat and were consequently afraid to venture too far out to sea, because they were scared they would fall off the edge of the world…. So what is not real has an effect on reality, in the same way that what does not yet exist has an effect on what already does exist. Or, to quote the sociologist W.I. Thomas: "If men define things as real, they are real in their consequences." The future as a "social construct" is an important explanatory factor for the behavior of people and organizations and in that area competes with history in terms of what has the greatest effect on the present. Someone who is obsessed with and ascribes predictive powers to history will not care very much about the future. But someone who suspects that tomorrow and the day after may be different from yesterday and today, will look for inspiration in the future.

It appears that, in recent years, more and more people are interested in the future. Abrupt social changes and new disruptive technologies have made the future a lot more interesting and relevant again. And even in science, there is an increasing appreciation for knowledge about the future, to the extent that there seems to be a futuristic change from "past-oriented sciences towards primarily future-oriented ones" (Poli, 2014, p. 15), and the knowledge about the future is even necessary for survival and reproduction (Seligman et al., 2013, p. 120). And we may assume that this knowledge about the future benefits from more knowledge about methods of foresight.

Approaches to the Future

The future can be approached in different ways. Different time preferences are reflected in three different approaches to the future: predictive, explorative and normative (Vergragt and Quist, 2011; Börjeson et al., 2006). The *predictive* approach to the future leans heavily on historical data and projects historical patterns onto the future, while the *explorative* approach assumes that the future is not an automatic continuation of the past and focuses more on what could happen in the future. The *normative* approach to the future is dissatisfied with the current state of affairs and sees the future above all as a possibility to fix things.

These three approaches are not separate entities, but are connected *cyclically* (see Figure 1.1). This cyclical *loop* can start in the past, with, for instance, predictions about the future being based on the past (*forward loop*). As mentioned above, the idea people have about the future then affects their thoughts and actions in the present. On the basis of that, they often look at the past differently as well (*backward loop*). But the cyclical loop can also start in the future. Based on a foresight study, people's thoughts and decisions in the present change (*backward loop*), after which it is possible that the past is seen in a different light. The normative

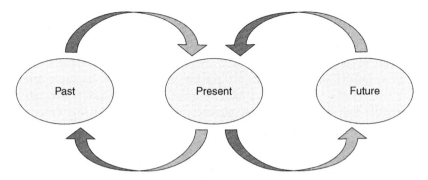

Figure 1.1 The past, present and future interconnected in a cyclical way.

approach to the future above all relates to the cyclical loop (*backward and forward*) between the present and the future, whereby the proposed future leads to a variety of possible *roadmaps* or *transition trajectories* that start in the present and envisage the realization of the proposed future.

An example to illustrate the *cyclical interaction* between past, present and future is the emergence of social media like Facebook and Twitter, which can be seen as a continuation of a historical pattern, with communication becoming ever more interactive and individual. Based on that, one can think about possible future forms of (social) media. For instance, the trend called "the Internet of things" means that not only do people send tweets, but that "objects" (like cars or copy machines) also send tweets about their maintenance status or about data they need to function properly. This image of the future in turn has an impact on the present, because businesses have to think about how to incorporate these future functionalities in their existing innovation processes. Finally, the image of the future also has an impact on how people look at the history of media, not so much in the sense that modern media show us how limited media were in the past, but above all in light of the fact that the highly networked nature of the new media offers an interesting perspective for looking at the history of media. For instance, traditional media (radio, TV, newspapers) are considerably less network-oriented and based primarily on broadcasting. This way, the past, present and future are connected cyclically and thereby inextricably.

The aim of connecting the past, present and future like this is to show that the predictive, explorative and normative approaches are both separate approaches and can be connected. Having said that, the modern history of looking at the future (say, after World War II) shows a shift away from the predictive toward the explorative and the normative.

The predictive and explorative approaches tell us something about how people can approach the future and what value they attach to the extent to which "the" past is seen as shaping "the" future. These two approaches are the best known approaches, but they are complemented by the normative approach, which is not based on what the future looks like or may look like, but what one *wants* the future to look like. What it has in common with the explorative approach is that there is a broad variety of possible futures. Whereas, in the case of an explorative approach, there can be many imaginable futures, in the case of the normative approach, there are many imaginable futures that one wants to realize. As a result, the difference between the two approaches is that the explorative approach has no value judgment about the quality or positivity or negativity of the future vision, while the normative approach results in a predominantly positive outcome. After all, it is a future that one desires, which means that it is normative. That also establishes the link to the predictive approach, because that also has but one future. Again, the normative approach yields a positive or desirable result, while that is not necessarily the case with the predictive approach. However, an important difference between, on the one hand, the explorative and the predictive approach and, on the other hand, the normative approach, is that the first two approaches are usually future visions of the environment of the subject (in most cases an organization), while the normative approach says something about the desired state of the subject itself. This leads to (yet) another difference, namely with regard to the decision that is made on the basis of the foresight study. In the case of the explorative approach, different decisions or strategies are linked to different future visions. In the case of the predictive approach, it is very difficult to establish a link between the future vision and a possible decision, because the predicted future is fixed and can no longer be influenced. And in the case of the normative approach, there are various possible decisions or strategies, but they all have to lead to the same future vision: all roads lead to Rome. As such, the normative approach can also be seen as a mix of the explorative and predictive approaches: the singular future vision is predictive in nature and the various ways in which it can be realized matches the explorative approach.

Foresight Methods

An approach to the future is no more than an approach unless it is worked out further. Between an approach and a study of the future, and the decision or action that follows, there is a no-man's land that needs to be worked out in greater detail. Between the approach to the future and the eventual futures study, there are various *methods* of foresight. It is the foresight method that makes the approach to the future concrete. The predictive approach is accompanied by a predictive method, the explorative approach is accompanied by an explorative method and the normative approach is accompanied by a normative method.

Figure 1.2 shows how the approach to the future leads to the choice of a foresight method, which then results in a futures study, on the basis of which a decision is made or action is taken. This path does not have to be linear in nature. It is quite possible that, on the basis of the preliminary results of a futures study, additional research is necessary using a different foresight method or a foresight method that is used in a somewhat different form. It is also possible to decide in advance what type of decision or action is needed. For example, if a company wants to decide in which technology it should invest, it makes more sense to use an explorative approach and method than to use the road-mapping method in which one more or less knows what the intended point in the future is.

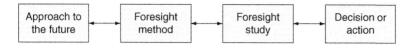

Figure 1.2 From approach to the future, via foresight method and study, to decision or action.

Determining which approach is the right one is not all that easy. In fact, a futures study is needed to determine which approach to the future to use! After all, the assumption is that the future is so uncertain that an explorative approach is needed, is in itself a prediction, as is the notion that the future is relatively certain, which means that a predictive approach can be used. To determine which approach is valid requires a kind of *pre-foresight* or *metaforesight*. One way to determine which approach is useful is to determine the time horizon. The more distant the future under examination is, the more sense it makes to explore the future. In the shorter term, it is possible to make unequivocal statements about the future, but, in the longer term, there is too much uncertainty and it is better to include various possible futures. I think that the normative approach lies somewhere in between, because the time horizon lies also somewhere in between: a longer time horizon does not match the predictive side of the normative approach, while a shorter time horizon does not provide enough time to realize the (challenging) normative vision of the future.

In this book, we describe seven foresight methods:

1 Scenarios
2 Delphi method
3 Trend analysis
4 Technology forecasting: quantitative trend extrapolation
5 Technology assessment
6 Backcasting
7 Roadmapping.

These seven methods can be linked to the three approaches to the future: predictive, explorative and normative (see Figure 1.3). The scenario method, for example, is meant to explore the future by setting up different possible futures, while technology forecasting can be used to predict the (technological) future, and backcasting and roadmapping are normative in nature.

It is important to emphasize that one cannot argue that one foresight method is better than another, because every method has a more or less different objective. The scenario method is designed to provide different images of the future and to give an organization insight into developments and events it had not previously considered but that can be very relevant to its organization and strategy. In the case of technology forecasting, and in particular quantitative trend analysis, the aim is not to identify multiple possible images of the future, but to predict the course of a technological development.

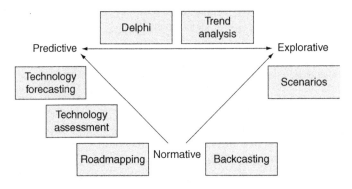

Figure 1.3 Foresight methods on the continuum from exploring to predicting.

The criteria for the application of foresight methods vary on the basis of the type of method, which means that, when selecting a method, it is important to keep in mind what the aim of the futures study is. Scenarios are suitable for "expanding" thought patterns, while technology forecasting is suitable for gaining insight into the development of a new technology. As such, there is no one size fits all, but there is a *contingency* principle. That is to say that the best method has to be chosen depending on the situation. In this context, the term situation refers to the goal and application of the futures study, the available data, the type of organization and sector, the specific questions that need to be answered, etc. So the success of a method not only depends on its actual application, but also on the question whether or not the method is suitable to the specific situation.

The foresight methods listed above have been chosen because they are the methods that are being used most frequently, although there are, of course, some similarities and even overlap. As far as their popularity is concerned, the scenario method has the best score. A study conducted in 2009 into the use of foresight studies by Dutch government ministries revealed that virtually all the respondents were familiar with the scenario method (Van der Duin et al., 2009). Another well-known method is the Delphi method, which is often used to consult large groups of experts regarding future developments. Roadmapping is a method that is often used by business, and in particular technological businesses, wanting to know how they can realize a future technological application. Immediately after World War II, when there was still considerable faith in the ability of technology to solve socio-economic problems, technology forecasting was a very popular method, and it is still used a lot to make decisions about new technologies. Technology assessment can be seen as a response to technology forecasting, after it became clear that assessing potential social consequences of the development and implementation of new technology is not entirely unimportant. In recent years, technology assessment has gained in popularity, thanks to the introduction of the concept of "responsible innovation" by the European Union, which is in fact a revamped version of technology assessment. In recent years, backcasting has become considerably more popular in identifying sustainable goals in the future and how to reach them. Trend analysis, finally, has always been popular, for the simple reason that mapping future developments is always useful for organizations that want to be ready for the future.

Trend analysis is a good example of different foresight methods complementing and overlapping each other. Scenario studies, for instance, often start by mapping relevant trends (trend analysis). Another example is the Delphi method, which can often be used as an element of a trend analysis.

Technology forecasting is the most predictive method. Technology assessment is closely linked, although as a method, it is less predictive, its focus being on the potential social consequences of new technological developments. Both roadmapping and backcasting take a *normative* look at the future. Their aim is not to explore or predict what will happen in the future, but to determine which future is desirable and which activities are needed to realize that desirable future. The Delphi method and trend analysis can be used in a predictive way. In the case of trend analysis, the emphasis will often be on identifying *certain* trends, while Delphi will try to find a consensus between the experts being consulted.[1] In this book, we are also interested in the explorative side of the two methods: also looking for uncertain trends and disagreement between experts. The scenario method is highly explorative in nature, because it examines what could happen in the future and looks for possible futures.

Terminology

In foresight literature, many different terms are used to describe the activity, including futurology, futures research, forecasting, futures studies, prognostics, foresight, futures explorations and future-oriented technology analysis. In all honesty, we should admit that the amount of terms being used in literature indicates that the area does not yet have an adult (academic) status. In physics, to name another area of science, there is not much discussion about what an atom is, let alone about the question whether or not physics is the right name for the discipline. In this book, we mostly use the term *foresight* to refer to the *activities* that are needed to conduct a futures study.

A definition of foresight is: "Foresight is the ability, the skill and art of describing, explaining, exploring, predicting and/or interpreting future developments, as well as assessing their consequences for decisions and other actions in the present" (Berkhout et al., 2007, p. 74). This definition states that exploring the future not only requires talent and creativity, but also a skill, in other words, a structured set of actions that can be learned. As such, exploring the future is not about gazing into a crystal ball, nor is it the exclusive domain of exotic characters, and foresight does not have to be a "black box," because there are methods available, as described in this book, that can be used to collect information and build knowledge about the future(s). This definition also makes it clear that foresight is not a goal in itself, but a way of making decisions based on different approaches to the future (including exploring and predicting), as discussed above.

Finally, I want to make it clear that, even though the application of method distinguishes the foresight professional from the tarot card reader, successful foresight requires more than being able to use methods. In fact, it is important not to engage in what the Dutch Scientific Council refers to as "method fetishism" (Van Asselt et al., 2010). The quality of foresight will not necessarily improve by developing yet more methods. It is better to improve the existing foresight methods by learning how they are applied in practice. It will undoubtedly become clear that, in addition to applying foresight methods, the human factor and organizational context also play an important role in understanding the future.

Structure of the Chapters

For the sake of readability and to allow the reader to compare the foresight methods discussed in this book, every method chapter more or less has the same structure.

1   Introduction: in the introduction, a description and short historical context is provided of the method. A simple characterization often quickly provides insight into the possible purpose of the method and the situations in which it can be used.
2   State of the art: a description of the core of the method: what are the central principles, what are the characteristics, what is the general structure of the method? In addition, insight is provided into when the method should be applied. A well-executed method that is used for the wrong purpose will not have the desired result, and the futures study will have little impact.
3   Structure: to apply foresight methods, it has to be clear what the different steps are. And for each step, there will be different goals and guidelines. What are the dos and don'ts of each method and of each step? How does one link the results of the foresight study to the decision that one has to make?
4   Finally: each chapter closes with a list of literature that has been used, as well as a list of literature for those who want to know more about the method in question.

In addition, to the seven foresight methods, this book also contains a number of "help techniques" or tools. Foresight methods to a large extent consist of the application of a number of tools that are common to multiple methods. For instance, both in trend analysis and in technology assessment, conducting interviews is useful. Another aspect that is common to several methods is the creation of causal diagrams that show the possible future relationships between different variables. In all, eight of these tools are discussed:

1   Interviews: the future is often imagined and determined by people, so consulting people directly is a very valuable source of information. Conducting interviews can be useful in providing insight into possible important future developments.
2   Workshops: an important source of input in the collection of information and knowledge with regard to the future is provided by workshops. Thinking

about the future together, sharing ideas and engaging in joint discussions can lead to surprisingly new and good insights.

3　Meta-analysis: in many cases, organizations cannot afford to conduct foresight studies. In those cases, it is also possible to use existing foresight studies in a smart way. By "recycling" existing studies, it is possible to acquire high-quality knowledge and information about the future, without having to spend a lot of resources (people, money).

4　The acceleration method: collecting many good ideas about the future quickly is not a luxury when conducting a foresight study. Using the acceleration method, participants in a foresight study can learn from and inspire each other quickly, because they immediately have insight into each other's opinions.

5　Creativity: the future cannot simply be calculated. The future is about "new things" that can sometimes be explored, and sometimes predicted. Using creativity makes it possible to discover and identify "new things."

6　Stakeholder analysis: the future is often the result of human thoughts and actions, which is why it is important to map actors that can or will play a role in the future, as well as the way they are interconnected.

7　Causal diagrams: for a good insight into possible futures, it is important to map the way changes are connected. Using causal diagrams makes it possible to visualize quickly how developments influence each other, and which variables are relevant to and decisive for the future.

8　Visualization: the future does not only consist of words, but also of images. It is especially the visualization of what may happen that can inspire people to engage in the future more. As with most other things, when we are thinking about the future, a picture says more than a thousand words.

Note

1　Of course, Delphi studies can also identify disagreement between experts (Van de Linde and Van der Duin, 2011).

References

American Council for the United Nations University, the Millennium Project, *Futures Research Methodology version 3.0.*

Asselt, M. van, A. Faas, F. van der Molen and S.A. Veenman (eds.) (2010). *Uitzicht: toekomstverkennen met beleid [Out of sight: looking to the future carefully]*. Amsterdam: Amsterdam University Press.

Berkhout, A.J., P.A. van der Duin, L. Hartmann and J.R. Ortt (2007). *The cyclic nature of innovation: connecting hard sciences with soft values.* Oxford: Elsevier.

Börjeson, L., M. Höjer, K.-H. Dreborg, T. Ekvall and G. Finnveden (2006). Scenario types and techniques: towards a user's guide. *Futures*, Vol. 38, pp. 723–739.

Duin, P.A. van der (2014). The crystal ball is not a black box: futures research in scientific and organizational perspective. *Journal of Futures Studies*, Vol. 19, No. 2, pp. 125–134.

Duin, P.A. van der, R. van Oirschot, H. Kotey and E. Vreeling. (2009). To govern is to foresee: an exploratory study into the relationship between futures research and strategy and policy processes at Dutch Ministries. *Futures*, Vol. 41, pp. 607–618.

Linde, E. van de and P.A. van der Duin (2011). The Delphi method as early warning: linking global societal trends to future radicalization and terrorism in the Netherlands. *Technology Forecasting and Social Change*, Vol. 78, pp. 1557–1564.

Poli, R. (2014). Anticipation: what about turning the human and social sciences upside down? *Futures*, Vol. 64, pp. 15–18.

Seligman, M.E.P., P. Railton, R.F. Baumeister and C. Sripada (2013). Navigating into the future or driven by the past. *Perspectives on Psychological Science*, Vol. 8, No. 2, pp. 119–141.

Vergragt, P.J. and J. Quist (2011). Backcasting for sustainability: introduction to the special issue. *Futures*, Vol. 78, pp. 747–755.

2 Developing Scenarios

Jan Nekkers

Introduction

Scenarios are a core product of foresight, because they embody two important starting points of the discipline:

1   We need to think about the future in a meaningful and structured way in order to be able to shape and prepare ourselves for that future.
2   At the same time, the future is often so uncertain that we cannot blindly trust predictions. A single prediction can never capture every possible future.

The word "scenario" comes from the world of theater. A scenario is the description of the story of a play or movie. In foresight, there are different kinds of scenarios. A scenario is a description of what the future may *possibly* look like. That is why we use a broad definition: scenarios explore potential futures that are deemed possible and the developments that may lead there and/or desirable futures and the developments that are needed to reach them (Dammers and Langeweg, 2013, p. 5).

Scenarios are *not* predictions, speculations or science fiction. A scenario is a story that describes a possible future end state in a horizon year, that also contains an interpretation of the events and developments in the present and their propagation into the future and that, finally, offers an internally consistent account of how a future world unfolds (Wright and Goodwin, 2009, p. 817).

We use scenarios because predictions usually do not become reality. There are many reasons for that: our knowledge of the world around us is limited. Theories about social developments are usually less "definite" than those about the physical world. Societies are reflexive: they respond to policy and, therefore, to predictions about the future. Social developments are often not linear and gradual, but abrupt and discontinuous in nature. To conclude with, society is often faced with unexpected disruptive developments: uprisings, natural disasters, accidents, turbulence and chaos.

Scenarios are not a goal in themselves, but a tool to think about the future. Scenarios can help us deal with cognitive complexity and uncertainty regarding the future. A good scenario taps us on our shoulder and says: "Look, this could be your future! Did you ever consider this to be possible? And most importantly: are you prepared for that future?"

Good scenarios are *plausible* and *relevant*, and they lead to *new insights*. They are plausible when we can imagine them becoming reality. This determines the credibility of the scenarios. They are relevant when they are geared toward the problems that organizations experience right now and when they offer leads for solutions for the future. Good scenarios also offer new insights. They present us with surprising new future realities. They encourage people to step outside their usual thought patterns, transcend the dominant culture in their organization and take action.

Ever since scenarios became popular, there is one scenario development method that has received the most attention: the scenario cross method, which is considered by both scenario developers and scientists as the "standard" for scenario-building (Van Asselt et al., 2010, p. 61). Its popularity is so great that many think it is the only way to develop scenarios. No matter how powerful a method it is, there are many other methods that can be used to develop good scenarios. In this chapter, we discuss both the scenario cross method and provide an overview of the other methods.

Types of Scenarios

Futures studies can describe the *probable* future, the *possible* future and the *desirable* future. These categories are not mutually exclusive, there is a degree of overlap.

Descriptions of the *probable* or *expected* future are predictions or prognoses (forecasts). They provide an answer to the question: what will happen? They do not fall under the definition of scenarios. However, some predictions are called scenarios. These are the so-called reference, baseline or business-as-usual scenarios in which currently dominant trends and developments are extrapolated into the future.

Descriptions of *possible* futures (foresights) answer the question: what could happen? They are scenarios in the strict sense of our definition. The scenarios are distinguished by the extent to which they explore uncertainties about the future. They vary from *What if*-scenarios to highly explorative scenarios.

What if scenarios show us what happens if a specified event were to occur in the near future. Such an event or development forms a so-called bifurcation point that causes developments to take place along different paths. An example of such a bifurcation point is a referendum about a fundamental issue. The "yes" or "no" result of such a referendum leads to two different scenarios.

Explorative scenarios describe situations in the future that diverge from – or even contrast with – the current situation, but that are still seen as possible futures. They create an extreme extrapolation of current developments, to explore the boundaries of what is possible. To map a broad range of possible futures, usually a set of multiple scenarios is developed. By presenting different scenarios, insight is provided into the uncertainty about the future development of a given issue. By picturing contrasting futures, explorative scenarios can help signal new developments and issues.

Normative scenarios answer the question: how can a certain goal be reached? Using roadmaps (preserving scenarios) and by posing a "daring" goal that can be achieved within the existing system, the steps are identified that can lead to the desired objective. These steps are concretized in business, project or policy plans.

Transforming scenarios answer the question as to how a certain goal can be reached if the current system blocks the necessary changes. Transforming scenarios have to do with fundamental social problems with a high degree of complexity, uncertainty and normative disagreement. Transforming scenarios paint compelling pictures of the goal in question, for instance a sustainable city in 2050, after which reverse reasoning (backcasting) is used to examine which system innovations and trend reversals are need to reach the desired situation.

Scenarios can be divided into two types: *external scenarios* and *object or policy scenarios*.

External scenarios focus on the factors that the relevant actors cannot influence. They describe what the environment of a company or organization may look like in the future. They make it clear that the world can change quickly and that that has consequences for one's organization. Neither the organization itself nor its strategy are a part of the scenario. External scenarios are very suitable as a framework for developing policy and strategy. A classic example is the scenario planning method whereby business strategies are developed that are robust in comparison to various future external scenarios.

Strategic scenarios indicate what the possible consequences are of strategic choices. They focus on the internal factors that the relevant actors can influence and examine how they affect future developments.

System scenarios are combinations of external and strategic scenarios. Within the normative scenarios, transforming scenarios are always system scenarios, while roadmaps are always strategic scenarios. Predictive and explorative scenarios can be either strategic or external scenarios.

History of Scenario-thinking

The scenario planning method has a history in military strategy. Since the dawn of time, soldiers have prepared for battles by reenacting future military situations.

Herman Kahn (1922–1983) is considered the godfather of scenario development. He created his first scenarios for the RAND Corporation, a think tank for

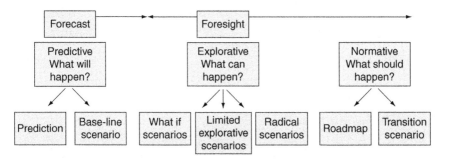

Figure 2.1 Kinds of scenarios.

military-strategic issues. Kahn's greatest contribution to foresight was that he used a system analysis to identify the mechanisms, patterns and structures that may lead to a future event, outlining a logical path of hypothetical events that lead to a certain end state. Kahn called it the "future-now" technique. He felt that the ultimate goal of these scenarios was: "thinking about the unthinkable."

With the exception of these first beginnings, the *predict and control approach* played a dominant role until the 1960s. With a scientific foundation, the future had to be predicted as accurately as possible. In the early 1970s, Shell broke with this way of looking at the future in a radical way. The director of the Planning Group, the Frenchman Pierre Wack, argued that scenarios should not explore the *certainties*, but that they should be based on the *uncertainties* regarding the future.

At the time within Shell, oil prices were considered to be one of the most certain and stable factors in the future. Wack and his team reached the conclusion, however, that oil prices may very well be the most uncertain factor. Overproduction of oil could develop into an oil shortage, which meant that huge fluctuations in oil prices could not be ruled out. In 1971, Wack created scenarios in which oil prices reached four times their current levels. The scenarios showed that oil-producing countries could limit oil production to drive up prices, which would cause oil prices to rise quickly in the 1970s.

The scenarios were ready just in time. On October 6, 1973, the Yom Kippur war started: a surprise attack by Egypt and Syria on Israel. In the aftermath, the Arab OPEC countries started to use oil as a strategic weapon against the West, causing the 1973 oil crisis. Because Shell had already captured these developments in scenarios, the company was able to respond more effectively and more quickly, which gave Shell a competitive advantage that lasted until the 1980s.

Former employees of the Shell Planning Group discovered a flourishing market for scenario planning. In 1987, they founded the Global Business Network (GBN). One of the founders of GBN, Peter Schwartz, wrote the first global bestseller about scenario planning (*The Art of the Long View*), in which the scenario cross method is presented as *the* method for developing scenarios.[1]

In 1996, Kees van der Heijden, former head of Shell's Planning Group, wrote the book *Scenarios: The Art of Strategic Conversation*. Van de Heijden argues that the main purpose of scenarios is to get decision-makers to enter into a strategic conversation about the future. This creates a shared language and collective understanding about which developments determine the future, which in turn will allow them to understand new developments better and anticipate more quickly. According to Van de Heijden, the strategic conversation about the scenarios is the core of the scenario method.

The Structure of a Scenario Project

A Scenario Project in Seven Steps

A scenario trajectory can be divided into seven steps. It is best to include all steps, but it is not necessary. Depending on the goal of the trajectory and the available means, more weight, time or attention can be assigned to certain steps.

The seven steps are:

1   Preparation
    • Why a scenario project?
2   Orientation
    • What is the question that has to be answered with the scenarios?
    • What is the time horizon of the scenarios?
3   Exploring the environment
    • What trends or developments are important for the future?
4   Determining scenario structure
    • How do you create a framework on the basis of which you can build different scenarios?
5   Building scenarios
    • What are the most important elements of the scenarios?
    • How can the scenarios be made radical and future-oriented?
    • What are the titles of the scenarios?
6   Using scenarios
    • What strategic conclusions can we draw from the scenarios?
    • What do the scenarios teach us about the future?
7   Monitoring scenarios
    • What scenario(s) are the actual developments in line with?
    • What are the early warning signs?

Step 1: Preparation

Scenarios are a tool for reaching a strategic goal. Before starting a scenario project, you have to ask yourself what it is you want to achieve with the scenarios that will be developed. The goal also determines the type of scenarios that are most suitable. If, for example, you want to examine which strategies are robust in an uncertain future, you would rather make use of external scenarios than strategic scenarios. On the other hand, when the aim is to start learning processes that will break through the dominant way of thinking within the organization, it is better to develop strategic scenarios.

Client

Every scenario project has a client and a developer. The client is a person or team entrusted with the development of the scenarios. To make sure the scenario project is effective, the client must have decision-making powers and influence in the area to which the scenarios relate.

Organization Scenario Team

The scenario team writes the scenarios. For most people, this is not a routine activity, which is why it is crucial to the success of the scenario team to make sure that the team members complement each other. A good scenario team is multi-disciplinary and includes a broad spectrum of people in terms of their age, professional education and working experience. Scenario writers need to be able to write vividly. A good scenario writer has the will and courage to engage in original and independent thought. In most cases, excessive expertise is actually a counter-indication.

Go/No-go

The most important question in the preparation is to assess critically whether scenarios are the right tool: should a scenario project actually be started? The checklist presented in Figure 2.2 can help to answer that question.

Step 2: Orientation

Scenario Question

As with any question: the answer is never better than the question you ask. In the orientation phase, it is important to formulate exactly what the question is that the scenarios are expected to answer. We call that the *scenario question*.

In most cases, the question for which scenarios are made are an unstructured problem, in other words, a problem to which no unequivocal answer is possible, due to the complexity and/or turbulence of the subject. Alternatively, it may be that the knowledge about the subject is incomplete or that there is disagreement about the values involved.

Determining Time Horizon

Most scenarios look about five to twenty years into the future. The time horizon depends on the dynamics of the environment. In extremely dynamic and complex circumstances, uncertainty about the future is greater than in stable unequivocal situations. When there is a lot of uncertainty, the scenarios will diverge quickly, in which case the time horizon can sometimes be less than one year.

Step 3: Exploring the Environment

The first step in exploring the environment is a broad orientation via the collection of information in different ways. Information that is available online about the subject is collected. People are interviewed. A more elaborate way of collecting information is by using a questionnaire, which can best be done after a little more is known about the subject. A future-oriented type of questionnaire is the Delphi technique.

Analyzing the Baseline

We make scenarios by connecting our knowledge of past and present with our imagination. To explore the future in a solid way, it is important to analyze the current state of affairs and examine how it came about. The analysis contains a

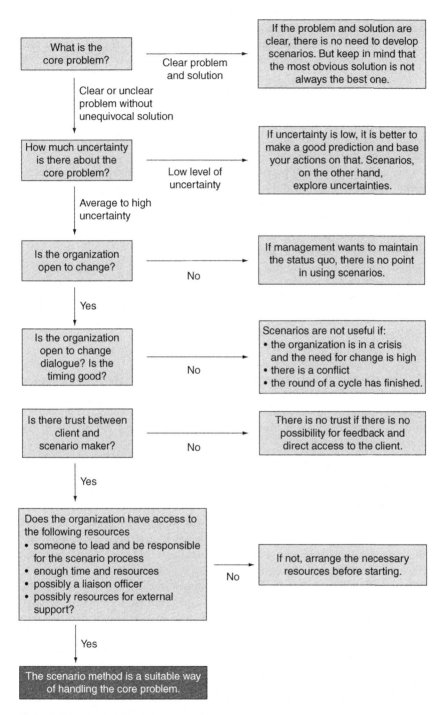

Figure 2.2 Go/no-go checklist.

description of the various forces or developments that affect the scenario question and the way they affect and relate to each other, in effect creating a (quantitative or other) model of the current situation. The analysis of the baseline can be used as a basis for a reference, baseline or business-as-usual scenario.

Identify Trends and Discontinuities

An important feature of the scenario method is that a distinction is drawn between elements that are predictable or predetermined and elements that are open to change in the future and, as such, uncertain.

In the environment of an organization or (policy) issue, there are social developments that have a major impact on the future. We call those: trends. Trends are extrapolations of developments in the present. They are slowly changing phenomena or projects that "is already in the pipeline" into the future. Like all phenomena from social reality, trends cannot be identified objectively. A trend is a trend because we perceive it as such.

Trends have the following characteristics:

• A trend can be distinguished in social reality.
• A trend has a certain direction and causes a change.
• A trend lasts for a longer period of time.
• A trend develops more or less evenly.

To be able to make meaningful statements about the future, we not only look at those trends that directly affect an organization or issue, but also at the "trends behind the trends" that occur in a wider social context. In doing so, we draw a distinction between trends in the transactional environment and trends in the contextual environment.

An important guideline in the exploration of trends is: *work from the outside in.* Businesses and organizations are systems that operate in a social environment. They have direct relationships and contacts with their transactional or work environment, which in turn is affected by the broad social developments in the contextual environment. In that sense, the transactional environment is a gateway for trends on the contextual environment. Once it is clear what trends there are in the contextual environment, scenarios can be made that show how the transactional environment will change in the future.

When looking in the contextual environment for the driving forces, the acronym DESTEP (demographics, economy, socio-cultural, technology, ecology and politics) is a good checklist to make sure you have taken all domains into account.

Because trends develop more or less evenly over a longer period of time, they can be used to say something about the future. However, future developments are never 100 percent certain. In reality, trends often develop in an unexpected manner. Trends can occur sooner or later than expected: uncertain in speed. Trends can deviate in their direction or even be reversed: pendulum uncertainty.

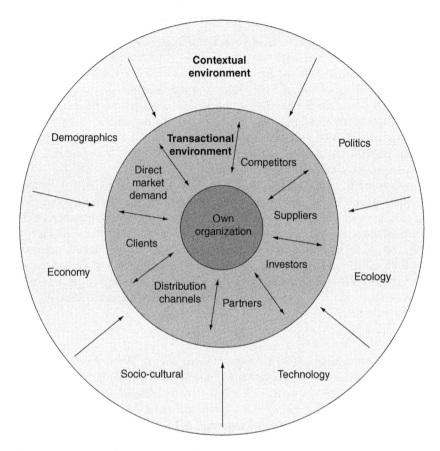

Figure 2.3 Contextual and transactional environment.

Trends whose future development is hard to predict are called *uncertainties*. They form the basis of scenarios, because the aim of scenarios is precisely to map uncertainties about the future. When creating scenarios, there is a special interest in what scenario thinkers call *core uncertainties*. The more uncertainties can develop in different and preferably contradictory directions, the more explorative scenarios become.

Discontinuities

Discontinuities are sudden disruptions in the existing development. Unexpected external developments can completely put the world upside down and force a trend reversal.

Wild cards are developments that are unexpected or considered to be unlikely and that have such a tremendous impact that a social development changes course definitively. Think of natural disasters like earthquakes or tsunamis. Terrorist attacks like 9/11 or the attack on Charlie Hebdo can also be considered wild cards.

Discontinuities can also be the result of technological innovations, which often display a fixed pattern, starting with a latent phase, followed by an eruption and a period of normalization. In the latent phase, an innovation is still in its pilot stage. Then the innovation breaks through, pushing established companies and technologies out of the market. Often, this is accompanied by extremely or even excessively high expectations: a bubble. After a while, expectations are tempered and the market becomes accustomed to the new technology. This development explains why the initial impact of new technologies is often overrated, and why its long-term impact is often underestimated.

Exponential developments are a specific type of discontinuities. A famous example is Moore's Law, which states that, when prices stay the same, processor chip capacity is doubled every 18 months. This law has proven to be correct ever since Intel introduced the processor 4004 in 1971, even though the period is not always exactly 18 months. Many products that are the result of IT developments can be described as an exponential development. An exponential growth curve rises very gradually and after a certain point (the knee in the curve) the dynamics increase. That explains why, at first, exponential trends remain "beneath the surface" and become manifest and dominant after a certain moment.

Discontinuities can be detected in their latent phase by being alert to "weak signals."

So-called bifurcations are a final form of discontinuity. Bifurcations are events whose developments can take one of two directions. Examples are referendums with a certain result, irreversible decisions, the success or failure of a given policy. Identifying future bifurcations offers the possibility to write a history book on the future (Dammers and Langeweg, 2013, p. 48), including an underlying timeline.

Step 4: Determining Scenario Structure

There are two ways to build scenarios: inductive and deductive (Van der Heijden, 1996, p. 196).

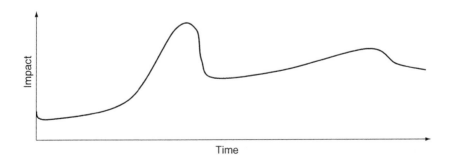

Figure 2.4 Impact of technological innovation.

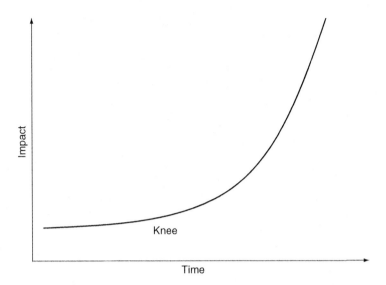

Figure 2.5 Exponential development.

In the case of the inductive way, separate trends, developments, continuities, discontinuities and future facts are brought together, after which they are clustered in coherent units and an attempt is made to identify chains of events in these clusters. Subsequently, storylines can be based on each of the clusters. Finally, the idea is to identify an underlying structure in the various storylines.

A famous example of inductive scenario-building are the Mont Fleur scenarios. In the early 1990s, many people were worried about how the transfer of power in South Africa would take place after the apartheid regime. The outbreak of a civil war was not unthinkable. In 1991 and 1992, in the conference center Mont Fleur, a group of influential South Africans came together, led by Shell's scenario planner Adam Kahane. The group consisted of leaders of the main

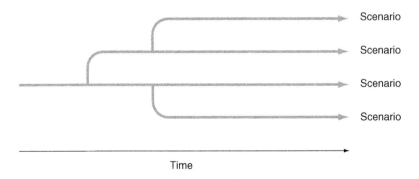

Figure 2.6 Bifurcations.

left-wing opposition groups, from ANC to the South African Communist Party, in addition to their life-long enemies; prominent members of the white minority (businessmen and scientists).

How was it possible to get these political opponents to make scenarios in a constructive way? Adam Kahane told the participants to brainstorm in small groups about possible scenarios for the transition. The central question was: "How will the future actually develop?" An added assignment was: "Do not give your vision about how you want the future to develop." The first brainstorming sessions yielded 30 stories, which were clustered and reduced over a number of rounds to four scenarios. Next, the underlying structure was analyzed. The four scenarios gave different answers to how the transition in South Africa could take place. They were presented in 1992 in a situation in which intensive negotiations took place about the transition toward a new society.

Three of the four scenarios showed how the transition could go wrong:

- Ostrich, in which the nonrepresentative white government sticks its head in the sand to try to avoid a negotiated settlement with the black majority.
- Lame Duck, in which there is a prolonged transition with a constitutionally weakened government which, because it purports to respond to all, satisfies none.
- Icarus, in which a constitutionally unconstrained black government comes to power on a wave of popular and noble intentions, and embarks on a huge and unsustainable public spending program, which crashes the economy.

Only the fourth scenario offered an attractive vision of the transition. It was the scenario called Flight of the Flamingos, in which the transition was successful because all the key building blocks were put in place, with everyone in South Africa rising slowly and together.

On closer analysis, it appeared that the underlying structure of the scenarios was the decision-making tree, shown in Figure 2.7.

With the deductive way of developing a scenario, a structure is determined in advance that is the framework within which the scenarios are developed. The framework is filled using separate elements (developments, trends, continuities, discontinuities) that were identified in the environmental analysis.

There are different ways to arrive at a scenario structure:

- qualitative models
- quantitative models
- scenario cross method
- morphological field.

Qualitative Models

In the case of qualitative models, the main causal relationships between variables are presented schematically, without quantifying them. The underlying dynamics

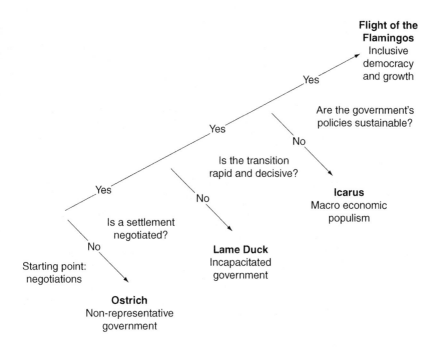

Figure 2.7 Scenario structures: Mont Fleur scenarios.

of the scenarios are visualized. By choosing from different variables, different scenarios are created. Figure 2.8 shows two causal models for sustainable packaging.

Quantitative Models

Quantitative models can also be useful to express the underlying dynamics of scenarios. Setting up quantitative models requires enough data and well-founded insight into the causal relationships. Demographic, economic and climatological developments are all very suitable for quantitative models. It is important to keep in mind that the models are used to create different possible scenarios, and that they do not lead to predictions.

An advantage of the quantifiable scenarios is that they are more plausible and convincing than scenarios that only contain qualitative terms. A disadvantage is that the scenarios can only focus on developments that are quantifiable. Another disadvantage can be that the scenario development will almost inevitably lead to a high, low and intermediate scenario.

Scenario Cross Method

The scenario cross method has been called the "golden tool" of scenario development (Van Asselt et al., 2010, p. 62). At any rate, the scenario cross method is

24   J. Nekkers

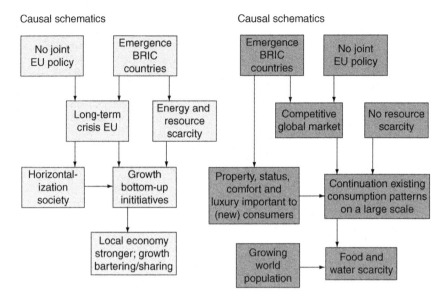

Figure 2.8 Causal schematics.

"a dominating model for scenario building around the world" (Lindgren and Bandhold, 2003, pp. 66–67), to the extent that many people believe, erroneously, that the scenario method is an indispensable element of scenario development.

A scenario cross is created by combining two core uncertainties in a 2×2 matrix, creating four quadrants by placing two dimensions with extremes opposite one another (see Figure 2.9). The quadrants distinguish themselves on the dimensions of the core uncertainties, as result of which each quadrant has two distinguishing characteristics. Each quadrant is the basis for a scenario.

The advantage of the scenario cross method is that it forces people to capture the complex future reality in, at the most, two main dimensions, forcing them to focus on the heart of the matter. Another advantage is that four scenarios are a good number. People working with more than four scenarios often cannot see the wood for the trees.

A precondition for a good scenario cross is that the core uncertainties are independent of one another. If the dimensions have a causal relationship, it will result in two rather than four scenarios.

Scenarios are often the most exciting when the dimensions create surprises, which is the case if there is friction in the combination of characteristics. At first, it is hard to imagine how such a combination can lead to a realistic scenario. Once people manage to imagine such a scenario, the result is often new and surprising.

How do you know if you have chosen the right axes that will yield the right future scenario? The honest answer is that you can never be sure. The main thing is to choose *usable* axes that can lead to meaningful scenarios, which is a matter of

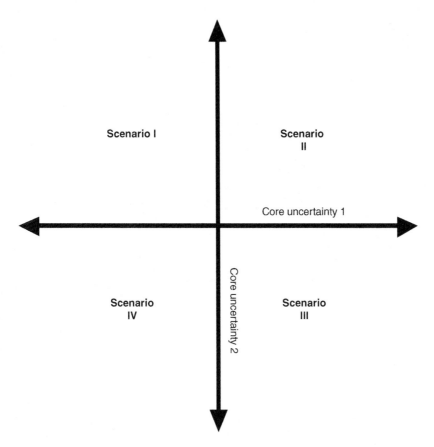

Figure 2.9 Scenario cross.

trial and error. In addition, it is a process that involves multiple people in a work-shop, because scenario development is an intersubjective affair.

A usable scenario cross is found by first looking at which of the trends and developments that have been identified has the greatest impact and uncertainties. That works as follows. In step 3, "Exploring the environment," a group of people have brainstormed about the trends and developments that may be relevant to their company or organization. These trends and developments need to be ranked in terms of their impact and uncertainty. That is not a scientific process. There are no fixed criteria to decide why one trend or development has a bigger impact than others. By discussing the various trends and developments intensively, the participants gain insight into each other's perspective on the organization and on the outside world, and are able to identify common ground. It is best to support the brainstorm session and the discussion about the driving and their ranking by working with stickers (moderation stickers or post-its). The first step is to divide the driving forces on the basis of their impact, the second step is to divide them on the basis of their predictability. The trends and uncertainties should first be ranked on a white board or flip-over on the basis of their impact. The result is shown in Figure 2.10.

The driving forces with the highest impact are the factors that are able to shake the company's or organization's foundations. In particular the discussion about which factors have a greater impact than others can – especially if opinions are extremely divided – lead to new strategic insights.

Next, the trends and uncertainties need to be ranked according to their level of uncertainty, which in this case is divided as the extent to which their future development is difficult to predict. This means that, at this stage, the stickers can only be moved horizontally, because they have already been ranked according to impact.

These two steps together produce the impact-uncertainty matrix shown in Figure 2.11.

The top-right corner shows the core uncertainties, in this case driving forces 1 and 3, which have the greatest impact on the organization and are at the same time the most unpredictable. Their uncertainty comes from the fact that their future development can take opposite directions.

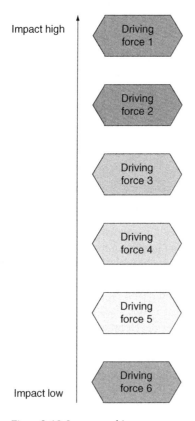

Figure 2.10 Impact ranking.

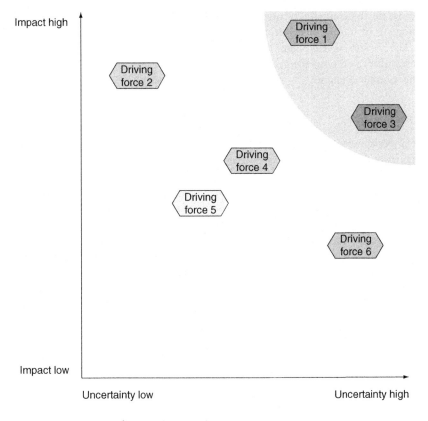

Figure 2.11 Impact and uncertainty matrix.

Driving force 2 is important to scenario development because it is a trend: the impact on the organization is high, but it is uncertain whether and how it will occur in the future. This trend will have to be included in all scenarios.

The core uncertainties that have been selected can be represented as opposites with extremes. Examples of core uncertainties are: centralized vs. decentralized, or economic growth vs. economic stagnation.

Combine the core uncertainties with the greatest impact and uncertainty into a scenario cross.

External or Strategic Scenarios

When the steps described above have been taken, that will result in core uncertainties for external scenarios. The core uncertainties determine what the most important dimensions are of the future environment of the company or organization.

To create strategic scenarios that show how a company or organization may develop in the future, a virtually identical approach is needed in workshops. It starts with brainstorming about the most important strategic choices and/or dilemmas for the company or organization. After that, the choices are ranked, not on the basis of uncertainty, but on the extent to which they are genuine dilemmas. The choices of real dilemmas exclude each other. The choices that have the biggest impact and pose the greatest dilemma are then used as core uncertainties for the strategic scenarios.

Morphological Field

General Morphological Analysis is a method to identify possible relationships or configurations for complex problems (Ritchey, 2011). The method starts by identifying the most important dimensions that determine a problem. These dimensions are called parameters. Next, values are assigned to the parameters. The morphological field consists of the collection of parameters and their assigned values.

The 2×2 matrix that is the result of a scenario cross is in fact a very simple morphological field. Whereas a scenario cross consists of two parameters that can take on two values, a morphological field consists of *x* parameters that can take on *y* values.

In the case of a morphological scenario model, the aim is to examine which configurations of values of the parameters can lead to a scenario. The main criterion for that is the internal consistency between the values. In a morphological field, the number of possible scenarios is the product of the number of values per parameter for all parameters. In the field mentioned above, that is $2 \times 2 \times 4 \times 2 \times 3 = 96$. The fact that it is possible to create a large number of scenarios in a morphological field is on the one hand its strength, but on the other hand, it is also a weakness.

Next, it is possible to examine which combinations of values have the highest level of coherence. Those are the dimensions of the scenarios. In practice, the best

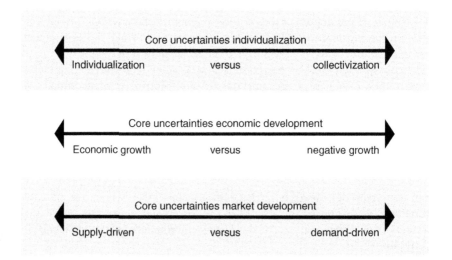

Figure 2.12 Core uncertainties.

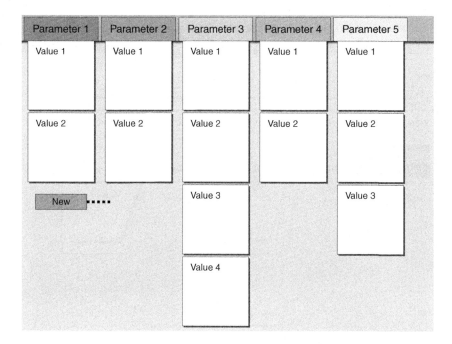

Figure 2.13 Morphological field.

way to find combinations is by ranking the parameters on the basis of their impact, from left to right, with the parameter with the highest impact on the left. Next, the aim is to look from left to right to see which consistent combinations are possible. That can be done by first outlining a scenario that is closest to the current reality and then outlining a scenario that is the most radical and future-oriented.

In the example presented in Figure 2.14, those could be the following combinations.

If the two parameters with the highest impact also have two values, the scenario cross method can be used to begin by exploring the four possible combinations, after which those combinations can be extrapolated to other values shown in Figure 2.15.

An important advantage of a morphological scenario model us that it is possible to produce a manageable number of scenarios, even with multiple dimensions. Unlike the scenario cross method, there is no need to reduce the complexity of reality to the two dimensions with the greatest impact and uncertainty.

Step 5: Building Scenarios

Filling in the Scenario Structure

At this point, we are about to fill in the scenario structure to create real scenarios. This is done by using imagination and logical reasoning to imagine future worlds.

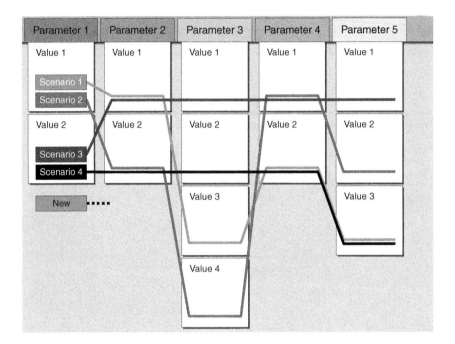

Figure 2.14 Scenarios in a morphological field.

In essence, it is the art of story-telling: connecting chains of events and consequences and combining various elements into a coherent story.

A useful instrument for that is the implication tree, which goes as follows. Imagine that the core of the scenario has become reality, what are the possible implications of this scenario? Write those possible implications on moderation stickers or post-its. Then, for each of the implications, brainstorm what its possible implications are. Systematically go through all first-order implications to identify the second-order implications, and possibly even the third-order implications. The final result looks like Figure 2.16.

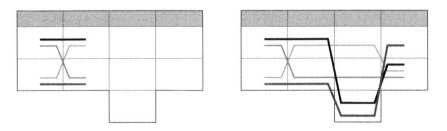

Figure 2.15 From scenario cross to morphological field.

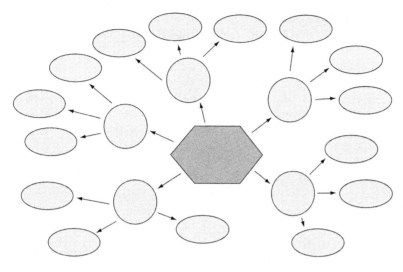

Figure 2.16 Implication tree.

The implications in the outer ring help in writing the scenario. They show the end state of a number of chains of cause and effect that were outlined with the implication tree.

When writing the scenarios, the end state is the starting point. What does the world look like in the year in which the scenarios are set? Next, write down which events have led to that end state, by placing the various elements according to their mutual relationships and temporal order. Two questions play an important role:

- How is it that the world was able to develop as it is outlined in the scenario?
- What is the relationship between the various elements of the scenario?

Use the results of all the work that has been done before. Take another critical look at the interviews, exploration workshops and impact-uncertainty matrices. In addition to the core uncertainties that were used for the scenario structure, the trends you have identified also need to be included in the scenarios. Trends will play a role in every scenario. For example, in every scenario on the future of health care, the aging population should be included as a trend. A future scenario without IT is virtually unthinkable. The way the trends will develop depends on the specific characteristics of the scenario.

Writing the Scenarios

Every scenario has a plot, which describes the core of the story of the scenario. At the start of writing a scenario, it is important to think of a plot, which can serve as the summary of the scenario. Write scenarios in the present tense and describe the future as though it were an actual reality. So no "perhaps" or "could be." Like any good story, a scenario should have a beginning, a middle and an end. A good beginning immediately puts the reader firmly in the future:

> Good morning diary. I really dread the idea of moving house. Next week I have to move to the Styx nursing home. The thing I fear most is the "senior wash" in the Styx: a human car wash. One push on the button and ten oldies are washed simultaneously.... You don't have privacy. Everything goes automatically, except getting dressed. You have to do that yourself because there is no staff.

Make sure to build in a flashback in every scenario, to allow yourself to outline the events and developments that have led to the future situation.

Next, in the middle section, describe the actual reality in the future, based on themes, which are aspects that are important when asking the scenario question. An example of a scenario question is: "How will consumers use energy in the future?" The following aspects are important: What kinds of consumers are there in the future? What are their lifestyles? What is their level of wealth? What types of energy are used in the future? Which energy sources are there in abundance? What do consumers use energy for in the future?

Describe the themes like the paragraphs with headers. Ideally, the same themes with the same headers can be included in all four scenarios. The contents of the paragraphs will vary for each scenario.

After writing the first draft, the text needs to be made more future-oriented by "radicalizing" all the elements, which can be done by constantly trying to make a relationship or situation more extreme. Make the elements a little more extreme, extrapolate the developments a little further and include new elements that fit the context of the radicalized scenario. By systematically and consistently making the text slightly more extreme, a different, more realistic future reality is created almost automatically.

Next, it is time to come up with catchy titles for the scenarios. Good titles are essential. They are short and provocative, and capture the precise essence of the scenarios. Examples of titles: "Quarreling tigers," "Gridlock," and "Dance of the lonely giants," for scenarios about development aid, and "Knowledge is power," "Knowledge for sale" and "Certainty guaranteed," for scenarios for a government knowledge institute. Beatles song titles have been used for scenarios about the labor market: "Eight days a week," "With a little help from my friends," "Come together" and "Help!". A good title will stay within an organization for a long time and be used to refer to the core of discussions.

Scenarios can be dry and written down as a kind of analytical outline. However, they have maximum impact when they are presented as a history of the future, which is done by dramatizing the scenarios into real stories in which actual people play the lead roles. Using characters in the scenarios who go through a dramatic development allows the users to connect to the scenarios on an emotional level. In addition to providing concise information about the future, scenarios also inspire a certain feeling, which is important, because strategic choices are based on both reason and emotion. It is possible to play on that emotion by presenting the scenarios as stories.

When the scenarios have been written, the work is not done yet. A good presentation is the finishing touch. Unfortunately, this is often forgotten in scenario projects. Using four sheets of paper simply stapled together is a waste of all the energy that the scenario team has put in. Use illustrations, drawings, pictures, graphs and tables. Choose the right lay-out, finish and paper to create a perfect and refreshing presentation.

To present the scenarios, you can use a PowerPoint presentation. Make sure not to champion one of the scenarios over the others. If the scenarios are presented multiple times, it may be worthwhile to present the core of the scenario in a video presentation. If you really want to make an impression, you could consider using actors. After all, projecting feelings and emotions is what they do. It may be a costly solution, but it will certainly make an impression.

Step 6: Using Scenarios

The strategic meeting is the core of the use of scenarios. That requires some explanation. Scenario theory assumes that people do not act in response to reality itself, but to their perception of reality. People learn the most when the reality they experience is different from the model in their head. That is when they adjust their frame of reference and start acting on the basis of something else. Organizations can learn as well, but for organizations it is even harder than it is for people.

In a strategic meeting, the learning processes are put in motion that may lead to new mental models about reality, which in turn may change people's behavior and actions. Scenarios help people let go of what is "trending" and learn to think in alternative images.

Structure of a Scenario Meeting

A strategic meeting usually takes place in the form of a workshop, in which the following rules apply:

- It is not a discussion, but a dialogue. It is not about being right. Nobody knows what the future will look like exactly, so nobody is wrong.
- The scenario has become a reality. Place yourself inside the scenario and pretend the present is set in the future.
- Stay within the framework of the scenario, so do not start designing an alternative future.
- Avoid criticism of the scenario. "Yes, but..." is not allowed.

It is the moderator's task to make sure the rules are obeyed.

External scenarios are discussed in two phases. The starting point of the first phase is: "The future is something that happens." In this part of the meeting, the characteristics of the various scenarios are discussed. What are the threats and opportunities in each scenario? What does your company or organization look like within the various future environments? In the second phase of the meeting, the starting point is: "The future is something that you make." The central question is: "Assume that the future scenario has become a reality, what choices do you have to make now to realize what you find attractive, and to avoid what you find unattractive?" At the end of the meeting, you examine whether there are opportunities that occur in multiple scenarios and set a summarizing agenda that indicates what decisions need to be made in the present.

Strategic Scenarios for Mission and Vision

In the case of strategic scenarios, the moderator asks the participants to place themselves inside the scenarios and ignore any resistance they may have to the scenario. Ideally, there are strategic scenarios that are the result of a deviation from the present course or even a break with the current dominant mindset within the organization. That will lead to resistance and irritation among some participants. Participants need to list the pros and cons of the scenario as objectively as possible and examine for themselves what values play a role in their assessment.

In the case of "the future is something you make," the participants assess the desirability of the various strategic scenarios and connect it to an argumentation. That way, the "basis" from which the various participants approach the scenarios becomes clear. Strategic scenarios help examine the mission and success formula, because they show that it is possible to do things differently and make people look into the mirror of the dominant mindset. Strategic scenarios provide answers to the questions: Why does the organization exist and what is the core of its success? What can the organization do that others cannot?

To be focused, the organization must have a coherent idea about where it wants to go. The vision shows what the future organization ideally looks like. It is preferable to shape the vision in a strategic meeting, so that the vision is shared by people in the organization. A vision can be developed by combing the desired elements from various strategic scenarios into a singly coherent scenario.

A more structured kind of scenario meeting is the so-called wind tunnel. In a wind tunnel, the prototype of a new airplane is exposed to various extreme conditions. It is only when the airplane has managed to pass all tests, that it will be put into production.

External Scenarios for Wind-tunneling

During wind-tunneling, the external scenarios are used as a stress test. The discussion can also be broadened by juxtaposing the possible options available with the scenarios. Which options are future-proof? Which activities had better be terminated and on which activities should we focus more?

A feature of wind-tunneling is that proposed policies are tested against one or more external scenarios. The main criterion in the meeting is the concept of *strategic fit*, which means that the organization of a company or organization has the best possible fit with its environment.

In a wind tunnel, robustness scores are given based on the strategic fit, which vary from very robust to very weak.

Participants give their scores independently, which are then added up to provide an overall robustness score (see Table 2.1).

Wind-tunneling is started by dividing the intended direction into separate policy options. The starting point of wind-tunneling is that all the external scenarios are equally likely. We do not know which scenario will become a reality. Make sure you always use external scenarios in wind-tunneling, otherwise you end up testing the strategic choice in relation to itself.

Policy options or strategic scenarios that have a robust score in all external scenarios are called robust or future-proof. They provide no-regret strategies that will work under any of the future scenarios. Options or strategic scenarios that are not robust in all the external scenarios can be a part of a provisional strategy. When you notice that social developments move in the direction of an external scenario in which the option is not robust, the development has to stop. When you know the external scenario in which the option is very robust will become a reality, you can accelerate its development.

Options that only have a maximum yield in one external scenario are the most interesting. It is possible to make a basic investment in such options, and scale it up quickly when the external scenario in question becomes a reality. Such strategies are used by real entrepreneurs and large corporations.

The outcome of the scenario meeting about robustness is a strategic portfolio containing the choices of certain options of strategic scenarios.

Step 7: Monitoring Scenarios

When the steps discussed above have all been taken and a strategy has been chosen, that does not mean that the process has come to an end. After all, time does not stand still. There are new developments in an ever-changing outside world, creating new threats and opportunities, and things change within the organization as well. Some goals are realized, while others are not. The organization has to ask itself continuously whether or not it is still on the right course.

An important goal of scenario-thinking is to increase awareness of what happens in the outside world and how to interpret that change. Most people look at their environment differently after taking part in a scenario project. Scenarios serve as lenses through which people look at reality. They have created a language to signal and look at the future and the underlying dynamics. That is what former Shell scenario planner Arie de Geus means when he speaks of scenarios as

Table 2.1 Robustness scores

++	Very robust
+	Robust
0	Neutral
−	Weak
− −	Very weak

"memories of the future," the aim being to create mental preparedness by anticipating multiple relevant futures.

The ability to detect change at an early stage, preferably before others do, and to recognize and connect developments, is a feature of a future-oriented and visionary leadership. That ability allows people and organizations to respond to changes in the outside world more quickly, and even to anticipate them. This increased future awareness can be anchored by introducing a monitoring and scanning system. Some organizations even set up a dedicated department, but it is also possible to have people within the organization who have knowledge of the scenarios to keep their eyes open and report periodically on the changes they observe.

Monitoring means scanning the environment for signals that point to a specific scenario. It is determined in advance which data are accepted as an *early warning sign*. A future-oriented monitoring mechanism selects those signals that provide indications about trends that will develop in the (near) future.

If scenarios have been developed using the scenario cross method, the scenario cross can be used as a two-dimensional space on which to plot future developments. By juxtaposing the scenarios and the actual developments, a path is created from the present to the future. The example in Figure 2.17 is based on the early warning system of the Dutch Ministry for Justice (Bottenhuis, Van der Duin, De Ruiter and Van Wijck, 2009).

With such a monitoring mechanism, it is possible to examine whether or not scenarios are still up-to-date and relevant.

A pitfall in the development of a monitoring system based on scenarios is that the focus is on the scenarios and that relevant developments outside the scenario framework are ignored, which is why it is important also to scan for weak signals of change, as well as to decode those signals to determine what they mean.

The scanning function is designed to serve as a radar to scan the environment for discontinuities, new trends and new business models. It focuses on matters that are not known in advance, so it is important to also examine signals that do not fit the scenarios. Detecting and decoding weak signals requires a very open

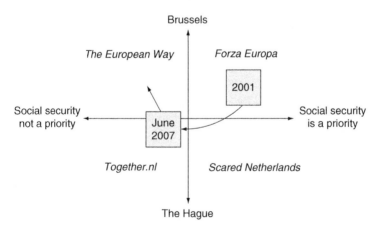

Figure 2.17 Monitor mechanism.

mind. Weak signals as an indication of major social change are hard to detect, with all the noise in the environment. It requires a broad mental framework to recognize them because, in many cases, they challenge existing thought patterns.

From Scenarios to Strategy

The scenario project provides the building blocks that can lead to concrete strategic choices. The transition from scenarios to strategies however, is not as clear-cut as sometimes suggested. Some emphasize that the transition from scenarios to strategy is an automatic and intuitive process, with decision-makers making choices based on the learning experiences via the scenarios. A condition for a fluent transition is that the scenario project is supported by the decision-makers, that it matches their urgencies and that it provides new insights.

Others emphasize that the transition from scenarios to strategy has to be shaped in a structured process. In their view, scenarios should be used to structure processes that lead to strategic choices. Wind-tunneling is a good example of that. It is a method that is used to develop a future-proof and flexible strategy instead of an approach based on intuition from a *single-point forecast*.

By using scenarios in the seven elements of strategy formation and by keeping the scenarios up-to-date, it is possible to make your company or organization future-proof. Not only does it allow you to anticipate future developments in a speedy and flexible way, but also shape the future by anticipating it.

Note

1 The development of the scenario cross method is ascribed to Jay Ogilvy, one of the founders of GBN and a friend of Peter Schwartz.

Further Reading

Peter Schwartz: *The Art of the Long View* (1991).
In 1991, Schwartz was the first to introduce scenarios to a wide audience with *The Art of the Long View*. He also wrote *The Long Boom* (1999) and *Inevitable surprises* (2003).

Kees van der Heijden: *Scenarios: The Art of Strategic Conversation* (1996).
The Art of Strategic Conversation is one of the first books to connect theory and practice of the scenario method. The book is considered *the* basic book on scenario planning for strategic issues. With core concepts like "business idea" and "strategic conversation," Van der Heijden connects scenario planning to strategy.

Mats Lindgren and Hans Bandhold: *Scenario Planning: The Link between Future and Strategy* (2003).
In this book, thinking about the future and scenario planning are connected for strategy formation. Lindgren and Bandhold provide a manual with various tools on how to put the scenario method into practice.

Bill Ralston and Ian Wilson: *The Scenario-Planning Handbook: Developing Strategies in Uncertain Times* (2006).
This handbook gives a detailed description of the scenario process in no fewer than 20 steps.

Shell International: *Scenarios: An Explorer's Guide* (2008).
Describes in a nutshell how to carry out your own scenario projects, not so much by suggesting specific scenario-building methods, but above all by guiding the aspiring scenario-builder through the process.

Thomas J. Chermack: *Scenario Planning in Organizations: How to Create, Use and Assess Scenarios* (2011).
This is the most comprehensive guide to scenario-planning available right now. Chermack provides a solid insight into the history and theoretical principles of scenario-planning, and gives a detailed description of the scenario method in five steps.

Woody Wade: *Scenario Planning: A Field Guide to the Future* (2012).
Beautifully illustrated book with one brief chapter in which the process of scenario-planning is explained, followed by scenarios, trends and future visions.

References

Asselt, M.B.A. van, J. Rotmans and D. Rothman (eds.) (2005). *Scenario innovation: experiences from a European experimental garden.* London: Taylor & Francis.

Asselt, Marjolein B.A. van, S.A. van 't Klooster, P.W.F. van Notten and L.A. Smits (2010). *Foresight in action: developing policy-oriented scenarios.* London: Earthscan.

Barker, J.A. (1992). *Paradigms: the business of discovering the future.* New York: HarperBusiness.

Bishop, P.C. and A. Hines (2012). *Teaching about the future.* New York: Palgrave Macmillan.

Börjeson, L., M. Höjer, K.-H. Dreborg, T. Ekvall and G. Finnveden (2006). Scenario types and techniques: towards a user's guide. *Futures*, Vol. 38, No. 7, pp. 723–739.

Botterhuis, L., P. van der Duin, P.A. de Ruijter and P. van Wijck (2009). Monitoring the future: building an early warning system for the Dutch Ministry of Justice. *Futures*, Vol. 42, No. 5, pp. 454–465.

Chermack, Thomas J. (2011). *Scenario planning in organizations: how to create, use, and assess scenarios.* San Fransisco, CA: Berrett-Koehler Publishers.

Cornish, E. (2004). *Futuring: the exploration of the future.* Bethesda, MD: World Future Society.

Dammers, E. and S. Langeweg (2013). *Scenario's maken voor milieu, natuur en ruimte: een handreiking.* The Hague: PBL.

Duin, P. van der (2006). *Qualitative foresight for innovation.* Delft: Eburon.

Geus, A. de (1997). *The living company: habits for survival in a turbulent environment.* Chicago, IL: Longview Publishing.

Gilad, B. (2004). *Early warning: using competitve intelligence to anticipate market shifts, control risk, and create powerful strategies.* New York: Amacom.

Godet, Michel (2001). *Creating futures: scenario planning as a strategic management tool.* London: Economica.

Heijden, K. van der (1996). *Scenarios: the art of strategic conversation.* Chichester, UK: Wiley.

Hines, A. and P. Bishop (2006). *Thinking about the future: guidelines for strategic foresight.* Washington, DC: Social Technologies.

Jong, R.J. de (2015). *Anticipate: the art of leading by looking ahead.* New York: Amacom.

Kahane, A. (2012). *Transformative scenario planning.* San Francisco, CA: Berret Koehler Publishers.

Kahn, H. (1965). *On escalation: metaphors and scenarios.* Piscataway, NJ: Transaction Publishers.

Kahn, H. and A.J. Wiener (1967). *The year 2000: a framework for speculation on the next thirty-three years.* New York: Macmillan.

Klooster, S.A. van 't and M.B.A. van Asselt (2006). Practising the scenario-axes technique. *Futures*, Vol. 38, No. 1, pp. 15–30.

Lindgren, M. and H. Bandhold (2003). *Scenario planning: the link between future and strategy.* Basingstoke, UK: Palgrave Macmillan.

Notten, P.W.F. van (2004). *Writing on the wall: scenario development in times of discontinuity.* Boca Raton, FL: Dissertation.com.

Petersen, J.L. (1999). *Out of the blue: how to anticipate big future surprises.* Lanham, MD: Madisson Books.

Pillkahn, U. (2008). *Using trends and scenarios as tools for strategy development: shaping the future of your enterprise.* Munich, Germany: Publicis Corporate Publishing.

Ralston, B. and I. Wilson (2006). *The scenario-planning handbook: a practitioner's guide to developing and using scenarios to direct strategy in today's uncertain times.* Mason, OH: South-Western Educational Publishers.

Raymond, M. (2010). *The trend forecaster's handbook.* London: Laurence King Publishing.

Ringland, G. (2002). *Scenarios in business.* Chichester, UK: Wiley.

Ritchey, T. (2011). *Wicked problems – social messes: decision support modelling with morphological analysis.* Heidelberg: Springer.

Ritchey, T. (2011). Modelling alternative futures with general morphological analysis. *World Future Review*, Vol. 3, pp. 83–94.

Ruiter, P. de (2014). *Scenario based strategy: navigate the future.* Farnham, UK: Gower.

Scearce, D., K. Fulton and the Global Business Network community (2004). *What if? The art of scenario thinking for nonprofits.* Berkeley, CA: Global Business Network.

Schwartz, P. (2003). *Inevitable surprises: Thinking ahead in time of turbulence.* New York: Gotham Books.

Schwartz, P. (1991). *The art of the long view.* New York: Doubleday.

Schwartz, P. (1999). *The long boom.* New York: Basic Books.

Shell International BV (2008). *Scenarios: an explorer's guide.* The Hague: Shell International.

Taleb, N.N. (2007). *The black swan: the impact of the highly improbable.* New York: Random House.

Vliet, M. van (2011). *Bridging gaps in the scenario world: linking stakeholders, modellers and decision makers.* Wageningen: Proefschrift.

Wack, P. (1985). Scenarios: uncharted waters ahead. Scenarios: shooting the rapids. *Harvard Business Review*, Vol. 63, No. 5, pp. 73–89 and pp. 139–150.

Wilkinson, A. and R. Kupers (2014). *The essence of scenarios: learning from the Shell experience.* Amsterdam: University Press.

Wade, W. (2012). *Scenario planning: a field guide to the future.* New York: Wiley.

Wright, G. and P. Goodwin (2009). Decision making and planning under low levels of predictability: enhancing the scenario method. *International Journal of Forecasting*, Vol. 25, pp. 813–825.

3   Trend Analysis

*Tessa Cramer, Patrick van der Duin and
Christianne Heselmans*

Introduction

Although many futures research methods are related to each other and can be
used in combination, trend analysis can be viewed as the most essential method of
futures research. Examining possible future changes is the most basic form of
looking at the future, because the future develops on the basis of trends. And
various aspects, like the uncertainty of trends, the role of experts in detecting and
identifying trends, and the emphasis on the predictability of the trends on quantitative terms, are addressing in various other forms of futures research (the scenario method, the Delphi method and quantitative forecasting, respectively). The
fundamental role of trends does not mean that trend analysis is a one-dimensional
method. The definition of a trend, the distinction of different kinds of trends and
the practitioners of trends are all very diverse, which is why the most important
purpose of this chapter is to show this diversity of trend analysis. To that end, we
first describe the available definitions of trends, subsequently how various trends
can be described, how trend professionals can be described and how trends can
be used in a decision-making process.

Trend Definitions

Ask ten random people what a trend is and you will get ten different definitions.
Many of those definitions will involve something related to fashion. People often
associate trends with the color, shape and materials of a new fashion season. On
the other hand, long-term economic developments are also mentioned. And
others might think about cultural and social changes, like globalization and secu-
larization. And in the business-minded community, trends are perceived as
changes in their own industry or sector and developments among competitors.

So despite the clarity of the question as to what is a trend, it is not always easy
to give a clear answer. And perhaps because trend is such a commonly used word
in everyday language, there are various definitions. To arrive at a clear and work-
able definition, we first provide a short overview of various definitions.

We start with the definition proposed by Kim Quaile Hill in the chapter
"Trend Extrapolation" in the voluminous *Handbook of Futures Research*, edited by
John Fowles. Hill (1978, p. 249) argues that "Trend itself is a tendency for the

values in a time serious to increase or decrease with some steady regularity." Right before that, he also provides a definition of trend analysis: "The analysis of trends is based on the empirical examination of some phenomenon with repeated measurements taken across time." As far is Hill is concerned, the emphasis is very much on measuring or extrapolating a "phenomenon" or "value" based on changes in historical series of data, which makes trend analysis primarily a quantitative affair. He prefers to reduce abstract concepts like "quality of life" and "economic wellbeing" to "measurable indicators."

The *Handbook of Forecasting* (Makridakis and Wheelwright, 1987) does not really provide a concrete definition of what a trend is, but describes "trend curves," which refer to the activity of describing and predicting (forecasting) trends, such as linear, exponential and S-shaped patterns (curves).

The *Futures Research Methodology* of the United Nations University speaks of "Trend Impact Analysis" (TIA), which not only involves extrapolating historical data, but also searching for "events" that influence the trend. In this approach, trends are primarily examined separately and connected to events that directly affect the future course of the trend: "TIA is a forecasting method that permits extrapolations of historical trends to be modified in view of expectations about future events" (p. 1). According to Theodore Jay Gordon, the combination of trends and events also means a combination of a quantitative predictive measures and "expert judgments," in other words, the combination of quantitative approach (based on statistical models that, in principle, can be used by anyone and should lead to comparable results in comparable situations) and an approach in which the personal, perhaps even subjective assessments of experts are included as a guide to future events.

In *The Trend Forecaster's Handbook* (2010), Martin Raymond defines a trend as "The direction in which values tend to move and which as consequential impact on the society, culture or business through which it moves." According to Raymond, a trend not only describes a change, but also the impact that that change has.

According to Henrik Vejlgaard, author of *Anatomy of a Trend* (2008, pp. 8–9), there are currently three definitions available: (1) a trend is a "progress of change," (2) a trend is product development or (3) a trend is a new product. Vejlgaard chooses the third definition, because he is primarily interested in how *trendsetters* are the first to try new products and thus help create a trend.

We want to emphasize that reading about what a trend is, is not just a semantic discussion without any practical goal. If, during the execution of a trend analysis, experts (or non-experts) are asked about trends, it needs to be clear in advance what we mean by trend. Is it really a large-scale change at a societal level, or is a new smartphone also a trend? Are we looking at changes over a 30-year period or at next year's summer? Based on the definitions discussed above and on our own experiences in carrying out trend analyses, we here describe what a trend is about. However, because it is impossible to capture that in one sentence, we mention seven relevant aspects.

1   A trend is about a change, which means it is aimed at innovation, the "new."
2   A trend can both be quantitative and qualitative in nature. We emphasize the qualitative dimension, because, if a trend is about what is "new," it is hard to

quantify. For quantitative trend analysts, historical data are proof that a trend exists, while, for qualitative trend analysts, data are meant above all to illustrate a trend. Trends are often about new personal and social values, and qualitative research is better for discovering those values than quantitative research, because quantitative research uses existing categories and concepts, which are not suitable for capturing new developments.

3   The focus on the qualitative dimension, changes and the "new" also means that basing a trend on historical data is not sacrosanct. We should not think that a trend is predictable in advance. After all, historical data do not always continue into the future. The change that is described by a trend actually means that those historical data only apply to the past, and not the future.

4   A trend has to "have a future," which relates to the expectation that a trend will last for a while. It should not be a hype, fad or some other kind of short-term change. How long *a while* is, is of course hard to determine. We want to emphasize that the concepts of short term and long term, which are often used in trend analysis, are relative concepts. For example, a ten-year time horizon is long for a company operating in the so-called *fast-moving consumer goods industry*, but short for a company operating in the infrastructure sector. The distinction between short term and long term is also reflected in the level of uncertainty of a trend. In the short term, a trend is more certain than in the long term, because in the long(er) term, the chance is greater that new trends will emerge that affect the trend that has been detected.

5   As such, a trend has a certain degree of uncertainty, because it is uncertain in advance whether a trend will in fact continue into the more distant future. But the level of uncertainty can also be determined by how one considers a trend. Some people will perceive a trend as certain, while others will not, which means that the level of uncertainty of a trend cannot just be determined objectively on the basis of a time horizon, but that there is also a subjective element due to the ideas people have about the possible course of a trend.

6   The subjectivity of a trend is also expressed in the concept of *counter-trend*, which means that different trends can occur side by side. An example is the trend of individualization: people want to be recognized as an individual and not automatically as a member of a group, which expresses itself, for example, in the fact that consumers increasingly demand customized products and services. *At the same time*, there are also trends that emphasize that people increasingly see themselves as part of a community. The truth is probably somewhere in the middle, but the fact is that trends do not have to be one-dimensional developments that apply to society as a whole. Trends (and counter-trends) can therefore be seen as so-called *tendencies*. The philosopher Roy Bhaskar uses that term to show that some laws are not as absolute as people think. An example from the social sciences is the (economic) law of supply and demand, which states that demand falls if prices increase (and vice versa). But, of course, there are plenty of products to which this principle does not apply, for instance, status symbols, the price of which rises when demand increases. That is another way to look at trends. Trends are certain

forces that have a certain influence on society, but that do not determine everything, which means that the future is not just determined by trends, but by trends and counter-trends.

7   A trend can be linked to an "event," i.e., a seemingly separate occurence that can be a symptom of a trend, and therefore a "weak signal." This means that an event can be a kind of tipping point at which a trend (or its value) transcends a certain critical value, turning it into something that can be a considered a real trend. It can also mean that an event is the start of a trend. The difference between these two functions of events also affects the shape of a trend. If the event is a tipping point, the trend is evolutionary in nature, while the trend is more revolutionary in nature and shape if the event signals the start of the trend.

A trend is never (physically) tangible, it is a *social construct* (made by humans). It is a direction in which society or a certain industry is expected to move. As such, a trend is a statement about a future situation that one expects, hopes or even fears will emerge. Of course, this statement is not made at random, but is often based on something that is tangible, or has existed, namely a historical development and/or an event in the present. So every trend has a history (the past), a starting point (the present) and a relevant future period (the future). With regard to the latter, an additional distinction can be made between the transition path toward that future situation and the future situation itself. For example, the trend that a larger portion of our energy will be provided by sustainable sources, like wind and sun, describes a change in the use of energy sources, in which some sources become less important, while other sources become more important. Ultimately, this can lead to a situation in which, compared to the past, the *energy mix* will have changed completely. It could even mean that certain energy sources (like nuclear energy) will have disappeared altogether, while other energy sources, that we currently do not know or use only marginally, will have been added. This new situation can be seen as a *bifurcation point* (or temporary plateau) from which new trends will develop.

Trends are not just changes in themselves or end situations, then, but in turn lead to other, new future situations. Look, for instance, at the consequences of digitization with regard to the way people deal with privacy. Privacy used to be something that needed to be protected at all times. But these days, more and more people are prepared to accept limitations to their privacy if that is compensated by something else, like increased social safety. In addition, digitization has accelerated people's daily lives. Nobody is willing to wait weeks for a proposition anymore. People want to know what's what at the click of a button. New generations will probably reinforce this attitude and behavior, because they are unaware of how important privacy used to be and have not developed the patience to live in that kind of world. And, of course, the question is how the future will develop from there on.

Needless to say, not every social change occurs with the same speed. Trend professionals examine signals of change. If, in 1980, a trend professional were to see a product for the first time that we nowadays call "sustainable," he would probably not see it as a "seed of change" or the start of a trend. However, if the trend professional were to read more and more articles about *sustainable* products, and were to be exposed more and more to sustainably manufactured products, overheard youngsters talking about their worries about the future of the planet and read government decisions promoting sustainability, the trend professional can conclude that social attitudes are changing and that there is a trend toward more sustainable solutions. All those "seeds of change" and signals are called *trend manifestations*. Ultimately, the different trend manifestations result in the description of a trend.

Trend Professionals

Trends do not just reveal themselves. They are not natural phenomena that occur independently of us, but developments that have a human or social origin.[1] And because trends are human made, they have to be discovered, identified and analyzed. And the people who (can) do that are difficult to capture in one word. Like trend analysis itself, the practitioners of trend analysis come in various shapes and sizes. As the reader will have noticed, in this chapter we use the term *trend professionals*. In practice other terms are used as well: trend watchers, trend analysts, futurologists or foresight experts.

In *The Trend Forecaster's Handbook*, Martin Raymond calls trend professionals *lifestyle detectives*. In other words, people who spend their time discovering patterns or changes in attitude and mentality. These changes can express themselves in the way people behave, communicate, act, eat, travel, buy, etc. In short, everything a human being does, thinks and decides. It is about a change in attitude in relation to what is or is experienced as "normal" at a given time. That change is motivated by the drive people have to move forward. That drive toward progress ultimately leads to changes in social values and standards.

Sometimes, trend professionals are jokingly referred to as people who gaze into crystal balls or predict the future. The trend professional still has a lot of explaining to do, the work has different associations with different people. It is often linked to marketing, because the difference between a marketer and a trend professional is not clear to everyone. Marketers want to know what is going on so they can sell products or services to a specific target group. Trend professionals do more than just map what is new. Trend research is about putting new products and services into context at a more abstract level. They examine changes in values and needs. Signaling new products and services is an essential element of trend research, but analyzing the change in values that they bring about is more important. The trend professional filters what is interesting in the client's sector, as well as beyond, in a broader sense, examining multiple sectors because the client often lacks the time. The marketer can then put that information to use, for instance to address the needs of new target groups more effectively. In essence, the difference between the marketer and the trend professional is also the difference between market research and trend research. Market research focuses on short-term developments in the market or sector of an organization, while the trend research (i.e., the trend professional) looks at long-term broader changes in society.

Although the practice of trend research has grown at a rapid pace, it has not yet been academically embedded. For a number of years, there are higher vocational courses that include trend analysis as an important element, like the Fontys Academy for Creative Industries in Tilburg (the Netherlands) and the Gent Hogeschool (Belgium), which offer a bachelor and post-graduate course, respectively. Perhaps this is caused by the diverse nature of trend research and the fact that it is applied in different research methods. So it is no wonder that the practitioners of trend analysis are a motley crew. Nevertheless, it is possible to distinguish various trend professionals on the basis of the following three elements.

1   *Spectrum of activities.*
    There is a spectrum of activities in which trend professionals engage. In *Road Trip to Innovation*, Delia Dumitrescu presents a pair of axes capturing the activities of trend professionals: from Watch to Interpret to Think to Act. In other words, from observing to interpreting to thinking to acting. The place within the four quadrants varies per individual. One trend professional focuses more on developing a vision, while another focuses on implementing a new idea. An automatic result of this is that there may be various end products. For instance, a trend professional can provide a vision or a concept for a new product to be marketed. Naturally, trend professionals can also move within the four quadrants.
2   *Timing.*
    In addition to the spectrum of activities, the concept of time can be used to categorize the different trend professionals. Second Sight, a Dutch trend agency, draws a distinction on the basis of time orientation. They distinguish "trend watching," with a focus on change in the present. Next, Second Sight identifies "trend forecasting," as an activity aimed at estimating changes

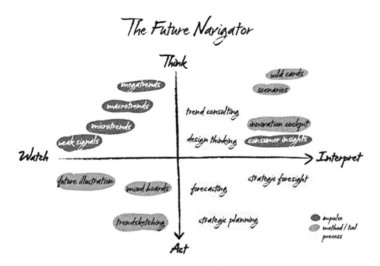

Figure 3.1 The future navigator (source: *Road Trip to Innovation* (Dumitrescu, 2012)).

within the next three to eight years. And, finally, they distinguish "futurists," who focus on the distant future, for instance 2025/2030. The time orientation indicates the scope of the research of the trend professional.

3   *Methods.*

Based on their experiences and practices, many trend professionals have developed a method of their own, with specific models and original titles. Information they are often unwilling to share with each other, due to the perceived risk of other people using the information for their own purposes. There are two categories of methods that are the most common: the intuitive approach and the use of an expert network.

Intuitive Approach

This approach is based on intuition and sees intuition as an instrument for detecting changes. The senses play an important role in every phase of this type of trend research. In this approach, it is important to be sensitive to the environment and novelty. The intuitive trend research reads a lot, hears a lot, watches a lot, lets it all sink in and tries to reflect on it. On the basis of a *gut feeling*, he or she then examines whether or not the trend can be genuinely relevant. Trend professionals can further develop this gut feeling. Through experience, it is possible to train one's intuition in such a way as to become an expert in one's field. In this approach, visual presentation is very important. A good example of that is Paris-based trend professional Lidewij Edelkoort, who uses a variety of images to visualize current developments, and who has a very specific and personal mental imagery. Often, it becomes clear very quickly when one is shown a presentation by Lidewij Edelkoort.

It is hard to capture intuition in numbers and statistics. And although the intuitive approach is not very methodical or scientific, it does match the creative nature of futures research in general, and trend analysis in particular. Trends cannot only be calculated (or that may even be totally impossible to begin with), they can also be understood with eyes and ears that are focused on what is new or unexpected, or does not fit within existing patterns.

Network of Experts

Many trend professionals do not work alone. They use the "wisdom of the crowds," which in this case does not consist of *average* people, but experts, or in other words, influencers and early adopters who are based all over the world. These selected groups of experts are all very much in touch with the "zeitgeist" and provide trend professionals with information about what is going on in the world around them. Often, for instance, their research of the new focuses on the city in which they live. In addition, trend professionals ask their network to answer specific questions on what is new, but also to give a general impression of the things that they notice around them. All this information is used as input for trend reports about current social questions and their possible future development. Generally speaking, these types of trend reports contain lots of examples of innovations. So, in this approach, the focus is not just on the knowledge and intuition of the trend professionals themselves, but more about the combination of what fellow experts signal and the findings of the network of the trend professional.

Organization of the Trend Landscape

Trend professionals are increasingly organized. There are various conferences and other meetings where they gather to discuss their area. An example of this is *La Futura*, an annual European event designed to bring trend professionals together and in which strategists, consultants and trend professionals participate. They are active in different parts of Europe. At the same time, there are local initiatives, like the Dutch Future Society, SwissFuture, Netzwerk Zukunftsforschung, Future Specialists Helsinki and the Association for Professional Futurists. The aim of these organizations is to allow professionals to learn more from each other. In a new area, this interconnection is crucial in order to find a common ground. During the La Futura meeting in Brussels in 2014, serious plans were developed to set up a joint association, the Global Trend Association. The reason for that is that trend professionals still feel underrepresented compared to other future professionals. In all their diversity, they feel the need to become a recognizable entity to their public.

Trend Research: Signaling, Analyzing and Applying Trends

Now that we have defined trend and described who or what trend professionals are, it is time to map the phases involved in using trends to get a clear idea of the future. After all, how do you signal change and how can it be analyzed? And how can trend research be applied? In the previous paragraphs, we briefly discussed a number of approaches by trend professionals. In terms of research, there are three phases in which trend analysis is applied and on the basis of which we can divide the activities of trend professionals: (1) signaling, (2) analyzing and (3) applying.

Signaling

Trends can be signaled in many ways. In Chapter 9, we describe how interviews can be used to gather information about the future, and in Chapter 11, we show how to conduct desk research into the future. That is why, in this subsection, we focus on an elementary activity of man that can be of great importance to the discovery of trends: seeing.

The start of trend research is about seeing. For many people, that in itself is a difficult task, because: where do you start looking? And what do you really see? On any given day, we see an immense number of things, but do we really absorb them and how is it possible to structure what we see?

In books like *How to be an Explorer of the World* and *On Looking*, various tools are provided. In *How to be an Explorer of the World*, Keri Smith provides practical tips and exercises on how to discover the world. Smith says: "Artists and scientists analyze the world around them in surprisingly similar ways" (2008, p. 6). Smith invites the reader to use the imagination, "to observe, collect, analyze, compare and notice patterns" (p. 7). The exercises consist of studying everyday activities, inviting the reader to pay attention when walking to the supermarket and, for instance, documenting what you see and hear on the way.

In *On Looking*, Alexandra Horowitz describes that, by focusing on specific elements, we keep the world understandable, but, in doing so, we overlook other things that happen around us. Her method of learning to look is based on two insights:

1   In the beginning, we can all *really* see, and Horowitz gives as an example that, when you buy a new house, you see that house in every detail. You absorb everything, the shapes, the structures and the space. But after a while, when you live there, you get used to the environment and you switch off that specific focus. You lose sight of the details, you even forget them. The same happens on our daily walk to the supermarket, you carry out that activity in sleep mode because it is so familiar.
2   Everybody has their own perspective and bias, and tends to see the world from their own frame, which is, for instance, formed by our profession. This means that an artist will walk around their neighborhood in a different way from a biologist. Horowitz illustrates those different perspectives by taking a walk with 11 different people.

Both Smith and Horowitz teach us that you can learn the skill of looking through renewed attention. On the basis of Smith and Horowitz, we formulate a number of basic tools to start looking:

•   Document everything you see: a sticker on a traffic light or that new coffee place may not seem immediately relevant, but they can later prove to be the missing link in your cluster.
•   Always bring a camera: it does not have to be a professional camera. The camera on a smartphone is compact and always handy.
•   Make notes about everything you see: it is hard to remember afterwards why something caught your attention.
•   Do not judge what you see: postponing your judgment can lead to surprising new insights.

With these basic tools in mind, the trend professional starts looking for signals of the "zeitgeist." By continuously observing on the street and, for instance by reading a wide variety of background articles, closely following the news, reading reports from renowned research agencies, visiting conferences and meetings, as well as exhibitions and museums, etc. As the trend professional does all this for a longer period of time, it is possible to build a personal archive that can be used for subsequent trend research.

In addition to personal observations, there are, of course, other *trend sources* as well. In Chapter 11, we describe how a meta-analysis (desk research) involving information about future developments can be carried out, while, in Chapter 4, we show how various experts can be consulted using a Delphi method. A fourth source is workshops in which different kinds of people talk and think about possible trends (see Chapter 10).

Naturally, it is perfectly possible to use these trend sources (personal observation, desk research, experts, workshops) separately, but they can also be combined or used at the same time. In the latter two cases, the question becomes how to combine and validate the acquired information.

Analyzing

Once signals of trends have been detected, the following step is to analyze them, which involves, among other things, determining what the meaning is of the signals and how they (may) relate to each other, and classifying them. There are various ways to analyze signals of trends. In this chapter, we merely specify the overall steps taken by virtually every trend professional during the analytical process.

Trend Levels

A trend consists of various levels of abstraction. Three levels can be distinguished, which influence each other and are directly interrelated. These levels have various labels, of which we mention two:

1   In *Road Trip to Innovation*, a distinction is made between the micro-, macro- and mega-level of a trend. According to Delia Dumitrescu (2012, p. 48), the micro-level is: "new, intelligent, a business model, mass market ready so you can scale it." She sees the macro-level as the result of "many forces" from our community that we cannot manipulate and that are based on changes in consumer needs. The most abstract level is the mega-level, which, according to Dumitrescu, consists of long-term developments: "collections of interlinked trends that will change the way people live and the technological products that they demand" (p. 72). Unlike the micro- and macro-level, this level is not fundamentally new, as it concerns concepts like sustainability and individualization.
2   The Dutch trend professional Hilde Roothart identifies the trend levels as micro, maxi and mega. With the way she organizes the trend levels, Roothart maps the time horizon, and with it the scope. Micro-trends are short-term trends and relate to developments in the market (products and services). Maxi-trends cover a longer time period and focus on value changes of the consumer, while mega-trends cover a period of ten to 30 years and focus on changes in society.

Analyzing with the Use of Trend Levels

Although there are various labels for trend levels, their essence is the same. The levels are interconnected and form a framework within which the analysis can take place. The question is then how you can use trend levels to analyze.

Every trend analysis starts with registering signals, or examples of the Zeitgeist. Usually, this is a mishmash of manifestations of a trend. Examples are the creation of the "Broodfonds" (translation: the Bread fund), in which self-employed professionals in the Netherlands create a joint safety net. And the minor Hacking by the Dutch Willem de Kooning Academy, where students are taught to research and adjust any type of system. Although it is tempting to focus on these manifestations, but the analytical phase is a fundamental element to transcend the product level and create one's own vision, because, it is only by creating distance that one can understand the core of the change.

One way to analyze the manifestations is to assign values to each separate manifestation. A value is something that is considered worthy of pursuit. Examples vary, from beauty to equality or independence. In 1973, social psychologist Milton Rokeach mapped a range of values, such as true friendship, freedom, equality, wisdom. A quantitative survey was used to have respondents rank which values were important to them. These values proved to be a reliable indicator for behavioral change, like political preference and religious convictions.

These values can help the trend professional to create more distance to the manifestations that are found. This is the link between Dumitrescu's micro-level and macro-level or Roothart's micro-level and maxi-level. For example, the creation of the above-mentioned Broodfonds can indicate attention to solidarity (= a value). The popularity of the new minor Hacking gives an idea about new ideas about intelligence (= a value). As such, a value can provide greater insight into the changed need that is at the basis of specific manifestations, which is not visible to the naked eye.

So it is possible to start untangling changes in people's needs by putting all the manifestations on one pile and assigning a value to each. You can assign one value, but it could also be more. After the values have been assigned, groups of manifestations emerge. For example, the value "independence" could be assigned to both the Broodfonds and the minor Hacking.

Based on those groups with similar values, the next step is to cluster them based on their relevance. Not every group of values is equally urgent. For example, the value "ease" can be assigned to almost anything, which means that its relevance is limited in the quest for innovation. A frequently used way to create an overview is to visualize clusters. Textual analysis on a computer is restricting, because meaning is assigned almost immediately. By visualizing a cluster of manifestations and making it tangible, it is possible to elicit the most innovative elements.

The question is, however: how does one determine whether a cluster of examples is innovative? That is very personal, every researcher has a different definition and different ideas. A good indicator is if the cluster still creates tension, which means that the central idea is not self-evident. It is exactly that uncertainty that makes the cluster an interesting subject for further study.

After studying the various clusters, the trend professional can proceed with filling in the structure of the cluster. In this phase, the information is examined further by looking for substantiation and additional evidence. For example, the trend professional collects more striking examples, interviews specific experts and looks for evidence to test whether the findings have a broader support.

Analyzing with the Use of the Trend Pentagram

The trend pentagram is a way to classify different trends and to value the *character* of the trend. To determine what the meaning is of the trends that have been found, there are five criteria that can be used:

1   *Possible*: is the trend possible in light of other trends or natural *laws*?
2   *Probable*: how great is the chance that the trend will actually develop?
3   *Desirable*: how much to like (or dislike) a certain trend? What are the interests or advantages of whether or not the trend will develop?
4   *Impact*: what are the (negative and/or positive) impacts of a trend, for example for an organization?
5   *Manageable*: to what extent can actors influence the course of the trend?

    The five criteria are related. For instance, probable trends are a subset of possible trends, because many trends are possible, but only a few trends will actually occur. And not all trends that have an impact will be manageable. Sometimes, there are developments that cannot or hardly be influenced or steered, for instance economic growth, the aging population of globalization. What is important here is from what perspective the trend is approached. A small company will be unable to influence most trends, but larger organizations, like national governments or companies like Apple, Shell and Google will be able to steer certain trends. For instance, a central government can affect economic growth through certain tax measures. If a country decides to increase government expenditures and finance those expenditures by levying taxes, in the expectation that that is favorable to economic growth, many companies will move their commercial activities abroad, which means that government will collect fewer taxes and the economy will shrink rather than grow.

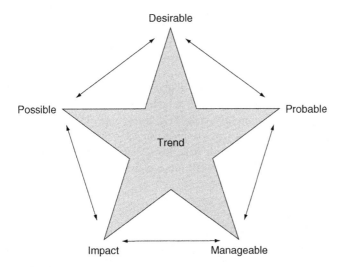

Figure 3.2 The trend pentagram.

The trend pentagram can be used in two ways:

1   To score a trend on all five indicators, so that the nature and meaning of the trend become clear. For example, if a trend has a high score on desirability, we consider the trend to be a good, positive development. And if the trend has a high score on manageable, we know that trend can be influenced (to some extent). And if the trend has a low score on probability, we know that there is a high level of uncertainty, and that it does not require immediate action, but that it does have to be monitored.

2   By combining the scores of trends on all five indicators. Because there are five indicators, there are too many possible combinations to discuss here, but we will take a closer look at some:

  •   Combination of a low score on probability and a high score on impact: the trends that fall into this category have a high level of uncertainty, but we do know that, no matter how these trends will develop, they will have a major impact on the organization or subject in question.
  •   Combination of a high score with regard to desirability and a low score on the level of probability: with regard to trends that fall into this category, it is important to examine how they can be influenced. Because it is hard to influence trends directly, the focus can be on how to influence the *trend drivers*. To determine that to some extent, it is also possible to look at how the trend scores on manageability.
  •   Combination of a high score on impact and a low score on manageability: trends in this category are a major problem for every organization, should the impact be negative, and also have a low score on desirability. The organization will be (virtually) unable to avert the danger.

The trend pentagram is not a method to detect trends, but to classify the various trends on the basis of one's position toward the trends. It is an analytical tool designed to value the nature of a trend.

DESTEP

Another way to separate the wheat from the chaff with regard to the classification of trends is by using the acronym DESTEP, which refers to the following social domains: Demographics, Economy, Social, Technology, Ecology and Politics. For a trend analysis, it is important to adopt as broad a view of the collected trends as possible. By checking if trends have been collected for every domain, one can make sure that there are no relevant subjects that are overlooked.

Trends in the Environment

Yet another way to analyze and classify trends is to determine how they relate to the organization. Trends are place in the environment of the organization (see Figure 3.3). A distinction is made between the *contextual* environment and the *transactional* environment. The contextual environment consists of *factors*, social trends (from the DESTEP domain) that have a long(er) time horizon and cannot be influenced by the organization. The transactional environment consists of developments at *actors* (like competitors, customers, suppliers, stakeholders) that have a short(er) time horizon and that are in relatively direct contact with the organization. The trends in this environment affect the organization, but the organization is also able to influence the trends.

Applying

After signaling and analyzing trends, it is time to apply them. There are various possible goals for which a trend analysis can be used, like the development of concepts, as input for innovation processes or to develop a future vision. The various goals of trend analysis make it clear that trend analysis is not a goal in itself, but a method that helps organizations get in touch with the future.

The application of trends means that trends are used in the decision-making process in organizations. In part on the basis of the goals described above, we distinguish two decision-making levels:

1   the innovation process
2   the strategic process.

The Innovation Process

Innovation, or the development of new products and services, takes time, depending on the type of innovation. Radical innovation processes take longer than incremental innovation processes. However, in both cases, it is recommended to use trend analysis, to make sure that the trends are used, because at the time when the first idea for an innovation emerges, the world will look different from the moment when the innovation is implemented, and the world has changed on the basis of a variety of different trends.

Trends can play a different role in different phases of an innovation process, like providing inspiration or for testing. Providing information includes questions like, in what direction does the future develop and what does the organization have to do to connect to all those trends? In the case of testing, relevant questions are whether or not the current concept is still *future proof* and, if not, how it can be adapted to changing circumstances.

Especially in the early phases of an innovation process, the goal of trend analysis will be to inspire, because, in this *fuzzy front end*, it is important to make the innovation idea as rich as possible, and trends play an inspiring role in that. This phase of an innovation process can be characterized as the *divergence phase*.

Later on in the innovation process, when the innovation idea is converted into a prototype and a business case is developed, the main purpose of the trend analysis will be for testing. In that phase, it is important to check whether the original trends are still relevant and whether new relevant trends have emerged that influence the prototype and the business case. This is the *convergence phase* of the innovation process.

During the innovation process, the type of trend will also change. These changes can be characterized on the basis of a selection of the tools discussed above:

- *Trend pentagram*: in the first phase, primarily trends will be used that have a high score on probability and impact, because the important thing then is to feed the future potential of an innovation idea. Later on in the innovation process, it will be more about trends with a high score on possible, probable and manageable, because at that stage, it is important to make realistic choices with regard to the further development of the innovation idea.
- *DESTEP/contextual-transactional environment*: trends based on DESTEP and in the contextual environment will primarily be used in the first phase of the innovation process. For the further development of the innovation idea in the second phase, trends in the transactional environment will predominantly be used.
- *Trend pyramid*: mega- and maxi-trends apply primarily in the divergence phase, while micro-trends are more suitable for the convergence phase of the innovation process. And, again, that has to do with the fact that broad trends with a long time horizon are a good source of inspiration, while *smaller* trends with a shorter time horizon are more suitable when it comes to specifying and implementing the innovation.

Consequently, the change in the use of trends and the type of trends to a large extent boils down to the application of broad, social trends in the divergence phase of the innovation process, and mainly of sector-oriented trends in the convergence phase. The inspirational function of the first innovation phase and the testing function of the second phase is reflected in this, as are the different time horizons of these social and sector-oriented trends. As such, in the case of radical innovations (with a long time-to-innovation), social trends will play a more prominent role than in the case of incremental innovations (with a short time-to-innovation).

The Strategic Process

The strategy of an organization can be described as the goal pursued by the organization and the decisions that the organization makes to realize that goal. In a sense, developing a strategy boils down to answering the following three questions:

1   Will our future business be the same as our current business?[2]
2   What will our business be in, say, ten years?
3   What strategic steps are needed to realize the strategy?

Because this goal will always be in the future, strategy and future (like innovation and future) are closely connected. This means that trend analysis can be used in determining and implementing the strategy of an organization. And, like innovation processes, trends can be used both for inspiration and for testing.

There are many different kinds of strategies and ways in which strategies are constructed (Mintzberg et al., 2009). It would go too far to provide a complete overview here. So we limit ourselves to two relevant dimensions (Van der Duin and Den Hartigh, 2009):

- Does the reasoning start from the market or from the organization? That is, is the future influencing the organization or is the organization influencing the future?
- Is the reasoning basically static or dynamic? That is, is the future linearly predictable, or is the future continually created?

We can link the former dimension to the environment model described above, with a contextual and transactional shell. Figure 3.3 contains an arrow pointing from the contextual environment toward the organization, which means that the reasoning starts from society and/or the market. This is also called *outside-in* thinking. There is also *inside-out* thinking, which means that the organization influences the environment. The latter dimension refers to the level of predictability of the future based on trends. If we combine the two dimensions, the model shown in Figure 3.4 emerges.

In every *strategic perspective*, the strategy process is different, depending on whether or not one thinks the environment can be influenced and how dynamic the environment is. Because the future has a different character in each of the four quadrants, the nature and role of trend analysis will also be different:

- Outside-in and static: trend analysis focuses above all on trends with a low level of uncertainty and on trends in the more immediate environment of the organization.

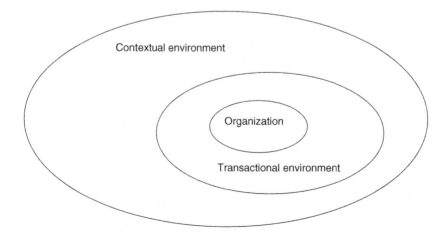

Figure 3.3 The contextual and transactional environment of an organization.

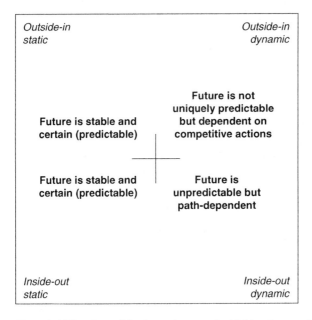

Outside-in
static

Outside-in
dynamic

**Future is stable and
certain (predictable)**

**Future is not
uniquely predictable
but dependent on
competitive actions**

**Future is stable and
certain (predictable)**

**Future is
unpredictable but
path-dependent**

Inside-out
static

Inside-out
dynamic

Figure 3.4 The place of the future in strategic thinking (source: Van der Duin and Den Hartigh, 2009, p. 340).

- Outside-in and dynamic: trend analysis focuses not only on social trends, but also on the strategic actions of the organization. The social trends and these strategic actions together shape the future.
- Inside-out and dynamic: trend analysis focuses above all on uncertain trends, because the future cannot be predicted, but the number of possible strategic actions is not limitless. The future is unpredictable and cannot be shaped, but the organization does preclude certain futures through certain strategic choices that were made at an earlier stage.
- Inside-out and static: trend analysis focuses above all on the certain trends in the immediate environment of the organization and on the strategic ambitions of the organization.

For the design of the trend analysis, it is therefore important first to determine in what kind of environment the organization operates and to what extent the organization can influence its environment. Outside-in strategic processes will focus more on using the inspirational function of trend analysis, while inside-out strategic functions will tend to emphasize the testing function of trend analysis. In addition, in a static environment, the trends in the more immediate (transactional) environment of the organization are most important, while, in a dynamic environment, the broader, social (contextual) trends have to make up the bulk of the trend analysis.

From the point of view of the trend pentagram, in the case of outside-in processes, the focus will primarily be on trend with a high score on possible and impact, while, in the case of inside-out processes, the focus is on trends that are manageable, probable and desirable.

Final Remarks

The order of the paragraphs in this chapter suggests that trend analysis is a linear process, in which trends first need to be signaled, then analyzed and finally applied. Although this is the most logical and common order, we want to emphasize that the trend analysis does not always have to be linear. It is also possible that, when applying trend analysis, a need emerges for other trends, for instance because trends need to be used for testing and the kinds of trends do not lend themselves for that. Or that the trend analysis shows that the current set of trends is incomplete and that certain trend categories are under- or overrepresented.

In addition, the different phases of the trend analysis can overlap or at any rate not always be easily distinguished. For example, the trend categorization proposed by Hilde Roothart can be used as a way to cluster and then analyze the trend manifestations. But at the same time, it can be used as a perspective for looking at possible seeds of change.

We also want to emphasize (again) that gathering and analyzing trends is not a goal in itself, but a way to improve the decision-making process. In this contribution, we looked at innovation and strategy, but there are other types of decisions for which trend analysis can also be used. This also means that, if we look at the distribution of time and effort among the three phases of trend analysis, most time should be spent on applying the trend analysis, because that is where the trend analysis stops being a goal in itself and becomes an instrument. Although signaling and analyzing trends is important, it is of little value if the results are not applied in practice.

Incidentally, the link between trend analysis and the decision-making process can have different levels of intensity. Roughly speaking, there are three ways (Van der Duin, 2006, p. 159):

- Ad hoc: in this case, trend analysis and the decision-making process are two separate activities, often also on an organizational level. Trends are applied incidentally, for instance during workshops.
- Integration method: trend analysis and the decision-making process are often different (organizational) processes, which is why it is often necessary to develop a separate tool or method for the application of trend analysis in the decision-making process.
- Full integration: in this case, trend analysis is a complete and integral element of the decision-making process. For example, in some organizations, it is mandatory to use trends in the decision-making process, making them an integral element.

Each level of intensity has its pros and cons. The ad hoc integration offers the trend professional a great deal of freedom to fill in his own agenda, but the drawback is that the link with the decision-making process is difficult and requires a lot of persuasion. The advantage of the integration method is that the link between trend analysis and the decision-making process is fairly intensive, but it is necessary to develop a separate instrument. A major advantage of full integration, finally, is that both the process and the results of trend analysis are taken seriously, but the integration into the decision-making process probably gives the trend professional less freedom and (therefore) fewer opportunities to signal *out-of-the-box* trends.

Notes

1 We are aware that this position is debatable. After all, is climate change not a trend that can be viewed as a natural phenomenon but that, at the same time, is considered by many to be the result of human activities? Perhaps trends in the natural environment are by definition not human made...

2 If the answer to this question is *yes*, the next two questions do not have to be answered. Incidentally, we do not think that, in the light of dynamics of the times in which we live, whenever a company answers this question in the affirmative, that company will not have the same business ten years from now, but no business at all...

References

American Council for the United Nations University, the Millennium Project, *Futures Research Methodology version 3.0.*

Duin, P.A. van der (2006). *Qualitative futures research for innovation*. Delft: Eburon Academic Publishers, PhD thesis.

Duin, P.A. van der and E. den Hartigh (2009). Keeping the balance: exploring the link of futures research with innovation and strategy processes. *Technology Analysis and Strategic Management*, Vol. 21, No. 3, pp. 333–351.

Duin, P.A. van der, R. van Oirschot, H. Kotey and E. Vreeling (2009). To govern is to foresee: an exploratory study into the relationship between futures research and strategy and policy processes at Dutch Ministries. *Futures*, Vol. 41, pp. 607–618.

Dumitrescu, D. (2012). *Road trip to innovation: how I came to understand future thinking*. Hamburg: TrendOne.

Fowles, J. (1978). *Handbook of futures research*. Westport, CT: Greenwood Press.

Gordon, T.J. (1994). Trend impact analysis. In *Futures Research Methodology version 1.0*, American Council for United Nations University – the Millennium Project.

Hill, K.Q. (1978). Trend extrapolation. In John Fowles (ed.), *Handbook of futures research*. Westport, CT: Greenwood Press.

Horowitz, A. (2013). *On looking: a walker's guide to the art of observation*. New York: Scribner.

Makridakis, S. and S.C. Wheelwright (1987). *The handbook of forecasting: a manager's guide*. New York: John Wiley & Sons.

Mintzberg, H., B. Ahlstrand and J. Lampel (2009). *Strategy safari*, 2nd edition. Harlow, UK: Prentice Hall.

Raymond, M. (2010). *The trend forecasters handbook*. London: Laurence King Publishing.

Rokeach, M. (1973). *The nature of human values*. New York: The Free Press.

Smith, K. (2008). *How to be an explorer of the world*. New York: Penguin Books.

Van der Duin, P.A., R. Drop and A. Kloosterhof (2001). *The world of future studies according to KPN Research*. Leidschendam: KPN Research.

Vejlgaard, H. (2008). *Anatomy of a trend*. New York: McGraw Hill.

4   The Delphi Method

Vincent Marchau and Erik van de Linde

Introduction

For decades expert judgments have been used to support decision-making and make predictions about the future within several problem areas (Gupta and Clarke, 1996). In particular, for those problems for which empirical data is not available and extrapolation from past observations is insufficient for valid forecasts, the expertise and insights of experts are considered to be of potential utility (Helmer, 1988). In practice, it is usually difficult to meet each member of a group of experts individually, as they might be distributed all over the world. Another option is to collect the group of experts at a single place at a single time. However, as experts are busy people it is often difficult to organize such a meeting from a logistical point of view. Furthermore, in such meetings communication among experts is generally stimulated. This has the advantage that divergent individual opinions, due to, for instance, misunderstandings, different perceptions, divergent knowledge etc., can be discussed straightaway. On the other hand, enabling communication between participating experts could also have some negative effects. For instance, some individuals might dominate other members of the group because of their professional position or vocal capabilities. Others might be less communicative or reserved within group settings, in particular when their individual opinion is extreme as compared to the general opinion.

The Delphi method concerns a specific way of surveying. It is a survey technique by which respondents are repeatedly and independently interrogated, usually by means of questionnaires, about issues under study. Initially, Delphi studies aimed at reaching consensus among experts on future technological developments, by confronting each expert in subsequent interrogation rounds with the differences of between his/her individual opinion and the group opinion and ask the expert to confirm or revise his/her individual opinion. The level of consensus as desired by the researcher mostly determined the number of interrogation rounds. The group opinion was then formed by the opinion in this latter round. Over the past years, the Delphi method has evolved into a method which is also useful to identify diverging opinions or dissensus among respondents. In this case, the Delphi method is not used to forecast technological developments but to identify possible opposing views on the solutions of a major policy issue (Turoff,

1975). This so-called policy Delphi may support a committee to decide on a policy issue by: exploring all different positions on this issue, estimating the impact and consequences of alternative solutions and estimating the acceptability of the preferred option (Steinert, 2009).

The Delphi method has often been used in practice as it has among others proven its forecasting capabilities and can be applied straightforwardly to several fields of interest (Parenté and Anderson-Parenté, 1987). In particluar, Coates (1975) labelled the Delphi method: "A method of last resort," a method to be used if all other methods would not deliver useful results.

Development of the Delphi Method

The Delphi method was originally developed for military applications at the RAND Corporation by Olaf Helmer and Norman Dalkey in the early 1950s. Next, the Delphi method became recognized as a useful method for technology forecasting by American business and industry. Since then, the Delphi technique has been applied within different problem domains across the world (for an overview of Delphi applications see, e.g., Gupta and Clarke, 1996; Linstone and Turoff, 2002).

The first published study by RAND to forecast technical and scientific developments using the Delphi method was written by Gordon and Helmer (1964): *Report on a Long Range Forecasting Study*. This is the first documented and publicly available application of the Delphi method with the aim to obtain the most reliable consensus opinion of a group of experts (Linstone and Turoff, 2002). The study focused on a specification of technical and scientific developments for the next ten to 50 years on topics including automation, space progress, war prevention and weapon systems. The Gordon and Helmer study inspired, among others, the establishment of the Netherlands Study Centre for Technology Trends (STT) in the end of the 1960s by the Netherlands Royal Institute of Engineers (KIVI). According to the KIVI, the Netherlands should have a similar think-tank for future studies. Later on, the Delphi method was applied in other areas within public policy-making (forecasting trends in, e.g., economics, health and education) and business (e.g., forecasting new product sales).

Initially, the main goal of the Delphi procedure was to reach consensus among a number of experts regarding the issue under investigation (Sackman, 1975). As soon as a desired level of consensus had been reached, the final group position was determined by calculating the average. While the Delphi method was initially applied for forecasting developments using expert opinions, nowadays the method is more characterized as a systematic, structured communication process – not limited to forecasting and not limited to the opinions of experts only. The underlying idea is that "more heads know more than one" if and only if the group opinion is formed in a controlled and systematic way. Today, there are different variants of Delphi studies, related to the purpose they serve, including:

- forecasting future developments within a certain problem area;
- identifying and exploring possible, future alternatives for a problem area;

- structuring the problem area in order to create the common ground to develop common policies.

Initially, Delphi studies were conducted by using paper and pencil, in which respondents had to write down their scores and their arguments for those scores. A typical question within a traditional Delphi study involved in which period the respondent thought that a particular development (e.g., geostationary satellites) would be feasible. Sometimes periods had to be estimated with probabilities of 10, 50 and 90 percent. The analysis of the response was limited to indicating the median and the distribution of the experts' opinions. As information- and communication technology became more mature, Delphi-online applications emerged, such as TechCast of the University of Washington and George Mason University. Many "group decision" and "acceleration" rooms can be considered as instrumented versions of the Delphi method. Over the past years, "real-time or e-Delphi" emerged, using computers, electronic devices and Internet to improve the speed, number of participants, scope and reliability at decreasing costs within Delphi studies (Gordon and Peas, 2006; Hsu and Sandford, 2012). However, it remains important to comply with basic scientific and procedural Delphi principles, such as the selection of participants, evaluations and the processing of arguments. Overall, the quality of the results of a Delphi-study is determined by: (a) the quality of the briefing and questions, prepared by the research team, and (b) the willingness of the participants to invest time and energy into answering the questions and supplying arguments for their opinions.

Pros and Cons of Using the Delphi Method

Each method to study the future has its pros and cons. The strength of the Delphi method is its ability to explore, independently and objectively, issues that require personal judgment (Gordon, 1994). Here the assurance of the participant's anonymity, controlled feedback and iteration and a statistical group response should result in reliable conclusions. The Delphi technique should provide more accurate judgments than those techniques which might be attained by interacting groups or by individuals (Rowe et al., 1991). In case a researcher has to choose between alternative forward-looking methods, the following reasons might support the choice for the Delphi method (Linstone and Turoff, 2002):

- The complexity of the problem is too large to be handled by analytical methods (e.g., modelling, simulation); it requires (subjective) opinions of experts and/or stakeholders.
- The participants required for studying the complex problem have different types of knowledge and expertise and are not (or scarcely) interacting about the problem.
- It is not possible, within the constraints of research time and budget, to visit the required participants individually or have group meetings.
- The interaction between participants can be improved through structured communication.

- The level of difference in opinions between participants requires anonymous communication.
- The heterogeneity of individual opinions should not be affected by group interactions. Think of a halo effect that develops when one or two individuals dominate the conversation, or a bandwagon effect, when participants are intimidated into silence or mask real opinions to be seen as agreeing with the majority (Tersine and Riggs, 1976).

In contrast, some researchers were very skeptical about the Delphi method. For instance, Sackman (1975) states that "The future is far too important for the human species to be left to fortune tellers using new versions of old crystal balls. It is time for the oracle to move out and science to move in." Over the years, some important points for attention should be taken into account when setting up and executing a Delphi study:

- The selection of experts should be handled with care. Given the objectives of the study, the variety of expertise pursued should be made explicit. The selection of non-experts could give a "garbage in garbage out" effect (Webler et al., 1991).
- Experts usually are extremely busy people. Consequently, the possibility and willingness of experts to participate in a Delphi study is often a problem together with the possibly increasing drop-out rate over subsequent question rounds (Jillson, 1975).
- The Delphi organizers deal with the interpretation of responses, intermediate feedback and final results. All responses are thus subjectively filtered through by the Delphi organizers before being seen by anyone else (Sackman, 1975).
- The reliability and accuracy of the results should not be overestimated (Woudenberg, 1991). The results are based on opinions with regard to future developments, to a high degree assuming a lack of surprises. Almost by definition we know that this assumption is not valid.
- Finally, the frequently used stopping criterion for the number of interrogation rounds in Delphi studies (a predefined level of consensus within the group) is arbitrary (Maasen and Van Vught, 1984). This measure does not give any information on the consistency of the individual answers over different rounds. Hence, at group level consensus might appear after a few interrogation rounds, whereas individual participants have given significantly different answers between subsequent rounds. As such some "false consensus" might exist within the group.

Throughout the years, several variants of the traditional Delphi technique have been developed and applied in order to improve the quality of the results by using, for instance, partial anonymity, a different number of iterative question rounds (ranging from two to ten), controlled feedback of opinions of specific groups within the panel (specialists versus generalists), statistical group responses varying from one single number to complete distributions of opinions, weighing opinions according to the degree of expertise, etc.

Doing a Delphi Study

Steps in a Delphi Study

In general, a Delphi study consists, by means of questionnaires, of a series of repeated interrogations or rounds of a group of individuals whose opinions or judgments are of interest. After the initial interrogation of each individual, each subsequent interrogation is accompanied by information about the preceding round of responses, usually presented anonymously. The individuals are thus encouraged to reconsider and, if appropriate, to change their earlier response in the light of replies of other members of the group. Hence, the Delphi method is used to facilitate communication on a specific task. Central characteristics of the Delphi method are anonymity of responses, iteration, controlled feedback to the participants and statistical group response (e.g., Rowe et al., 1991):

- Anonymity: participants are approached and act anonymously, as social interaction among participants could negatively influence the individual opinion. Anonymity should enable participants to judge the subject of interest on its merits only, without possible dominance of some experts or group conflicts. It should provide more accurate judgments than those produced by techniques which involve interacting individuals.
- Iteration: the Delphi method consists of a number of repeated interrogations or rounds. After each round participants are allowed to modify an earlier reply. The number of repeated interrogations usually depends on the degree of consensus defined by the Delphi organizers.
- Controlled feedback: after each round participants are confronted with both the group opinion and their individual opinion. Participants are hereby encouraged to evaluate their earlier replies with respect to the group opinion. The intermediate group response is often represented by some descriptive statistics (frequencies, median, mean, variance, etc.), although arguments underlying individual opinions can also be included.
- Statistical group response: after the final round the group opinion is represented by an adequate measure for the central tendency of opinions. Often, the dispersion of opinions is given as well, as this indicates the degree of consensus among the experts.

Hence, the main steps of the Delphi method are:

1 the selection and briefing of participants;
2 the anonymous interrogation of participants;
3 the analyses of and feedback of (intermediate) results.

In practice, conducting a Delphi study, requires many more (small) steps, including (e.g., Linstone and Turoff, 2002):

1 The composition of a research team.

2   The selection of participants – based on the type and level of expertise required to handle the problem.
3   The design of a draft questionnaire.
4   The pretest of the draft questionnaire (e.g., on unambiguous language, clearness of questions, length of the survey).
5   The distribution of the revised questionnaire among the participants (first round interrogation).
6   The analysis of the responses given in the first round.
7   The design, pretest and distribution of the second round questionnaire showing: (a) the first round opinion of the specific participant and (b) the first round, group opinion. Next, participants are asked to evaluate their earlier answer with respect to the group opinion.
8   The analysis of the responses given in the second round.
9   Repetition of steps 7–9 over subsequent rounds in order to obtain a predefined level of stability in the answers (note: not necessarily consensus).
10 Reporting the final results.

Practical Considerations when Doing the Steps in a Delphi Study

The implementation of the steps above depends to a large extent on the budget, facilities and time frame available for the study. For instance, some research groups have advanced group facilitation tools at their disposal. If so, the questions can be pre-programmed using these tools and the participants can submit their answers from a terminal. In this case, anonymity is considered less important as compared to the speed and efficiency of data collection. Moreover, unwanted interactions among participants are limited, as each participant has his own terminal for giving his/her opinion. Other research organizations have access to a web-based application for collecting (expert) opinions. The big advantage of such a tool is the independence of time and place for data collection. A Dutch example of such an Internet-based tool is Synmind (www.synmind.com), which collects opinions and argumentation regarding predefined statements. The opinions are displayed in "Synmind graphs," which give an overview of the differences and similarities of opinions. Opinions can next be adjusted by the participants.

Selection and Briefing of Participants

The selection of experts is always considered an important issue in the set up of a Delphi study, as the quality of a Delphi outcome strongly depends on the quality and completeness of the input. In general, the selection of experts is guided by (Helmer, 1988): (a) the determination of the variety of expertise needed for the problem under study, and (b) the identification of the experts for each part of this variety. Once the participants have been selected, it might be useful to explain and discuss the problem definition in more detail. This should ensure that all participants have a similar problem definition. Ideally, if time and budget allow, the participants are interviewed in advance in order to improve the quality of the questionnaire. Moreover, the interviews can be used to emphasize the importance of participation in the Delphi study. Experience shows that, in this way, the participation improves in terms of willingness to participate and quality of responses given. Finally, in order to maximize the completeness of the panel, each interviewee can be asked to name the main experts he or she knows in this field. If these recommended experts are not already selected, they can be included in the panel.

Anonymity and Willingness to Participate

Next to anonymity, other incentives are often required to stimulate individuals in participating in a survey. In order stimulate participation, a final report with all the results of the survey can be promised and/or a price can be offered through some lottery. Filling in two or more rounds of questionnaires requires a serious effort of the participant. The question is why one would participate if he/she remains anonymous? The reasons include (a) that an expert is motivated by the fact that his/her expertise is required to study the topic surveyed, and/or (b) the expert is interested in the opinions of other experts on the topic surveyed. Finally, participation can be stimulated by unambiguous questions, with clear response options, and of an appropriate length. Salancik et al. (1971) calculated that a sentence length of 20–25 words works best.

Analyses and Feedback

The analysis and feedback of the (intermediate) results involves, in essence, a confrontation between the opinion of the individual participant and the (distribution of) answers within the group. Often a scoring scale is used in this context (most used are a five- or seven-point scale). Based on some measure for central tendency (e.g., average, median) respectively distribution of all scores (e.g., standard deviation, interquartile range), the individual participant can quickly position his/her score and, if necessary, reconsider his/her opinion in a subsequent round.

Delphi researchers often state that statistical analysis and feedback only has no meaning without the underlying arguments for these scores. Feedback is only useful if it stimulates a participant to rethink his/her original argument in light of the arguments of other participants and, if necessary, adjust this score. Here, a balance has to be found between the amount of feedback and the length of the survey (as this can easily explode over subsequent rounds if all arguments are included). Finally, the frequently used stopping criterion for the number of interrogation rounds in Delphi studies (a predefined level of consensus within the group) is arbitrary (Maasen and Van Vught, 1984). This measure does not give any information on the consistency of the individual answers over different rounds. Hence, at group level consensus might appear after a few interrogation rounds, whereas individual participants have given significantly different answers between subsequent rounds. As such some "false consensus" might exist within the group. In order to avoid "false consensus," first the consistency of individual answers between rounds should be checked. Several experts might change their judgments substantially between two rounds, whereas the average group opinion as well as the dispersion of opinions does not change, due to compensating effects at the individual level. Only if the individual answers are consistent between consecutive rounds, can the consensus indicator be validly interpreted. A way to operationalize and measure this individual consistency is given by Chaffin and Talley (1980) using the so-called "individual stability of answers": the idea that the response frequencies of two subsequent rounds do not differ significantly from each other.

Examples of Delphi Studies

In this section, three Delphi studies are presented in short for illustrative purposes. The first study involves the Long Range Forecasting Study by Gordon and Helmer (1964) being the first published Delphi study. The second study involves an exploration of the future of electronic driver support systems (Marchau and Van der Heijden, 2000), as this study did not focus on predicting (vehicle) technology futures but on the uncertainties surrounding those predictions (and how to handle these uncertainties). Finally, the study of Van de Linde and Van der Duin (2011) entitled "The Delphi method as early warning" is presented, because it uses the Delphi method to detect early signals of future developments – a new application.

Report on a Long Range Forecasting Study

This study aimed at specifying important events or items for the next 50 years. Six broad themes were distinguished: scientific breakthroughs, population growth, automation, space progress, probability and prevention of wars, and future weapon systems. The results of this study included predictions, the motivation of participants for their predictions, the variation in opinions among participants, the convergence among participants' opinions after getting feedback and, of course, the shortcomings of the Delphi method and ways to improve this. Some resulting predictions were: (1) a territorial conflict will emerge about parts of the Earth that are covered by water; (2) another world war is highly likely and ways of preventing this are lacking; (3) continued automation will lead to social turbulence, indicating the need for regulations; (4) the development of nonproperty destroying weapons that attack on a biological or psychological level; (5) the unbalanced distribution of energy, food and raw materials, stimulating global tensions.

For each of the six themes, a separate panel of experts was composed. Of the 150 invited people, 82 participated in the study of which 35 were RAND employees, seven were RAND consultants and the other 40 were not affiliated with RAND (six of them were European). There were four rounds of questions, the time interval between two successive rounds was about two months. Per theme, experts were questioned in the first round on what they thought would become important items or events for their theme. In the next round, each panelist had to indicate when they expected that the item or event would happen.

For example, the panel on scientific breakthroughs indicated after the first round that 49 possible items could have a major impact on society in the coming 50 years, three of which were:

1   molecular biology: chemical control over heredity;
2   popular use of personality control drugs;
3   reliable weather forecasts.

In the second round, respondents were invited to estimate the probability of actual implementation of these items for the different time-intervals shown in Table 4.1.

Given each respondent's probability distribution the year was determined for which the respondent thought an item would be implemented with a probability of 50 percent. Next, the median and quartiles of these "50 percent-years" were determined. For the items presented above this gave the results shown in Table 4.2.

So, one-quarter of the respondents estimated that reliable weather forecasts will occur before 1972 with a chance of 50 percent; half of the respondents thought this would be before 1975, and a quarter of the respondents thought this would be after 1988. Given these findings, the researchers concluded that for ten out of the 49 items "reasonable consensus" existed. This consensus was fed back in the third round and respondents were asked to give a motivation if they disagreed with the majority consensus. Of the remaining 39 items (about which there was unreasonable consensus), the researchers selected 17 items of which they thought to be of interest for further exploration. These were represented also to the respondents in the third round (together with the level of consensus) and a request for motivating disagreement from the majority. Some items were rephrased as the researchers assumed that ambiguity of the original phrasing had partly caused the lack of consensus. After round 3, the median was found to shift a little earlier or further in time. No explanation was presented for this shift. But, more important, the dispersion decreased, or in other words, the consensus increased. For round 4, a similar procedure as for round 3 was followed: some items were left out (still no reasonable

Table 4.1 Panel on scientific breakthroughs, second round results

1963–1965	1972–1978	1997–2013
1965–1968	1978–1986	later than 2013
1968–1972	1986–1997	never

Table 4.2 Panel results

	Median	Quartiles
Molecular biology: chemical control over heredity	1993	1982–2033
Popular use of personality control drugs	2050	1984–2050
Reliable weather forecasts	1975	1972–1988

consensus), announcement of sufficient consensus about some items and some items were rephrased. The consensus in the responses of round 4 was considered sufficient, and these estimates were taken as final.

Figure 4.1 presents the final estimates of the panel on scientific breakthroughs. Note that the panel showed considerable consensus about the fact that some items will only happen in the far future or even never. In addition, the panel expectations

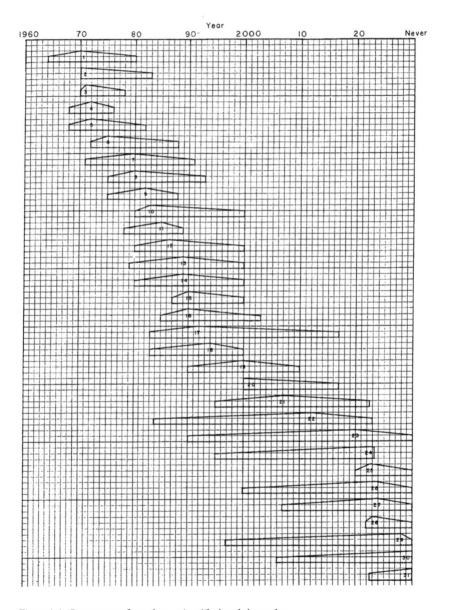

Figure 4.1 Consensus of panel on scientific breakthroughs.

Key
1 economically useful desalination of sea water;
2 effective fertility control by oral contraceptive or other simple and inexpensive means;
3 development of new synthetic materials for ultra-light construction;
4 automated language translators;
5 new organs through transplanting or prosthesis;
6 reliable weather forecasts;
7 operation of a central data storage facility with wide access for general or specialized information retrieval;
8 reformation of physical theory, eliminating confusion in quantum-relativity and simplifying particle theory;
9 implanted artificial organs made of plastic and electronic components;
10 widespread and socially widely accepted use of non-narcotic drugs (other than alcohol) for producing specific changes in personality characteristics;
11 simulated emission ("lasers") in X and Gamma ray region of the spectrum;
12 controlled thermo-nuclear power;
13 creation of a primitive form of artificial life (at least in the form of self-replicating molecules);
14 economically useful exploitation of the ocean bottom through mining (other than off-shore drilling);
15 feasibility of limited weather control, in the sense of substantially affecting regional weather at acceptable cost;
16 economic feasibility of commercial generation of synthetic protein for food;
17 increase by an order of magnitude in the relative number of psychotic cases amenable to physical or chemical therapy;
18 biochemical general immunization against bacterial and viral diseases;
19 feasibility (not necessarily acceptance) of chemical control over some heredity defects by modification of genes through molecular engineering;
20 economically useful exploitation of the ocean through farming, with the effect of producing at least 20 percent of the world's food;
21 biochemicals to stimulate growth of new organs and limbs;
22 feasibility of using drugs to raise the level of intelligence (other than as dietary supplements and not in the sense of just temporarily raising the level of apperception);
23 man–machine symbiosis, enabling man to extend his intelligence by direct electromechanical interaction between his brain and a computing machine;
24 chemical control of the aging process, permitting extension of life span by 50 years;
25 breeding of intelligent animals (apes, cetaceans and so forth) for low-grade labor;
26 two-way communication with extra-terrestrials;
27 economic feasibility of commercial manufacture of many chemical elements from subatomic building blocks;
28 control of gravity through some form of modification of the gravitational field;
29 feasibility of education by direct information recording on the brain;
30 long-duration coma to permit a form of time travel;
31 use of telepathy and ESP in communications.

about relevant items seemed clearly influenced by the background of the RAND employees in the early 1960s. This involved a military background, as is clearly noticeable, for example, in the opinions of the respondents about a possible next war. Some items and opinions seemed to have been strongly influenced by the spirit of the age, some seemed more stated as self-fulfilling or self-denying prophecies and some seem now up to date. The reader may judge for himself. Space limitations do not allow us to give an overview of all the results of this study. These can be found in the full report at: www.rand.org/pubs/papers/P2982.html.

Finally, a methodological reflection was presented for this study on typical Delphi characteristics (such as dispersion, confidence intervals and other elements) to underline the limited validity of the results. These elements include the changing composition of participants in the panels (resulting in dropouts), the two month period among subsequent interrogation rounds (too long), wording of stated items (some theorems proved to be ambiguous) and expertise panelists (specification and assessment of the level of expertise of respondents appeared difficult). In addition, the implementation period of several items seemed hard to predict as their implementation followed a gradual, developing pattern. Also, a claim was made that respondents with diverging opinions should have been challenged more to come up with convincing arguments. Without those arguments, the other participants appeared not willing to take these "outliers" seriously. It is concluded that consensus could be controlled for some items while for other items differences remained or were even strengthened. Altogether it was concluded that, although the method used had quite some shortcomings, these issues were not that fundamental to disqualify the Delphi method in general.

Policy Aspects of Driver Support Systems Implementation: Results of an International Delphi Study

In the 1980s and 1990s, driver support systems were generally assumed to contribute to public traffic goals. However, much uncertainty existed about their future: technology development, market introduction and impacts on driver and traffic behavior. An international Delphi study, collecting expert opinions on these issues, was performed in the late 1990s to reduce these uncertainties (Marchau and Van der Heijden, 2000). In three interrogation rounds opinions were collected from 50 experts from the USA, Japan and Europe.

The study focused on those functions which are generally considered to be a first steps toward fully automated driving, as well as on the autopilot itself. They included (see Figure 4.2):

- Speed/time headway support or adaptive cruise control senses the presence and relative velocity of vehicles ahead of the equipped vehicle, and provides

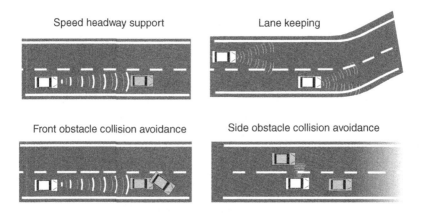

Figure 4.2 Basic driver support systems toward automated driving.

warnings and/or adjusts the speed of travel to maintain a correct separation between vehicles. Vehicle speed is adjusted either by downshifting, throttling or braking.

- Front obstacle collision avoidance support senses the presence and speed of vehicles and objects in front of the equipped vehicle and would provide warnings and/or control of the vehicle speed (downshifting, throttling or braking) to minimize risk of collisions with vehicles and objects in the vehicle's lane of travel.
- Lane keeping support provides assistance to the driver through lane monitoring and determining the safe speed for road geometry in front of the vehicle. Drivers are advised and/or the vehicle is temporarily controlled in order to avoid impending road departure.
- Side obstacle collision avoidance support monitors the lane position, relative speed and position of side objects and advises the driver and/or controls the vehicle steering in case of a potential collision during a lane-change maneuver.
- The autopilot automates all driving tasks. Steering, throttling and braking are fully taken over by technology, allowing hands-off and feet-off driving.

In the questionnaire, among others, experts were asked to indicate the period of market introduction and the user costs for each of these systems. Furthermore, respondents had to indicate for which type of user groups and for which specific roads a system will become available at initial market introduction. The next step was to assess the importance of the barriers for a system's market introduction and/or further developments, using a five-point scale. Several barriers were presented based on a review of recent literature. Respondents however could add missing barriers during the first round of interrogation. Finally, the experts indicated the relative importance of several public policy measures to overcome these barriers.

Experts were selected based on: (1) expertise needed for this study (technology development and implementation in the field of driver support systems); (2) prominent persons with recent publications in these fields; and (3) additional experts recommended by the initial selected experts. As stated above, the number of rounds of a Delphi study depends on the reaching of a sufficient degree of consensus. After two rounds consensus within the response group was considered to be sufficient on most issues. Where consensus was lacking, respondents were invited to review their opinion in a third round and, irrespective of changing their previous answer, to comment on their final choice. In the first round 117 participants were invited to participate, 65 of which returned a filled-in questionnaire. Of the 65 questionnaires sent out in the second round, 50 were returned; 40 of them answered the questionnaire in the final round. These response rates were quite satisfying, given the considerable amount of work asked from the respondents for filling in the questionnaires. In Table 4.3 the response is further specified in terms of the participants' geographic background and affiliation.

The degree of expertise of the selected participants was measured on a four-point scale (see Table 4.4). Between 86 percent (for speed headway keeping) and

Table 4.3 Response with respect to geographical background and affiliation

Background respondents	Questionnaires sent out	First round response	Second round response	Third round response
Europe	58	39	30	21
North America	42	16	13	12
Japan	17	10	7	7
Government	12	7	6	6
Industry	31	16	13	9
Consultancy	35	24	17	12
University	39	18	14	13
Total	117	65	50	40

58 percent (side obstacle collision avoidance) of the response group indicated to have at least average expertise on a system. Only three respondents (6 percent) indicated that they had limited expertise on each system.

With regard to the (further) introduction of driver support systems, the study confirmed the evolutionary implementation process (see Table 4.5). In the short term, i.e., before 2005, there was consensus that various warning devices for driving support would enter the market, next to vehicle following systems with limited deceleration capabilities.

In summary, the Delphi study suggested that the, often expected, evolutionary development of driver support systems was not at all obvious. There still existed many barriers which obstructed successful implementation. Only for the short term, i.e., before 2005, did there exist a strong consensus that warning devices for speed headway keeping, lane keeping and obstacle avoidance would become (further) available, next to vehicle-following systems with limited deceleration capabilities. The introduction of more advanced systems taking temporary control of the vehicle in dangerous situations was still considered to be uncertain. Overall, systems were initially expected to be of use on motorways only, and to be adopted by professional drivers and fleet operators. The study further pointed out that the contribution of most support systems to road capacity gains and reduction of environmental impacts were (highly) uncertain. Moreover, safety improvements may be achieved but these were strictly limited to those driving

Table 4.4 Expertise of response group with respect to different systems ($n = 50$) (%)

System expertise	Speed headway keeping	Front obstacle collision avoidance	Lane keeping support	Side obstacle collision avoidance	Autopilot
(1) Major	38	24	24	16	30
(2) Average	48	52	46	42	34
(3) Minor	14	24	28	36	32
(4) No expertise	0	0	2	6	4

Table 4.5 Expected period of market introduction of each system (n = 50)

System	Speed headway keeping		Front obstacle collision avoidance		Lane keeping support		Side obstacle collision avoidance		Autopilot
	Warn	Control	Warn	Control	Warn	Control	Warn	Control	
Period Median[2]	1[1]	2	2	3	2	3	2	4	4.5
Interquartile range[3]	(1–2)	(1–2)	(1–2)	(2–4)	(2–2)	(3–4)	(2–3)	(3–4)	(4–5)

Notes
1 1 = before 2000; 2 = 2000–2005; 3 = 2005–2010; 4 = 2010–2020; 5 = after 2020; 6 = never.
2 Group opinion: half of the respondents score lower, half of them higher.
3 Dispersion of opinions: interval containing the middle 50% of the scores.

situations for which the system was designed and these could easily be counter-measured by more risky driving behavior. Furthermore, for each type of support various systems could become available with different operating characteristics. It was unclear how this diversity would affect total traffic performance. Most uncertain seemed the implementation of the auto-pilot, due to various technical as well as non-technical arguments. As the implementation of more advanced driver support systems appeared to be very uncertain, a stronger focus on systems that could be implemented in the short term was required. For the mid-term, i.e., up to 2010, the Delphi study pointed out that the implementation of the first driver support systems would be dominated by market opportunities for these first systems. Therefore, it was important to gain insight into the preferences of the market and the willingness of potential users to purchase such driver support systems.

The Delphi Method as Early Warning

In the first decade of this century, the Netherlands (among others), was confronted with its share of terrorism. Examples were the murder of columnist and film producer Theo van Gogh, the murder of politician Pim Fortuyn, and threats to the lives of other politicians, among others Geert Wilders and Ayaan Hirshi Ali. In response, the need for fighting terrorism increased. To do this efficiently and effectively, a thorough understanding of the preceding process of radicalization was needed. In other words, to understand what goes on in the minds of people for them to become radicalized to the point of terrorism. In particular the Dutch government stated the following research question: Which global societal trends relate to future radicalization and subsequent terrorism in the Netherlands? In order to answer to this question, a study was performed based on the Delphi method (Van de Linde and Van der Duin 2011). The reasons for applying the Delphi method were that this method seemed particularly suited for the purpose of study, required limited means and a short time frame, and published literature on exploring future terrorism using the Delphi method was lacking.

An inventory of 200 global societal trends and a literature study of radicalization together served as input for the participants in the Delphi study, including:

- trends in demography, ecology, natural resources (e.g., climate change, shortage of drinking water);
- trends in Politics-Institutions (e.g., increase of failed states and lawless territories, politicizing Islam, commercialization of the media (shallower political debate));
- social-economic trends (e.g., increasing differences in GDP per capita between countries, China will economically outgrow the USA, the difference between low and high income will continue to rise);
- science and technology trends (e.g., broadband communication networks connecting everyone and everything, speech recognition and speech synthesis, tropical diseases migrate to Western countries);

• trends in culture, rules and regulations, values (increasing pressure on universality of human rights, decline of liberal market orientation – as centrally regulated economies perform better, globalization challenges local culture).

In the first round, which was conducted in writing and anonymously, participants were asked to score all of the 200 trends with a score of 1–5 indicating the expected level of influence on radicalization processes, "1" representing no influence at all, and "5" representing a very strong influence. Also, when a score higher than "1" was given, they were asked to provide supporting arguments for that score. Of 167 trends the median score was between 1 and 2, indicating consensus among participants that most trends had no influence on radicalization, and they agreed on almost all of those trends. Thirty trends showed a median score of 2–3.5, indicating some influence on radicalization. Of these, five trends scored 3–3.5. Only three trends resulted in a median score of 3.5–4, indicating a strong influence on radicalization. These were: (1) increasing hatred against Israel, (2) politicizing Islam and (3) globalization of Jihadism. When broadly summarizing the consensus of the first round, six themes emerged (in decreasing order of priority):

1   tensions between church/state: politicizing Islam, globalization of Jihadism (median 4);
2   demography: megacities, migration, homeless, overpopulation (median 3);
3   economy: joblessness (especially youth), difference in growth (median 2);
4   infrastructure and basic needs: scarcity of food and water (median 2);
5   governance: failed states, lack of trust (median 2);
6   culture: confrontations between "the West" and "the East" (median 2).

Although this consensus points at very likely or indeed existing relationships between trends and radicalization, that result was of limited interest to the client, as these relationships were already known. Also, in this round no additional trends were suggested. In this study, the differences of opinion (dissensus) was further focused on. The differences in scores between participants was striking. Some hardly ever scored higher than "2," whereas others used scored "4" and "5" quite often. In 50 trends, there were participants that scored "1" while all others scored at least two scores higher. In 20 additional trends, there was one participant who scored at least two scores higher than others.

In round 2 the trends in which strong dissensus was found were subjected to reconsideration and reargumentation. The feedback given consisted of a limited selection of seven to eight trends per participant in which they were confronted with an either much higher or much lower median score. They were asked to reconsider their scores and then either to change them, or not to change them. In the latter case, they were asked to provide a convincing argument against changing. As a result, 30 scores were changed and no longer showed strong differences and 40 scores were unchanged and continued to show strong differences, all but four with associated argumentation of mostly one short sentence of ten words on average. It was hypothesized that the 30 scores that were adjusted were to be considered "noise," while the remaining 40 were not. Also, ten additional trends were provided including reasons to add them. Clearly, participants were better stimulated to provide additional trends in round 2 than in round 1, as in round 1 they did not provide additional trends at all.

In the second round, participants were also asked to indicate which trends they would prefer to discuss in the focus group meeting. The idea here was that, in this way, optimal participation in the focus group as well as a most lively exchange of thoughts would be stimulated. In summary of the answer to that question, we could propose the following general discussion topics (in order of participant preference):

- social and cultural tensions and confrontations between "the West" and "the East";
- disfunctioning and failing states;
- politicizing Islam, and globalization of Jihadism;
- unemployment and major differences in economic growth.

The focus group meeting was a three-hour, face to face meeting with an independent chairman (a professor of future research) in which participants discussed the limited set of topics defined by the dissensus analysis. This provided a large number of interesting statements, arguments, views and insights relative to the need of the customer. When, for instance, stating that social and cultural tensions and confrontations between "the West" and "the East" can cause radicalization and terrorism, six participants agreed and three disagreed, all with associated arguments. Arguments in favor were, among others: this is exactly what is going on right now, multipolarity of global powers strengthens conflict dynamics, new world powers have anti-Western sentiments, tensions are a direct result of the interest of the West in oil. Arguments against were, among others: no clear relationship between globalization and global tensions, migrants are primarily focused on improving their own situation and urbanization leads to greater tolerance and solidarity. Each "dissensus topic" was discussed in this way in the third round.

In conclusion, in this Delphi study on radicalization and terrorism for the National Coordinator for Counterterrorism of the Netherlands, it turned out to be possible to obtain new notions of future radicalization using differences in opinion regarding the relationship between global societal trends and radicalization processes. Such notions were the boy problem (surplus of boys in selected countries may lead to radicalization of young men that cannot find work or marry), the gender problem (emancipation of women in selected countries may lead to radicalization of men that cannot accept the new status of women), differences in human rights between East and West, the black-and-white modern media, etc. It emphasized the importance of exploring divergence of opinion with the Delphi method as an early warning research tool, as opposed to convergence ("consensus"). This study hypothesizes that in those cases where the opposite views that were discussed kept their ground, this Delphi study may have found early warnings of future radicalization. The essence of this study is that it is possible, with limited effort, to get a handle on the complex and poorly defined subject of global societal trends influencing future radicalization. Application of the Dissensus Delphi method provided a selection of early warnings that may be looked into with future research.

Practicalities when Applying the Delphi Method

After more than 50 years of experience with the Delphi method, some dos and don'ts emerged for researchers that are planning to use the Delphi method:

1 The researcher should not provide his/her opinion regarding the subject under study to the participants, i.e., he/she should stay as neutral as possible in the instructions, questions and feedback.
2 The Delphi method is not always a good approach for communication within a group (some problems might require more in-depth interaction on opinions to specify underlying arguments, perceptions, etc.).
3 The researcher should be careful with summarizing or rephrasing opinions and arguments of participants as this might induce bias. Often, it is better to use the original answers.
4 Attention should be paid to all the opinions and arguments of all participants, including those of outliers.
5 Participants often invest a lot of time and effort in giving their opinion; rewarding participants supports the response rate and quality.
6 The results of a Delphi study are often at disposal of policy- and decision-makers, but the participants are not responsible for the policy chosen or decision taken.
7 The time periods among different interrogation rounds should be as short as possible.
8 Opinions and arguments should not be led to the participant from whom these originate. Anonymity of the participants can only be stopped based on personal approval.
9 Logical propositions/questions and self-explanatory, intuitive scoring scales should be used. In addition, ambiguity in the phrasing should be avoided as much as possible.
10 In addition to questions about the subject under study one should also ask for certainty about the opinion, the level of expertise, etc.
11 The communication with respondents should be handled with care; attention should be paid to courteous and clear feedback to the participants, including formal letters, etc.
12 If there is a final, non-anonymous round included in the Delphi study, an independent chairman with natural authority is required.

Once the Delphi study has been done, attention should be paid on how to link the outcomes to decision-making. There is a clear distinction between the role of a Delphi study within a decision-making process and the study itself. Participants in the study do not have no responsibility for the decision-making process and the resulting decision. If this principle is not followed, opinions and arguments are likely to be influenced and the resulting opinions unreliable and/or reflecting strategic behavior of participants.

Some Last Reflections

We already reflected on the pros and cons of using the Delphi method to gather expert opinions. In summary, the disadvantages of the Delphi method are typically related to the aims and the set-up of the study. If one for instance tries to forecast the market introduction of future technologies, focusing on reaching consensus among experts, the results might be disappointing. Instead, the opinions of experts might be more useful to identify and evaluate barriers to technology implementation, as well as to research underlying reasons for different opinions. A problem is the limited number of experts usually included in a Delphi study, and therefore not enabling for statistical grounding of the arguments. Furthermore, the degree of consensus on aggregate level might be misleading as a stopping criterion for the number of rounds. Instead, one should focus on the individual stability of expert opinions over different rounds and explore the reasons for diverging opinions. Other pitfalls related to the execution of Delphi studies have been mentioned and it appears that many of these disadvantages can be handled by taking appropriate measures when setting up a Delphi study.

On the other hand, as compared to other expert opinion techniques, the Delphi method can be considered most appropriate, due to its proven validity, in terms of consistent results of the different studies, and limited use of research resources. Furthermore, the Delphi method appears to be a well-established tool which can be applied straightforwardly. More than 50 years after the first application of the Delphi method, there is still no end to the application and development of the method. Much effort has been spent over the last years on the use of ICT to improve the speed of data collection and include a larger group of participants, independent of time and place. At the same time, there is still a substantial level of "handwork" required. For example, the selection, recruiting and retaining of participants requires a serious effort. Also, the development of criteria for consensus and dissensus are not given by ICT. But, the Delphi method has the distinctive advantage of the arguments and the iterative feedback.

References

Chaffin, W.W. and W.K. Talley (1980). Individual stability in Delphi studies. *Technological Forecasting and Social Change*, Vol. 16, No. 1, pp. 67–73.

Coates, J.F. (1975). Review of Sackman Report. *Technological Forecasting and Social Change*, Vol. 7, No. 2, pp. 193–194.

Gordon, T.J. (1994). The Delphi method. In J.C. Glenn (ed.), *Futures research methodology*, Version 1.0, American Council for United Nations University – The Millennium Project, Washington, DC.

Gordon, T.J. and O. Helmer (1964). *Report on a long range forecasting study*. Santa Monica, CA: Rand Corporation.

Gordon, T.J. and A. Peas (2006). RT Delphi: an efficient, "round-less" almost real time Delphi method. *Technological Forecasting and Societal Change*, Vol. 73, No. 4, pp. 321–333.

Gupta, U.G. and R.E. Clarke (1996). Theory and applications of the Delphi technique: a bibliography (1975–1994). *Technological Forecasting and Social Change*, Vol. 53, No. 2, pp. 185–211.

Helmer, O. (1988). Using expert judgement. In H.J. Miser and E.S. Quade (eds.), *Handbook of systems analysis: craft issues and procedural choices*. New York: John Wiley & Sons.

Hsu, C.-C. and B.A. Sandford (2012). The Delphi technique: use, considerations, and applications in the conventional, policy, and on-line environments. In C.N. Silva (ed.), *Online research methods in urban and planning studies*. Hershey, PA: IGI Global.

Jillson, I.A. (1975). The national drug-abuse policy Delphi: progress report and findings to date. In H.A. Linstone and M. Turoff (eds.), *The Delphi method: techniques and applications*. Boston, MA: Addison-Wesley.

Linde, F.J.G. van de and P.A. van der Duin (2011). The Delphi method as early warning: a brief study on future radicalisation and terrorism in the Netherlands. *Technological Forecasting and Societal Change*, Vol. 78, pp. 1557–1564.

Linstone, H.A. and M. Turoff (eds.) (2002). *The Delphi method: techniques and applications*. Boston, MA: Addison-Wesley.

Maasen, P.A.M. and F. van Vught (1984). The Delphi methode: voorspeltechniek en beleidsontwikkelingsinstrument. *Beleidsanalyse*, 13e jrg, no. 13 (in Dutch).

Marchau, V.A.W.J. and R.E.C.M. van der Heijden (2000). Introducing advanced electronic driver support systems: an exploration of market and technological uncertainties. *Transport Reviews*, Vol. 20, No. 4, pp. 421–433.

Parenté, F.J. and J.K. Anderson-Parenté (1987). Delphi inquiry systems. In G. Wright and P. Ayton (eds.), *Judgmental forecasting*. Chichester, UK: John Wiley & Sons.

Porter, A.L., A.T. Roper, T.W. Mason, F.A. Rossini and J. Banks (1991). *Forecasting and management of technology*. New York: John Wiley & Sons.

Rowe, G., G. Wright and F. Bolger (1991). Delphi: a reevaluation of research and theory. *Technological Forecasting and Social Change*, Vol. 39, No. 3, pp. 235–251.

Sackman, H. (1975). *Delphi critique, expert opinion, forecasting and group processes*. Lexington, KY: Heath.

Salancik, J.R., W. Wenger and E. Helfer (1971). The construction of Delphi event statements. *Technological Forecasting and Social Change*, Vol. 3, No. 1, pp. 65–73.

Steinert, M. (2009). A dissensus based online Delphi approach: an explorative research tool. *Technological Forecasting and Social Change*, Vol. 76, No. 3, pp. 291–300.

Tersine, R. and W. Riggs (1976). The Delphi technique: a long-range planning tool. *Business Horizon*, 51–56.

Turoff, M. (1975). The policy Delphi. In H.A. Linstone and M. Turoff (eds.), *The Delphi method: techniques and applications*. Boston, MA: Addison Wesley.

Webler, T., D. Levine, H. Rakel and O. Renn (1991). A novel approach to reducing uncertainty: the group Delphi. *Technological Forecasting and Social Change*, Vol. 39, No. 3, pp. 253–263.

Woudenberg, F. (1991). An evaluation of Delphi. *Technological Forecasting and Social Change*, Vol. 40, No. 2, pp. 131–150.

5 Technological Forecasting

Scott W. Cunningham and Jan H. Kwakkel

Introduction

This chapter discusses technological forecasting. Technological forecasting at its heart is a systems approach to analyzing emerging technology, and anticipating future growth and trends. As such technological forecasting is not associated with any one method. Rather, technology forecasting is a discipline that uses a variety of techniques for studying and anticipating the emergence and diffusion of new technologies. However, this chapter provides an in-depth example of trend extrapolation, one of the more emblematic approaches used in technological forecasting.

Technological development itself is discontinuous. Freeman and Perez hypothesize that there have been five major waves of technological development in the modern world. Like Kondratieff and Schumpeter postulated before them, these waves restructure economies and reshape national infrastructures. These waves have been variously postulated to be economic, demographic or innovative in character. The first industrial revolution involved steam, canals and the cotton gin. The second involved steel and railways. The third wave consisted of electricity and industrial chemistry. The fourth wave was composed of automobiles and petrochemicals. By this theory, we are in the long winter before the newest information age of the economy.

The role of technology forecasting depends on where in the wave one finds oneself. Late in the wave of new technologies, when markets are saturated and growth is deeply uncertain, technological forecasting approaches have typically thrived. Interest often continues well into the "spring" of the new wave of technology, until trends become clear, and new opportunities become locked into the system. Later, when markets are mature and prosperous, planning for the future typically stagnates.

The chapter provides a brief historical background of technological forecasting. The chapter then transitions into a more detailed accounting of trend extrapolations of new technologies' work. More specifically a brief discussion of the dynamics of technological change, following the famous work of Frank Bass, is provided. An extensive example of growth curve modeling is presented, using the case of broadband Internet adoption in the Netherlands. The chapter demonstrates how simple Excel modeling tools can be used to perform non-linear regression, and thereby to anticipate future growth trends given a technological time series. The illustration also shows how to provide a robust forecast by considering a range of possible explanatory models for the same data set.

Historical Background of Technology Forecasting

Technology forecasting has its roots in the late nineteenth and early twentieth century. This is the period in which the modern nation state emerged. This came with a variety of challenges, such as the administration of professional bureaucracies, the governance of large economic and technical networks, and a growing awareness of the mixed character of technological progress. The methodological origins of technology forecasting were derived from statistics. Early statistics involved the systematic tabulation of demographic and economically significant data. Such data was essential to the functioning of emerging national governments and bureaucracies. Statistics became increasingly coupled with probability – the analysis of uncertain events. What remained a challenge at the onset of the twentieth century was the reasoning back from observed events to their presumed natural causes. One prominent school, based on controlled experimentation and the neutrality of the researcher, was developed at this time. This approach, called frequentism, still informs the design of trend analysis and regression techniques.

The early emphasis on data collection and analysis was soon remedied with a variety of alternative technological forecasting techniques. During World War II and its aftermath, applied mathematics became strongly coupled to state interests. Military planners and, later, think tanks, were some of the earliest innovators in the field of technological forecasting. This close alignment of technologists and the state later led to the critique that professional bureaucracies were closed, technocratic and endorsed only a limited set of potential values.

Many of the modern techniques of technological forecasting were laid down in their present form in the 1960s to late 1980s. Advances were made in many fronts – in the area of expert opinion, modeling and simulation, monitoring, scenario analysis and trend extrapolation. Related work in systems thinking, strategic planning and serious gaming also saw pioneering use in the field of technological forecasting. With respect to trend extrapolation, Fisher and Pry (1971) and Bass (1969) worked on adapting and modifying bio-statistical techniques to the needs of technology analysis. In the 1960s to 1980s, technology forecasting became a discipline. This is also reflected in the emergence of a number of academic journals including *Technological Forecasting*, and a number of prominent reference books, including books by Martino (1972) and Porter et al. (1991).

Arguably the field is currently in a period of adaptation and recoup. Concern with planning and the future diminished through the 1990s as the principle technologies of the age of petroleum and automotive reached maturity. Worldwide economic shocks, and an awareness of the need for sustainable use of current petroleum energy reserves, have set the stage for a long winter decline. We may feel already familiar with the information age, but the true social and economic transformations of the age may still be ahead. A series of choices are emerging for the new technological revolution, including green energy, nanotechnology, smart networks and devices, localized production and worldwide Internet adoption. Revolutionaries, with cell phones in hand, have acquainted the world with the transformative power of publicly sourced media. As the recession of the late 2000s recedes, we foresee a new sense of optimism and a desire to make progressive choices in the face of technological uncertainty.

It is rapidly becoming clear how technological forecasting will grow to adapt to these changes. The Internet is increasingly used as an instrument for forecasting. A broader range of data is being used for monitoring and analysis. A new social awareness has been introduced to technology forecasting. Prediction markets are informing expert opinion techniques. The analysis of social and economic networks is rapidly being incorporated into technological forecasts. New modes of technology governance are being entertained, including radical systems of design and innovation. There may be a renewed emphasis on the analysis of argumentation and discourse, emphasizing the role of practical and pragmatic forms of communication in shaping technology. Necessary for this analysis may be a coherentist approach that examines whole systems of ideas, beliefs and propositions. Any single proposition succeeds or fails only in proximity to other claims about society and technology. Thus, the early methodological choices made by the logical positivists may have come full circle.

The State-of-the-Art in Trend Extrapolation Methods

There is a vast and multi-disciplinary literature on technological diffusion. A subset of this literature builds upon the modeling of technological diffusion, noting the following stylized fact: technological diffusion typically follows an S-curve. If this is in fact the case, it should be possible in principle to track growth and anticipate future developments using extrapolation methods.

The leading model of technological diffusion is the generalized Bass model (Bass et al., 1994). This model is best fit using non-linear regression (Meade and Islam, 2006). Although the Bass model is the best, all-purpose model for forecasting diffusion, there are many others. Meade and Islam (2006) list 18 others. Resistance to the use of the Bass model stems from the fact that more parameters are required for estimation than some of the simple alternatives. Simpler models are often better in use for actual forecasts (Martino, 2003).

In the remainder of this section a review of the state-of-the-art in technology adoption and diffusion is provided. This review leans heavily on three recent review papers (Meade and Islam, 2006; Peres et al., 2010; Geroski, 2000). The review is motivated by Geroski (2000) which notes "if we are going to think creatively about public policies toward diffusion, we may need to think reflectively about how we think about technology diffusion." As a result, Geroski provides three different mental models which underlie models of technology diffusion: epidemic modeling, choice modeling and population modeling.

Epidemic models regard technological diffusion as if it were an innovative outbreak, which is spread to others through a process akin to contagion. These models place the features of the technology in a central role. The epidemic process may behave differently at different stages of the life cycle (Peres et al., 2010). As is the case in real epidemics, some new technologies fail to reach a critical threshold. Serious models of technological diffusion ought to consider failure of adoption as a real possibility. Epidemic outbreaks occur with multiple variations of the main pathogen. And, like any real epidemic, technologies emerge on the market in multiple variation. Future such models should consider the fact that technologies come to market in multiple variations (Geroski, 2000).

Choice models emphasize the central role of the adopter in making the choice to utilize a new technology. Users are heterogeneous, with a small population being early adopters and having a very low threshold to accepting new products. Rogers was among the first to consider technological adoption in heterogeneous populations (Rogers, 1962). Other choice modeling approaches require that we consider diffusion in social networks, and consider network externalities (Peres et al., 2010). Given the importance of social networks and culture it is not surprising that there should be cross-national effects in technological diffusion (Peres et al., 2010; Meade and Islam, 2006). And, since choice plays a central role in these models, features such as price, performance or marketing can and should be incorporated (Meade and Islam, 2006). Note that Bass argues that price and advertising are already implicitly subsumed within the generalized form of the model (Bass et al., 1994).

Population modeling regards the population of firms disseminating the technology as the central feature that should be modeled. The number and health of these firms in turn determine the success with which products diffuse through the marketplace. In the ecological literature, such a phenomena is known as density dependence. Geroski (2000) argues that the analogous technological and economic processes involve competition and legitimation. The competition effects on growth are well acknowledged with a large body of applied models (Peres et al., 2010). Other significant models in this space invite a more detailed modeling of technological generations, and also technological substitutions.

Current research activity, and indeed future activities, will continue developing on these three fronts of epidemic, choice and population modeling of technological diffusion. These three models place, respectively, the technology, the consumer and the supplier in a central role when conceptualizing the societal activity of technological diffusion. In addition, we expect continued growth in the applied literature, where these models are actually put into practice. Finally, we expect there will be a heightened emphasis on using technological diffusion models despite missing, or limited, data sets (Meade and Islam, 2006).

Description of the Technique

Technology forecasting then attempts a comprehensive, whole-parts analysis of the relationship between technology and society as a whole. It does not endorse a single methodology, but rather entails a multi-methodology combining the strengths and weaknesses of a number of methods. The approach used for critiquing forecasts is based on case studies and so-called "natural" experiments (Cook and Cambell, 1979).

Somewhat confusingly this systems methodology behind technology forecasting is being used in service of a range of distinct problems. The resultant approaches share much of the systems methodology in common; yet bear different names depending on the specific problem being addressed. Table 5.1 shows a range of *problématiques* and the somewhat more specialized discipline, which has emerged to address these specific kinds of technological forecasting problems.

Technology forecasting is broad both in method, as well as in its attempted framing of technological problems. For this reason the material which follows will focus more narrowly on one of the five principal methods of technology forecasting mentioned earlier. In particular, we will provide a sharper focus on trend extrapolation techniques. As will be discussed below, a general and data-oriented approach to technology forecasting delivers many different kinds of trend extrapolation models. We focus more narrowly on a class of trend extrapolation models informed by a theory of technological growth, adoption and change.

Trend extrapolation is not the principal method of technology forecasting, but it is among the oldest. It has certainty been shaped by the discussion of analyticity, reductionism and the role of empirical data in futures planning. Many of the critical assumptions of technology forecasting are embedded in trend extrapolation. When we are reflective of the strengths and weaknesses of trend extrapolation as a method, we can also reflect on the status of technology forecasting as a discipline.

Central Principles of Trend Extrapolation

Technology serves a set of functional needs for both consumers and society as a whole. Trend extrapolation techniques require us to evaluate and measure the functional capability of new technologies. The technique assumes that technological progress is often quite orderly, and therefore that past technological progress

Table 5.1 *Problématiques* and the analysis of technology

Name	Problématique
Foresight	Supporting national and public decision-makers in anticipating the early stage of technological growth, and thereby directing policy in the support of national goals.
Tech mining	Supporting decision-making in the private sector by electronically monitoring a range of publicly available sorts of information about science, technology and innovation.
Technology assessment	Anticipating the unintended consequences of new technology. The approach is not limited to environmental impacts, although this is a major field of interest.
Technology roadmapping	Enhancing coordination between diverse public and private actors with the goal of achieving a common, desirable set of technological achievements.

may be a good indicator of continuing future progress in technological development. These assumptions of continuity are somewhat troublesome, and are discussed further below. Despite these concerns retrospective evaluation of trend evaluation techniques reveals that it delivers relatively affordable, actionable and objective results to decision-makers.

The needed investment in delivering a trend extrapolation model depends in part on the purposes for which it is used. There are five different levels of trend modeling: descriptive modeling, naive modeling, causal modeling, predictive modeling and strategic modeling. Descriptive models summarize previous progress, often with simple numerical or graphical techniques. Naive models attempt to recognize trends or patterns in the data. Such simple trends might be an accurate description of the future, but are subject to trend breaks or discontinuities when underlying forces change. Thus the next level of causal modeling attempts a causal explanation of the changes in technological performance. Additional modeling rigor is needed to attempt an explanation of technological change under new, unforeseen future circumstances. A final level of modeling requires strategic analysis. Technological outputs are often jointly determined by the collective choices made by producers and consumers. Future plans made by the decision-maker with a technological forecast in mind will often be acted upon and compensated by the choices of other stakeholders in the system.

The technique is quite demanding with regard to data. Adequate historical data is needed for a given technology. Hard rules to evaluate data sufficiency are not available, and perhaps cannot be formulated even on first principles. Roper et al. (2011) offer the following pragmatic advice. Extrapolate only as far as

$$F = \frac{H^2}{16}$$

where H is the number of historical periods available in the dataset, and F is the number of periods which you choose to forecast into the future. For instance, if you have eight years of historical data, this heuristic recommends only forecasting four years into the future. Later in the chapter we provide some practical, spreadsheet-oriented techniques for assessing the robustness of forecasts in light of your data.

Further, the correct technological attributes of progress must be selected, which in turn requires some technical knowledge involving the technology itself. Technological functionality can be measured either directly or indirectly. Direct measurements of technology involve performance characteristics. Performance characteristics can be in terms of good attributes – such as velocity, processing speed or energy output. Performance characteristics can also be in terms of reducing bad outputs – such as fuel consumption, cost or pollution output. Direct measurement and extrapolation of technological performance is often known as trend extrapolation or technometrics. These models are usually descriptive or naive in character.

Indirect measures of technological performance are possible as well. Total adoption of a given technology is often a measure of whether the technology is adequately meeting societal needs. The total adoption of a given technology can be measured using units such as total units shipped, or total numbers of households subscribed. Indirect measurement of performance, using adoption measurements, is often known as growth or adoption modeling. When two technologies are being compared, and one is over-taking the other, the approach may be called technological diffusion modeling. These models are often causal in character, and with sufficient additional rigor may be suitable for predictive or strategic purposes.

The following sections provide a detailed example of using a model to anticipate technological diffusion. In particular, we use a growth model to anticipate the penetration of broadband technologies across households in the Netherlands. This narrower focus affords a more detailed, in-depth example of technological forecasting using one particular trend extrapolation approach. Despite the narrow focus, the Bass model discussed below, is among the most general purpose extrapolation techniques available. The approach used in estimating the model, nonlinear regression, can be re-applied to alternative model forms. Furthermore, the technological dynamics behind the Bass model incorporates some of the simpler models of technology adoption and diffusion. The technological dynamics of the Bass model are discussed further below.

Technological Dynamics and Bass's Model of Diffusion

Early attempts to understand technological dynamics were opportunistic, and somewhat haphazard in character. Potentially relevant models from biology or demography were adapted to the purposes of technological forecasting. While sometimes startlingly accurate depictions of technological growth resulted from these models, they were poorly formulated in terms of the underlying causal forces of technological growth, and therefore how these forces might be affected or altered by the tactics of technological decision-makers.

Everett Rogers offered an early and comprehensive account of technological diffusion. Rogers's book, *Diffusion of Innovations*, was a pioneering contribution to the field of sociology of technology. In particular, Rogers attempted to explain why certain technologies and ideas diffused more rapidly through society than others. Technological diffusion, as Rogers explained, is strongly influenced by the positive word-of-mouth across peers in a social system.

Frank Bass sought to transform Rogers's qualitative and sociological theory into a mathematical model of technological diffusion. A mathematical model can enable us to understand technological diffusion, and possibly predict or shape its future course. The resultant paper, which characterized technological diffusion, is considered one of the most influential works in the field of management science. Bass attempts to explain the fraction of new consumers adopting a new technology in a given year.

Bass explains and predicts this fraction with two terms. First, he presumes that there is a fixed pool of potential technological consumers which will adopt the technology only once during the full life cycle of the technology. This means that those who have already adopted the technology limit future growth. Second, he presumes that adoption is driven by word-of-mouth. There are always consumers who will buy a new technology without consulting peers. But there is also a group who wait to be persuaded by the positive experiences of others.

Bass's formula is derived as follows, where A is the cumulative number of adoptions over time, and the derivative of A is the yearly adoption rate of the technology:

$$\frac{dA}{dt} = \text{(pool of available customers) (word-of-mouth)}$$

We must further formulate the pool of available customers, and the word-of-mouth component of the model. Let M be the total size of the potential market, in terms of consumers, shipped units or households, as appropriate. Then the pool of available customers at any given time is the total available market minus those who have already adopted the technology.

$$\text{(pool of available customers)} = (M - A)$$

Decomposing the equation still further, word-of-mouth is offered by some fraction of the total potential market who will purchase the technology regardless of the word-of-mouth. Then there is a fraction of those who purchased the technology, q, who will provide a positive word-of-mouth encouraging others to also purchase. In this formula the parameter p, which is unconditioned on actual purchase, is known as the co-efficient of innovation. The parameter q, which is conditioned on the number of customers who have already purchased the technology, is known as the co-efficient of imitation.

Multiplying through, we have the following differential equation which given specific parameters to the model fully determines the ideal trajectory of technological adoption and diffusion:

$$\frac{dA}{dt} = (M - A)(pM + qA)$$

This differential equation may be solved using differential calculus. This results in the following equation of technological adoption as a function of time.

$$A(t) = \frac{M - Me^{-(p+q)(t+t_0)}}{1 + \frac{q}{p}e^{-(p+q)(t+t_0)}}$$

In this equation e is an exponent, and t is a measurement of time. Most practical examples involve time in years or in quarters. In many real world examples we will have a partial time series – that is, we will begin monitoring a technology after diffusion is underway. Thus, the first year of our available data is not the first year the technology is introduced to the marketplace. This equation has an adjustable parameter, t_0, which can be adjusted to estimate the first year of the technology being introduced.

This equation will be further utilized in the example below where we forecast the cumulative adoption of broadband technologies in the Netherlands. Yet another useful form of the Bass equation is the following:

$$\frac{dA(t)}{dt} = \frac{(M(p+q)^2 e^{-(p+q)(t+t_0)})}{(p+qe^{-(p+q)(t+t_0)})^2}$$

This equation might be used if the data was provided in terms of yearly shipments. Consider for example radio frequency identification (RFID) tags which are used to tag consumer goods, baggage or even livestock. World shipment of these devices is reported in terms of millions of units shipped per year. On the other hand, we don't know the cumulative units shipped over all years that RFID tags have been produced. The yearly form of the equation (shown above) is therefore useful for this purpose.

As noted above, the Bass dynamics are quite complex, and encompass several simpler models. When the potential market is very large, and the technology is newly introduced, the Bass model represents a pattern close to that of exponential growth. When the coefficient of innovation is very low, the Bass model approximates the dynamics of a Pearl curve. The Pearl curve, adopted by analogy from biology, represents a symmetrical S-shaped pattern of growth. When the coefficient of imitation is very high, the Bass model approximates a Gompertz curve. The Gompertz curve, adopted by analogy from demography, represents an asymmetric pattern of growth. More of the adoption occurs earlier, since consumers are not awaiting further information from their peers.

Model Estimation and Software Support

The Bass account of growth is deterministic. In reality data is noisy and information is incomplete. We need to introduce noise into Bass's framework in order to determine the best possible fit of data given Bass's dynamic theory of technological diffusion. The simplest and easiest approach is simply to add a source of noise on top of Bass's model (see equation below).

$$A(t) = \frac{M - Me^{-(p+q)t}}{1 + \frac{q}{p}e^{-(p+q)t}} + N(0,\sigma^2)$$

This model lends itself to non-linear regression. Given a source of data about technological adoption (A), our goal is to evaluate the Bass model parameters (M, p, q). During the course of fitting the data it becomes possible to evaluate the degree to which there is uncertainty in the model (represented by the variance σ^2).

There are many merits to using spreadsheet programs, such as Microsoft Excel, for growth curve modeling. Spreadsheets provide a structured and visual approach for analyzing data and communicating the results to decision-makers. Further, programs such as Microsoft Excel have built in optimization capabilities, as well as the capabilities to support the robust decision-making through searching through an exhaustive space of possible models given the data. The next section provides a hands-on approach to using the non-linear optimization and Monte Carlo simulation features of Excel in order to do a small, but complete, growth curve analysis.

Illustration

The following section provides an example of trend extrapolation in service of technological forecasting. The typical steps in trend extrapolation are:

1   gathering of the data;
2   setting up the worksheet;
3   estimating the trend;
4   interpretation of the results;
5   robustness and sensitivity analysis.

In this illustration we will follow these same steps.

Gathering the Data

There is extensive data regarding broadband penetration across the world (OECD, 2015). Broadband access involves high bandwidth access to data, video or voice; a level of access which was previously not available. In this example we choose to forecast future penetration of broadband Internet in the Netherlands. The Netherlands is interesting as a case because of a highly urbanized corridor in the west of the country where broadband has spread extremely rapidly. Although the example uses Netherlands data, the procedure shown is completely general and could be applied to data from any nation or region. The figure of merit used in the forecast is penetration – the percentage of Dutch households that have adopted broadband Internet services.

Technological forecasting is in service to decision-making. In this instance, a decision-maker interested in the future of broadband Internet could be either a public or private actor. The public sector is often concerned with broadband penetration, as it is an enabling technology for supporting a range of information age industries and services. Further, regional authorities may have a vested interest in monitoring the progress of broadband adoption, perhaps with an intention of providing additional stimulus if broadband adoption falls below desired levels. A final public service interest may be in enhancing public accountability. The appropriate design of electronic governance services or websites may require knowledge of future public acceptance of broadband technologies. Private sector parties may be interested in providing future network access. Alternatively, a private sector decision-maker may be a content provider who needs information about the future development of broadband communication among consumers.

Table 5.2 shows the penetration of broadband in the Netherlands. This is a cumulative measure of Dutch households with broadband Internet service access in a given year. We wish to know the total number of households that will eventually subscribe to broadband, and the speed with which new subscribers adopt broadband.

Table 5.2 Broadband penetration in the Netherlands

Year	% of Dutch households
2002	6.3
2003	9.8
2004	14.7
2005	22.4
2006	29.0
2007	33.1
2008	35.8
2009	37.7

Setting Up the Trend Worksheet

A useful first step is to plot the data. This gives you a feeling for whether there is a trend worth forecasting, and if there is a trend, where the trend might be leading. For this data, there appears to be a clear trend (Figure 5.1). Yearly subscriptions have been in decline in recent years. Observing the data we might naively assume that a maximum of 50 percent of all Dutch households will one day have broadband connections. Eyeing the data we might assume that this adoption plateau may be reached within ten years.

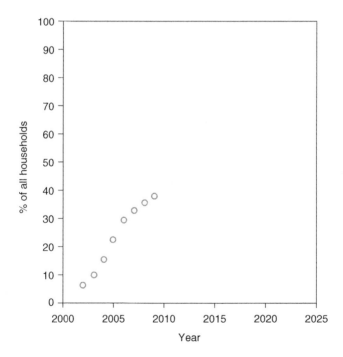

Figure 5.1 A plot of broadband penetration in the Netherlands.

The next step is to enter the data into Excel as a preparation for trend analysis. Figure 5.2 shows the table of data entered into Excel. Note that we recode the year as a way of easing the computations for Excel. In this example, we recode the year 2002 as year 1, and then each year thereafter increases by 1. Although we don't have data for the years between 2010 and 2020, we include these years on the spreadsheet in anticipation of extrapolating the data.

The next step is to introduce some estimates of the Bass curve that we are trying to fit. These are only estimates, but it eases finding a solution should you get them close to the correct answer. The parameters of the Bass model are

- *M, the limits of growth*, which we set to about 100;
- *p, the coefficient of innovation*, which we set to about 0.10;
- *q, the coefficient of imitation*, which we set to about 0.10;
- *t, the first year of introduction*, which we set to 0.

These values are entered into the spreadsheet and labeled in Figure 5.3. In Figure 5.3 we are using a feature of Excel called "named cells." Note the circled data entry point where we enter the value "M." This provides a name for cell M3; we

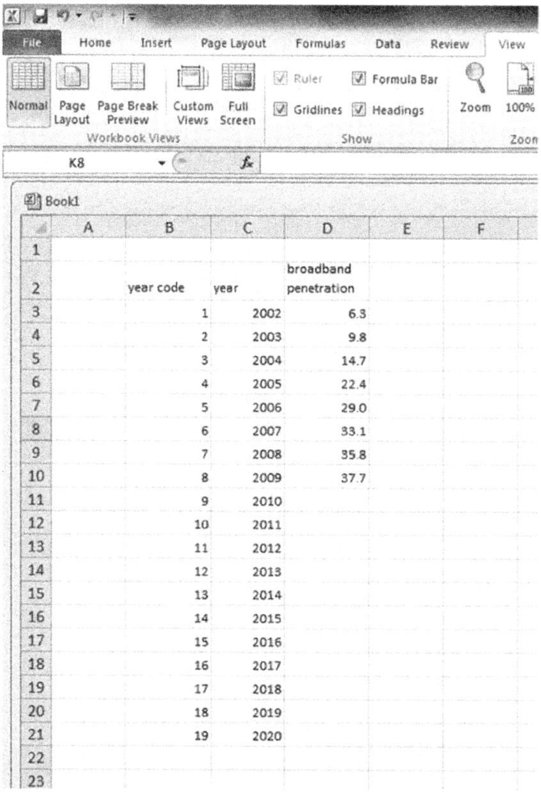

	A	B	C	D	E	F
1						
2		year code	year	broadband penetration		
3		1	2002	6.3		
4		2	2003	9.8		
5		3	2004	14.7		
6		4	2005	22.4		
7		5	2006	29.0		
8		6	2007	33.1		
9		7	2008	35.8		
10		8	2009	37.7		
11		9	2010			
12		10	2011			
13		11	2012			
14		12	2013			
15		13	2014			
16		14	2015			
17		15	2016			
18		16	2017			
19		17	2018			
20		18	2019			
21		19	2020			
22						
23						

Figure 5.2 Raw data entered on the worksheet.

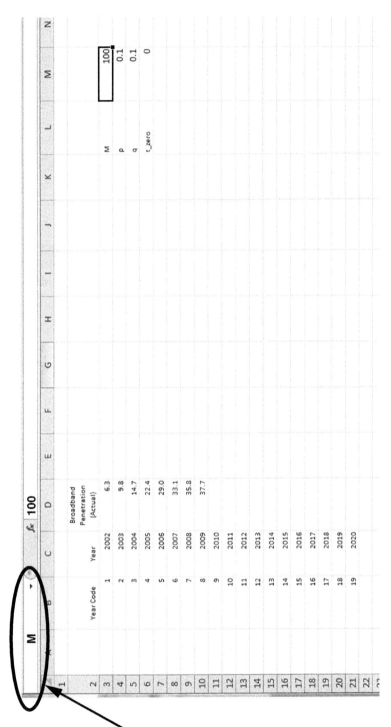

Figure 5.3 Labeled parameter estimates for a Bass diffusion model.

may now refer to this cell by its name in the Bass diffusion model. We do the same for the coefficients p, q and t, entering names in the appropriate entry.

Note that we can also name whole columns of data. In Figure 5.4 we name the recoded years "year" to ease the translation of the Bass diffusion equation into Excel formula. We can't call the column "t" because that is a reserved for the name of a statistical distribution in Excel functions. Note how the whole and corresponding column of data has been selected in the figure.

The next step is to transform the parameters of the Bass diffusion model, and the coded year, into a estimate of the cumulative diffusion of the technology. We enter in the numerator, and the denominator, of the Bass model and then divide through the numerator by the denominator to get the full model. Recall how we have named the appropriate parameters. This allows us to use the following, easily read formulas.

N, Numerator: $= M * (1\text{-EXP}(-1 * (p + q) * (\text{year} + t\_\text{zero}))$

D, Denominator: $= (1 + (q/p) * \text{EXP}(-1 * (p + q) * \text{year} + t\_\text{zero}))$

B, Bass Cumulative: $= N/D$

Figure 5.5 displays the spreadsheet once the equations have been entered. Note that we also name the columns containing the numerator and denominator "N" and "D" respectively. The formulas for the named column "N" are visible in the worksheet.

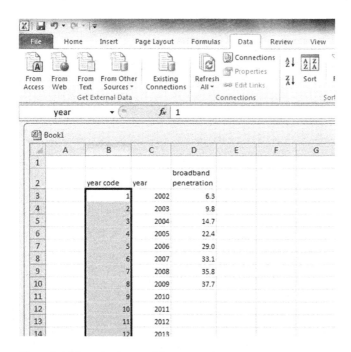

Figure 5.4 Named column of data.

N =M*(1-EXP(-1*(p+q)*(year+t_zero)))

	A	B	C	D	E	F	G	H	I	J	K	L	M	N
1														
2		Year Code	Year	Broadband Penetration (Actual)	Bass Cumulative (Estimate)		N	D						
3		1	2002	6.3	9.97		18.13	1.82				M	100	
4		2	2003	9.8	19.74		32.97	1.67				p	0.1	
5		3	2004	14.7	29.13		45.12	1.55				q	0.1	
6		4	2005	22.4	37.99		55.07	1.45				t_zero	0	
7		5	2006	29.0	46.21		63.21	1.37						
8		6	2007	33.1	53.70		69.88	1.30						
9		7	2008	35.8	60.44		75.34	1.25						
10		8	2009	37.7	66.40		79.81	1.20						
11		9	2010		71.63		83.47	1.17						
12		10	2011		76.16		86.47	1.14						
13		11	2012		80.05		88.92	1.11						
14		12	2013		83.37		90.93	1.09						
15		13	2014		86.17		92.57	1.07						
16		14	2015		88.54		93.92	1.06						
17		15	2016		90.51		95.02	1.05						
18		16	2017		92.17		95.92	1.04						
19		17	2018		93.54		96.66	1.03						
20		18	2019		94.68		97.27	1.03						
21		19	2020		95.62		97.76	1.02						
22														

Figure 5.5 Bass diffusion equations.

The nice thing about working in Excel is that you can try out various alternative forecasting models in terms of their parameters in order to see the match
between the estimated diffusion and the actual data. Our initial guess of (100, 0.1,
0.1, 0) for the parameters is graphed in Figure 5.6. These values are close to other
Bass models as published in the literature. The Bass diffusion curve for these
parameters is given in a solid line in the figure. As before in Figure 5.1 the data
are plotted using small circles.

The estimate of 100 percent penetration appears overly optimistic. The real
goal of this exercise however is not just to guess at the parameter estimates, but to
have the closest possible overlap between the data and the actual points. There
are various ways of defining this distance between the points and the diffusion
curve. Here we are adopting a standard measure, involving the least squared difference between the data and the Bass model. Suppose we name the columns as
follows:

Broadband Penetration, Actual

Bass Cumulative, Estimate

E, Error: $= (\text{Actual} - \text{Estimate})^2$

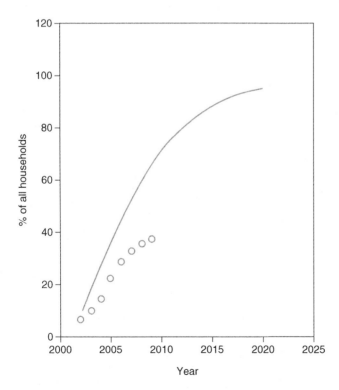

Figure 5.6 Penetration of broadband, naive estimate.

The column labeled Broadband Penetration is named "Actual." The column labeled Bass Cumulative is named "Estimate." A new column, where the error is calculated, is introduced. The formula used for calculating the squared difference between the actual and estimated column of data is given.

The current state of the worksheet after introducing an error column, with the formula given above, is shown in Figure 5.7. Note that we only need to calculate the error for every year where there actually are data. Also introduced in the worksheet is a "Sum of Error" cell where the new Error column has been summed.

Estimating the Trend Model Using Non-Linear Optimization

We now use Solver, an Excel Add-in which ships standard, to calculate the best parameters for the model. Best in this case means those parameters which minimizes the sum squared of error. Thus, we are looking for the closest possible fit between the model and the data. Ensure that the Excel Solver Add-in is active by taking the following steps. Go to the "File: Options" menu. Go to the "Add-Ins" menu where you will see the screen shown in Figure 5.8. Make sure that the Solver tool has been selected. This is shown in Figure 5.9.

In the "Manage" and "Excel Add-Ins" chooser, hit "Go." You will then see the screen shown in Figure 5.9. In this screen, make sure that the Solver Add-in is checked.

Once this is complete, you will be able to find and use Excel Solver under the "Data" and "Analyze" menus. Select "Solver" to see the Solver input screen given in Figure 5.10. There is a lot to be seen on this screen, and also a lot to be learned about Solver. This chapter only covers some of the basics of using Solver. A useful intermediate reference is given by Ragsdale (2011).

Our goal here, in short, is to minimize the error on the current data by changing the parameters of the Bass model. There are four things which must be entered into Solver to accomplish this goal. First we must select a cell which contains the objective. Here we enter the "Sum of Error" cell. Second, we determine whether we want to maximize or minimize the objective. Our goal is to minimize the error, so we select "Min." Third, we select the parameters of the model which we can change. The Solver window contains the absolute references for the three cells which contain the parameters M, p and q. Fourth and finally, we introduce a constraint that none of the parameters can go below zero. This is accomplished by ensuring the "non-negative" box has been checked. Once these four things have been added, we then hit Solve. The resultant model is equivalent to a non-linear regression procedure, which you might find in a complete statistical package such as SAS, Minitab or SPSS.

In our model, Solver rapidly converged to the following parameters:

- M, 39.7238
- p, 0.0117
- q, 0.6436
- Sum of Error, 2.0454.

	Year Code	Year	Broadband Penetration (Actual)	Bass Cumulative (Estimate)		N	D		Error				
3	1	2002	6.3	9.97		18.13	1.82		13.45		M	100	
4	2	2003	9.8	19.74		32.97	1.67		98.75		p	0.1	
5	3	2004	14.7	29.13		45.12	1.55		208.26		q	0.1	
6	4	2005	22.4	37.99		55.07	1.45		243.20		t_zero	0	
7	5	2006	29.0	46.21		63.21	1.37		296.24				
8	6	2007	33.1	53.70		69.88	1.30		424.56		Sum of Error	2715.3413	
9	7	2008	35.8	60.44		75.34	1.25		606.97				
10	8	2009	37.7	66.40		79.81	1.20		823.90				
11	9	2010		71.63		83.47	1.17						
12	10	2011		76.16		86.47	1.14						
13	11	2012		80.05		88.92	1.11						
14	12	2013		83.37		90.93	1.09						
15	13	2014		86.17		92.57	1.07						
16	14	2015		88.54		93.92	1.06						
17	15	2016		90.51		95.02	1.05						
18	16	2017		92.17		95.92	1.04						
19	17	2018		93.54		96.66	1.03						
20	18	2019		94.68		97.27	1.03						
21	19	2020		95.62		97.76	1.02						

Figure 5.7 Spreadsheet after introduction of error column.

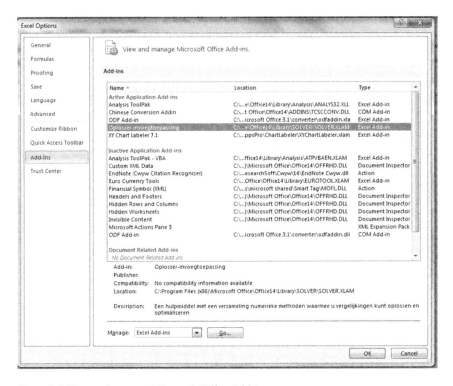

Figure 5.8 View and manage Microsoft Office Add-ins.

A pressing problem which you might encounter if starting the model from a different initial set of parameters is the fact that the Bass model results in extreme values as p, the coefficient of imitation, goes to zero. Ultimately, this results in a division by zero error in Excel, represented by the code "#DIV/0!" An additional constraint, which requires that p be greater than one part in a million, prevents this numeric underflow.

Note that Solver cannot guarantee that it finds the single set of values which have the lowest overall error. Those parameters, across all possible parameters of the model, which result in the minimum value are known as the "global minimum." Instead, the algorithm finds the best possible solution across a limited search of possible solutions, known as the "local minimum." Sometimes immediately restarting Solver with the last available parameters can result in still further improvements in optimization.

For this reason it is a good idea to run the model from a range of values and compare the results. Here are a number of outcomes which result from starting the procedures from different starting conditions. These starting and finishing values, with the sum of error, are given in Table 5.3. In these examples, it took several starts and restarts on each run. However the final parameter space appears quite robust.

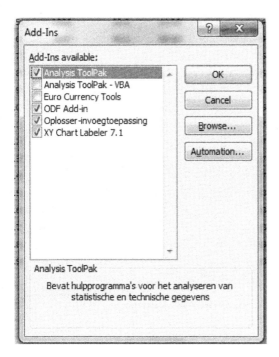

Figure 5.9 Manage Microsoft Add-ins.

Interpretation of the Results

The projection resulting from model run 3 is given in Figure 5.11. The model presents a bearish forecast for broadband growth in the Netherlands. Penetration is forecasted to peak at 40 percent of households in the Netherlands. Currently the growth is already nearing 38 percent of all households, affording growth only to another 2 percent of all households. It may be easiest to set broadband connections in the highly urbanized regions of the Netherlands – the Randstad for instance contains approximately 43 percent of all households. The more distant and rural population centers may be more expensive to connect. Its also useful to

Table 5.3 Alternate model runs of Solver non-linear regression

	Model Run 1		Model Run 2		Model Run 3	
	Starting	Finishing	Starting	Finishing	Starting	Finishing
M	100.0000	39.6216	186.2623	39.6200	84.5138	39.6201
p	0.100	0.0001	0.0827	0.0000	0.1230	0.0000
q	0.100	0.6843	0.0080	0.6846	0.0114	0.6846
t_zero	0	9.1480	0.8701	11.3643	−1.6152	10.998
Sum of Error	2715.3413	1.6242	15,366.9583	1.6216	328.6352	1.6218

Figure 5.10 The Solver window.

note that the time series is apparently truncated – the best fitting model suggests broadband diffusion in the Netherlands began as early as 1995. (See the further model runs in Table 5.6, below.)

In the traditional Bass model technological "word-of-mouth" determines whether additional consumers adopt the technology. Broadband Internet is actually a "club good" – it is largely excludable from non-paying customers, and yet the group experience is made better when there are more subscribers delivering news, content and discourse for others to access. Further, it is not viable for individuals to access broadband, unless a supporting infrastructure has been developed which permits access for whole neighborhoods and cities. Like other patterns of diffusion for high-tech media, broadband shows a very low innovation parameter, and a very high imitation parameter. These parameters are a natural outgrowth of the technological characteristics of broadband as a networked industry delivering club goods. Table 5.4 shows some other Bass models as reported in Bass's original 1969 work.

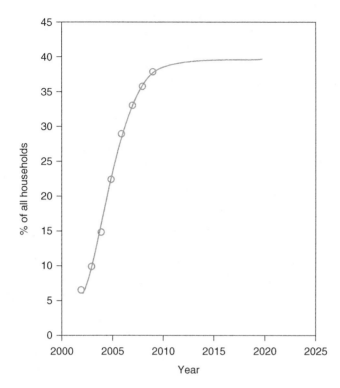

Figure 5.11 Penetration of broadband, best point forecast.

Much of the work of identifying plausible parameters is now complete. As new data become available, the forecaster can easily incorporate this into their model, updating the estimated diffusion parameters. A gentle drift of parameters is perhaps the most likely course as new data become apparent. Bass himself argued that the model parameters were probably not constant over time; his model is a useful first approximation (Bass, 1969).

Robustness and Sensitivity Analysis of the Trend Model

Experience teaches us that it is best not to take a single model as the definitive forecast. The best forecasts usually mix a range of possible, yet still plausible models of growth. Forecast which results from mixing multiple, plausible models, are less precise. Nonetheless the apparent precision in trend extrapolation forecasts is only allusory anyhow. It is better to have a less precise, but more robust, forecast which can be used for decision-making and planning.

This is in sharp contrast with the frequentist approach to building models. The frequentists argued that there is but a single model which, as a hypothesis, can be confirmed or denied given the presence of data. While this perspective has its

Table 5.4 Sample Bass model parameters

Technology	M (millions of US households)	p	q
Electric refrigerators	40	0.0026	0.216
Home freezers	22	0.0181	0.171
Black and white television	96.7	0.0279	0.251
Water softeners	5.8	0.0177	0.297
Room air conditioners	16.9	0.0104	0.419
Clothes dryers	15.1	0.0172	0.357
Power lawnmowers	44.8	0.0092	0.338
Electric bed coverings	76.6	0.0059	0.244
Automatic coffee makers	58.8	0.0171	0.301
Steam iron	55.7	0.0286	0.328
Record players	21.9	0.0248	0.654
Cable television	7.6	0.0125	0.514

place, for instance in the design of experiments, it is not especially useful in the open and fluid world of social statistics (Gill, 2007).

Analysts should be concerned with three kinds of uncertainty when producing a forecast. They should address structural uncertainty – "Was Bass the correct model to use on this data?" They should address variability uncertainty – "How much yearly variation in the data is there?" They should address parameteric uncertainty – "What is the range of plausible scenarios?" Structural uncertainty is best addressed by considering the dynamics of the model (discussed previously) and its match to the specifics of the case. Variability uncertainty and parametric uncertainty can be addressed using statistical and spreadsheet modeling techniques. Here is an example of how to use spreadsheet models to develop a rigorous, probabilistic forecast using the data and an estimated model.

The variability uncertainty can be estimated by finding the average root-mean square of the errors from the spreadsheet. In our example of Dutch broadband, when we "backcast" our model in an effort to reproduce historical data, the model fits the data within +/–0.5 percent. So for instance if the 2011 forecast is for 39 percent penetration of broadband, we could in fact expect anywhere from 38.5 percent (on the low end) to 39.5 percent (on the high end) depending upon yearly variation in the data. This is not much inherent variability in the forecast; clearly the basic assumptions of the Bass model are suitable here. There are additional sources of uncertainty in the forecast however – these are discussed further below.

As noted earlier the goal is to take into consideration a full range of the most likely explanations of the data. The likelihood of the model is in direct proportion to the forecast error associated with the model (see equation below). Relative likelihood can be scaled as needed (using the constant c). The most important issue is sampling from a range of models in accordance to their over-all likelihood. For instance, we might scale the likelihood so that 25 models sum to 100 percent likelihood.

Relative Model Likelihood $L = \exp(-cs^2)$

In our previous examples we showed that the optimum fit to the data discovered models with a forecast error (s^2). Since models diminish rapidly in likelihood as their fit also diminishes, we will want to search for models within a fairly narrow range of error. For instance, we might examine only those models which vary from seven units of error to our best in class 1.6 units of error. The model with eight units of error is 74 times less likely than a model with 20 units of error. More implausible models with higher errors could be included, but these models would have correspondingly less chance of actually being sampled. A lesser chance of being sampled means these models are unlikely to make an impact on the final forecast.

It is straightforward, albeit laborious, to seek out a range of plausible alternative models using Excel. The technique of Monte Carlo simulation allows us to examine a range of possibilities. Excel's random number generators are useful for generating a range of possible scenarios. We can then test these models by simply cutting and pasting the proposed model into the spreadsheet developed earlier.

Trial and error reveals that the inverse log normal distribution in Excel (see equation below) is useful for generating sharply focused values within a range of interest. Once we have generated a few points of interest (for instance from Table 5.1), we can continue searching that region in the parameter space to find more plausible model runs. We then keep the likely model runs, discarding implausible results, and further refine our strategy for generating future plausible results.

Random Draw for Parameter = LOGNORM.INV(x,mean,standard_dev)

Experimentation reveals that the following Monte Carlo simulation parameters are useful for generating potential model runs (Table 5.5). In principle the range of parameters is mutually dependent. For instance, a high value of the market parameter (M) might be associated with lower values of the innovation parameter (p) in the space of plausible models. Or, as a further example, the innovation parameter (p) might always be higher than the imitation parameter (q). In practice we can ignore such constraints, in order to make an exhaustive search (Table 5.5). This requires more exhaustive searching, but affords a relatively easy search strategy.

Table 5.6 shows 25 of the most plausible runs discovered through Monte Carlo simulation. These scenarios can be tabulated any number of ways. They could be sorted in the order in which they were found; or they could be ranked in terms of relative likelihood from most likely to least likely. Table 5.6 sorts the results according to the market coefficient, from smallest to greatest market.

Table 5.5 Monte Carlo simulation of potential models

	x	*mean*	*standard_dev*
M	RAND()	3.681	0.004
p	RAND()	−8.659	0.135
q	RAND()	−0.380	0.011
t_zero	RAND()	2.136	0.008

These alternative model runs are highly multivariate. It is not clear therefore necessarily how to sort the data for further presentation. However, we choose to sort the data on the market parameter (M) as this parameter has the largest effect on future growth and penetration. This value therefore has particular significance for decision-making, at least in this case.

There are subtle dependencies between the parameters in this case; in other examples they may be more readily apparent. For instance, there appears to be tradeoff between imitation and the year of first introduction. One explanation is that broadband has been available relatively longer, but that consumers are not especially innovative in its adoption. An alternative explanation is that broadband has been around somewhat less long, but individual consumers have more enthusiastically adopted it earlier in the technological life cycle.

Now that a range of plausible models has been created, we can use these scenarios in two ways. We can produce probabilistic forecasts of the model parameters themselves. The total size of the market (parameter M) is particularly decision-relevant. The second use of the robustness analysis is to present a plausible range of future growth scenarios in order to help the decision-maker plan for a range of possible outcomes. We present both model outputs below.

Table 5.6 Twenty-five likely model scenarios

Case	Market coefficient (M)	Coefficient of innovation (p)	Coefficient of imitation (q)	Year of introduction (t_zero)	Forecast error (s^2)	Relative likelihood of forecast
1	39.340	0.000177	0.671	8.509	6.758	0.0050
2	39.372	0.000163	0.678	8.591	3.596	0.0352
3	39.424	0.000172	0.684	8.390	3.828	0.0305
4	39.475	0.000187	0.685	8.513	5.707	0.0096
5	39.475	0.000178	0.675	8.557	2.089	0.0893
6	39.481	0.000202	0.671	8.540	2.725	0.0603
7	39.552	0.000160	0.679	8.499	7.248	0.0037
8	39.574	0.000155	0.688	8.676	3.124	0.0471
9	39.577	0.000185	0.698	8.302	5.243	0.0127
10	39.618	0.000170	0.684	8.357	5.029	0.0145
11	39.618	0.000205	0.684	8.357	4.979	0.0150
12	39.620	0.000180	0.685	8.294	3.914	0.0289
13	39.622	0.000206	0.681	8.412	5.285	0.0124
14	39.625	0.000197	0.691	8.285	3.589	0.0354
15	39.627	0.000196	0.684	8.125	6.248	0.0068
16	39.627	0.000196	0.684	8.453	6.360	0.0064
17	39.636	0.000193	0.684	8.317	1.627	0.1187
18	39.666	0.000121	0.692	8.801	2.367	0.0752
19	39.797	0.000170	0.683	8.413	2.749	0.0594
20	39.830	0.000193	0.685	8.329	2.256	0.0805
21	39.838	0.000148	0.699	8.508	2.793	0.0578
22	39.844	0.000186	0.673	8.382	5.040	0.0144
23	39.893	0.000175	0.680	8.480	1.730	0.1114
24	39.918	0.000166	0.691	8.476	3.008	0.0506
25	39.970	0.000179	0.675	8.397	4.577	0.0192

Figure 5.12 presents a probabilistic forecast of the total market penetration. This graph is derived from Table 5.3. On the y-axis we present the sorted scenarios for the total market penetration (parameter M). On the x-axis we cumulate the relative likelihood of the various scenarios. Note that they have been scaled to sum to 100 percent. The results are then presented graphically.

This figure may be used to ask the question "What is the probability that the Dutch market is no more than X households?" Note that the frontier of market size and cumulative probability is still somewhat ragged; continued exploration of the parameter space would smooth out this curve substantially. The curve may actually be linear – thus there is a uniform probability across the model runs being considered. The model runs vary from a low of 39.3 percent of Dutch households, to a high of 40 percent. Note that there are 7.5 million households in the Netherlands as of 2011. The forecast therefore shows a swing of about 50,000 households which may or may not ultimately get broadband connections. We may also combine the objective data with expert (or subjective) data concerning the eventual growth parameters of the model. Growth scenarios might be constructed around both the joint space of models which are both empirically plausible, and deemed most plausible by experts.

Figure 5.13 is also based on the Monte Carlo analysis of Table 5.3. Like previously, we rank the scenarios from least to greatest growth, and calculate their

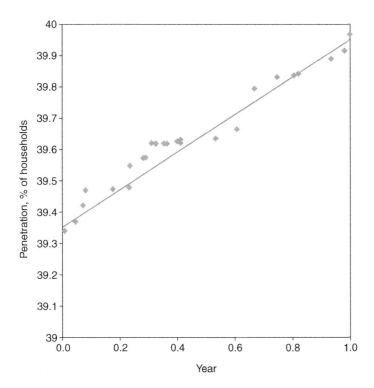

Figure 5.12 Probabilistic forecast of total market penetration.

cumulative likelihood of occurrence. We isolate five scenarios for further presentation – the scenarios associated with 5, 25, 50, 75 and 95 percent cumulative likelihood. It is customary to produce the 5 and 95 percent likelihood scenarios; we could easily choose more extreme scenarios if we wanted a more complete picture of possible uncertainties.

Again, the cumulative probability across these scenarios rather raggedly distributed. Some of the simulated scenarios are much more plausible than others. Repeated Monte Carlo simulation could refine the boundaries more tightly. Nonetheless, this suggests to take a closer look at scenarios 2, 7, 16, 20 and 23. We enter these scenarios into our previous spreadsheet, and take and plot the growth trajectories (Figure 5.13).

This model offers a remarkably accurate fit to historical data. The variability of the data given the model is less than one part in 1000. For instance, the original 11 technologies investigated by Bass showed variability of about one part in two. More formally, these models averaged an explained variance (R^2) of about 64 percent. As previously noted, the various kinds of uncertainty are coupled. A higher variability uncertainty also permits greater parametric uncertainty – there is a greater variety of plausible alternative explanations of the data.

In the example shown above, the principal variation is the ultimate size of the Dutch broadband market. In other cases the uncertainty is expressed as a classic

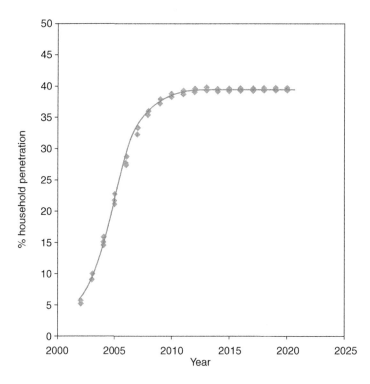

Figure 5.13 Robustness analysis of future growth.

"trumpet" of uncertainty. There is the least uncertainty around the central year of the data – as we extrapolate forward in time the uncertainty grows ever greater. Small variations in initial conditions have a greater opportunity to play out in substantively different trajectories of growth.

Concluding Remarks

Our forecast of Dutch broadband suggests a relatively small number of households may still be subscribing to broadband in the coming few years. This total amounts to fewer than 50,000 households. In yearly growth terms, the broadband industry can expect an average of about 1.2 percent yearly growth through the year 2020. Growth might be as low as 0.6 percent or as high as 2.0 percent. Most of this uncertainty is parametric in character; roughly one part in five stems from the external economic or demographic environment. The principal parametric uncertainty concerns the eventual size of the Dutch broadband network. Additional information can be incorporated into the forecast as 2010 and 2011 subscription data becomes available.

This chapter is only a brief in-road into quite a vast literature on growth curve modeling. Many researchers have expanded the Bass model. Some of the most exciting findings involve the explicit use of decision-making variables, such as pricing or promotion, in predicting future adoption. The literature on analyzing technological trends in general is still broader. Readers interested in learning more about the quite extensive field of technological forecasting might wish to investigate academic journals such as *Technological Forecasting and Social Change*, or *Futures*. Roper et al. (2011) provide an updated account of the current status of technology forecasting, including a broad-based examination of a range of forecasting methodologies including trend extrapolation.

References

Bass, F. (1969). A new product growth model for consumer durables. *Management Science*, Vol. 15, No. 5, pp. 215–227.

Bass, F.M., T.V. Krishnan and D.C. Jain (1994). Why the Bass model fits without decision variables. *Marketing Science*, Vol. 13, No. 3, pp. 203–223.

Cook, T.D. and D.T. Cambell (1979). *Quasi-experimentation: design and analysis issues for field settings*. Boston, MA: Houghton Mifflin Company.

Fisher, J.C. and R.H. Pry (1971). A simple substitution model of technological change. *Technological Forecasting and Social Change*, Vol. 3, pp. 75–88.

Geroski, P.A. (2000). Models of technology diffusion. *Research Policy*, Vol. 29, pp. 603–625.

Gill, F. (2007). *Bayesian methods: a social and behavioral sciences approach*. Boca Raton, FL: Chapman & Hall/CRC.

Martino, J.P. (1972). *Forecasting for decision making*. New York: Elsevier.

Martino, J.P. (2003). A review of selected recent advances in technological forecasting. *Technological Forecasting and Social Change*, Vol. 70, No. 8, pp. 719–733.

Meade, N. and T. Islam (2006). Modelling and forecasting the diffusion of innovation: a 25-year review. *International Journal of Forecasting*, Vol. 22, No. 3, pp. 519–545.

OECD (2015). *Broadband portal.* Retrieved from www.oecd.org/sti/ieconomy/oecdbroad-bandportal.htm.

Peres, R., E. Muller and V. Mahajan (2010). Innovation diffusion and new product growth models: a critical review and research directions. *International Journal of Research in Marketing,* Vol. 27, No. 2, pp. 91–106.

Porter, A.L., A.T. Roper, T.W. Mason, F.A. Rossini and J. Banks (1991). *Forecasting and management of technology.* New York: John Wiley & Sons.

Ragsdale, C.T. (2011). *Managerial decision modeling,* 6th edition. Canada: South Western Cengage Learning.

Rogers, E.M. (1962). *The diffusion of innovations.* New York: The Free Press.

Roper, A.T., S.W. Cunningham, A.L. Porter, T.W. Mason, F.A. Rossini and J. Banks (2011). *Forecasting and management of technology.* Hoboken, NJ: John Wiley & Sons.

6   Technology Assessment

Karel Mulder

Introduction

The state of technology is often used to characterise societies: the names of Stone-, Bronze- and Iron Age reflect this. The twentieth century has been called the "Automobile Age" (Flink, 1990), and our own time is often referred to as the "Information age" (Castells, 1997). Technology appears as a major determinant of society. This suggests that technical change has more far-reaching consequences than just replacing a device with something better: technological change creates structural change in society, which leads to new opportunities for some and new threats to others. Impacts of new technology are often unforeseen. At the moment of introduction, new technologies are generally just perceived as replacements of inferior predecessors. Impacts that a technology might have for society at large, as well as impacts that affect specific groups in society often come over time and unnoticed. An early awareness of these impacts might prevent later problems.

However, it is not only relevant to assess impacts of new technology; it might be as important to translate societal problems into challenges for technological innovation, and involve stakeholders in the technological innovation process to create opportunities to mold innovations to their needs. The "fit" between technology supply and societal demand for new technology could be improved and social resistance might be prevented. *Technology Assessment (TA) aims at societally optimizing the process of technological change.*

This chapter will first examine how various debates on technologies gradually broke the grounds for Technology Assessment in the 1970s (the second section of this chapter). Afterwards, Technology Impact Assessment is discussed, which aims at systematically analyzing the impacts of new technologies (the third section). These impact studies signaled problems, but were insufficient to guide developments toward solutions. Stakeholder involvement might both lead to adjustments of a technology and to more stakeholder appreciation of the technology. Some new technologies are important for everybody, as they relate to core human values. Especially in those cases it is very important to involve the general public in the debates. Stimulated public debates on emerging technologies are covered in the fourth section. Improving the fit between emerging technologies and the (future) stakeholders, called Constructive Technology Assessment, requires imagination and analysis as it is about a "world coming into being" and is covered in the fifth section.

The Origins of Technology Assessment

In the twentieth century, society has perceived technology from different angles: technological optimism and pessimism alternated repeatedly. After World War II, technological optimism dominated. Technology was perceived as identical to social progress. An example of this technological optimism is the 1935–1982 corporate slogan of the chemical multi-national Du Pont: "Better Things for Better Living ... Through Chemistry."

Technological innovation was supported by the general conviction that technological change was a "positive sum game," that is, an activity that leads to redistribution in society, but where the ultimate overall benefits are greater than the costs. "Innovation" was synonymous to "progress." In the 1960s, the positive sum game conviction quickly turned into a negative one. A wave of criticism in regard to various technologies emerged. Critics declared "technological progress" as an autonomous force in society that threatened civilization (Ellul et al., 1964). In particular, the book *Silent Spring* by Rachel L. Carson (1962) was of major influence. It was a powerful statement against pesticides, as the wildlife damage created by these chemicals was regarded much larger than the increased agricultural yields that it contributed to. Various controversies emerged: the (nuclear) arms race was fueled by new technologies, computers created threats to privacy, biotechnology could create new epidemics (Bauer, 1997), unemployment was due to automation (Busse, 1978) and drinking water fluoridation was considered as a first step toward government control of individual health (Hicks, 2011). Nuclear power became the focal point of technological controversy.

The positive sum game was no longer self-evident. In the academic world, the propelling mechanisms of technological change became of interest. Scholars initiated studies regarding the social interests that were behind the apparent neutral character of technologies. Could the dichotomy between technological optimism and pessimism be solved empirically? In the United States the aviation pioneer Charles Lindbergh was lobbying for "Technology Assessment." In 1973, the US Congress Office of Technology Assessment (OTA) was established. Ideally, the effects of new technology on American society were to be studied scientifically and submitted to Congress prior to the adoption of that technology: "Technology assessment is an attempt to establishment an early warning system to detect, control, and direct technological changes and developments so as to maximize the public good while minimizing the public risks" (Cetron and Connor, 1972). In this definition, TA was primarily an instrument that had to protect societal interest. However, in other definitions, the political pitfalls that were hidden in this definition were left to policy-makers:

> Technology Assessment is the systematic identification, analysis and evaluation of the potential secondary consequences (whether beneficial or detrimental) of technology in terms of its impacts on social, cultural, political, economic and environmental systems and processes. Technology Assessment is intended to provide a neutral, factual input into the decision-making process.
>
> (Vary Coates in: Smits and Leyten, 1988)

Technology Assessment was not primarily aimed at forecasting the future development of a technology. It rather focused at analyzing the various social impacts of its development and implementation, and options to modify them.

In Europe, parliamentary Technology Assessment offices were created after OTA. From the mid-1980s parliamentary TA institutes were created for instance STOA (European Parliament), OPECST (France), TAU (Austria), TAB (Germany), POST (United Kingdom), Rathenau Instituut (Netherlands) (Smits, 1990). Due to strong anti-Washington bureaucracy sentiments, OTA was dissolved in 1995.

A number of corporations were engaging in TA as well. Liability issues, the potential threat of the introduction of new legislation and public image issues were important drivers for them (Mulder, 2001)

The Control Dilemma: Ignorance and Lack of Control

Predictions regarding the impacts of emerging technologies are commonly made by many people. However, impacts of the new technologies of the past were hardly predicted accurately, not even by experts. Still, assessing the impacts of new technology in an early stage is important: once the impacts of new technology have materialized it is hard to do anything about them; the technology has connected to various habits of individuals and groups who adjusted their lives to it, and has been accommodated by institutional adaptations. Sunk costs (fixed investments related to the technology) are another factor. The experience gained by using the technology further diminishes the desire to change. Together, these factors create a strong preference for the established technology, and induce resistance to change or adaptation. So after a technology is introduced, its success implies that it becomes *entrenched* in society. Entrenchment and lack of accurate Impact Assessment in early stages lead to the control dilemma:

> attempting to control a technology is difficult, and not rarely impossible, because during its early stages, when it can be controlled, not enough can be known about its harmful social consequences to warrant controlling its development; but by the time these consequences are apparent, control has become costly and slow.
>
> (Collingridge, 1980)

The history of leaded gasoline is a good example. Around 1930, tetra-ethyl lead was the cheapest chemical gasoline additive that could prevent engines from "knocking." In the early 1970s, it became clear that the lead emissions from cars inflicted enormous health hazards, especially upon children in large cities. However, it took 25 years and billions of dollars to introduce a (cheap) unleaded gasoline additive.

The merit of Technology Assessment is not just to take better decisions as the impacts of a new technology are better understood; it is also aimed at preventing decisions that cannot be undone anymore when better options might become available.

Technology Impact Assessment

In the early 1970s Impact Assessment was an existing methodology that focused on identifying social and economic impacts of policy measures. Especially in infrastructure development the socio-economic effects that governments aimed for, required careful analysis. In principle, this seems like a clear cut methodology: to map all impacts and calculate a price tag for each. By quantification of impacts one could draw clear conclusions. Such a quantitative comparison is also known as a social cost/benefit analysis.

Technology Impact Assessment was intended to provide a similar analysis of advantages and disadvantages of new, emerging technologies. The control dilemma makes clear that there is much uncertainty regarding impacts. Moreover, determining price tags is not easy: what is the price tag of pollution (economic damage, wildlife, costs of clean up...)? The price tag of a threat to privacy is hardly to be expressed in monetary value. But even if not all impacts could be quantified, it might still be useful to provide an inventory of impacts that is as complete as possible. A reminder in the form of a checklist might be a useful tool:

The Technology Impact Assessment Checklist (Mulder, 1996) comprises three parts:

A   research and development
B   product
C   manufacture.

A: How acceptable is the research and development work that is involved in the creation of the new product and the related manufacturing process?

1   Might this research create direct threats to its environment?
2   Is there social resistance against the methods used in the research and/or development, or is there resistance against collection/storage of certain data?
3   Is the research/development of scientific interest? Could it provide new knowledge that might contribute to science/other technologies?

B: How acceptable is the new product by itself?
Normative:

1   Are there social values attached to the product itself, or the product it replaces?
2   Is the product objectionable in the system of values and norms of specific religious or cultural groups?

Social acceptance:

3   Will the probable cost of the new product raise objections?
4   Are there (safety) risks for the user of the product, or for others?

5 Is the foreseen use of the product in line with ingrained behavioral patterns of large groups of people?
6 Are there financial or psychological barriers that hinder acceptance of the product?

Secondary social effects:

7 Does the product create options for new (economic or other) activities? (positive/negative)
8 Does the product create a threat to existing activities which create a certain social or cultural value?
9 Does the product affect communities? (family, local community, cultural region)
10 Does the product have other possibilities of use than the ones that are intended?

C: How acceptable is the manufacture of the new product?
Within the company:

1 Are there standards or values at stake in production?
2 Are the working conditions in manufacturing acceptable?

Local environment:

3 What are the impacts of the production facilities for its environment?
4 What are the expected (primary and secondary) employment effects (local/regional/national) of manufacture? What level of education is required for staff?
5 What might be other consequences of manufacture for the local area?
6 What are the social consequences of production for the local community?
7 Is there a strong breeding ground for local activism?
8 Is it possible to limit adverse effects (C5–C7) by the choice of a suitable location?

Company:

9 Which (existing or planned) economic activities are threatened by manufacture of the new product?
10 Are existing power relations influenced by manufacturing the new product? These include relationships:

a between employees (or unions) and employers;
b between different manufacturers;
c between producers, buyers and suppliers;
d between government and industry;
e between government agencies.

11 Are relationships between global trading blocs affected by manufacture of this new product? What does the new product imply for the development of third world countries?

In practice, the mapping of all impacts of a new technology turned out to be a huge task. Quickly it became clear that focus was required in TA projects. A framework was needed to guide the search for impacts. Policy documents and strategic plans could provide such a framework. But this solution was far from "neutral" and "scientific." Moreover, as one of the TA definitions states, the main aim of a TA study is identifying new issues for the policy agenda...

OTA tended to deal with these issues in an "ad hoc" way. Checklists were developed containing impact factors like economics, demography, geography, social, administrative/legal, technology, environment, education. As a real systematic method for Impact Assessments did not exist, the OTA proclaimed "Technology Assessment is a craft, not a science." It developed its own quality evaluation system, which had to protect it in the political arena (Office of Technology Assessment, May 1993). Quality control of OTA reports was strict.

Impact Assessment was not only politically sensitive. Impacts were uncertain because of a more fundamental reason: the impacts of a new technology do not directly emerge from a new technological artifact or system. These impacts emerge in interaction between the new technology and its social environment. After all, technology that is not being used does not produce any impact. However, the use of new technology is often not as intended by its creators. Computers were not intended as "game machines," the Internet was designed for robust (military) data exchange and text messages (SMS) were intended to enable communication between maintenance engineers of telephone companies. The unforeseen use of technology can create new options and challenges. *First order impacts* which are directly caused by the introduction of a new technology, create *second order impacts* (changes in behavior as a result of the availability of a new technology), which in turn might create new impacts, but also adaptations of the new technology. Obviously higher order impacts are not caused solely by the introduction of a new technology. There is not a clear cause–effect relationship between a single cause and its impacts. Technology and society co-evolve, and it is therefore impossible to construct a strict causal chain linking a single technology to higher order changes.

> The birth control pill was designed to prevent undesired pregnancies. This technology decoupled sexuality from reproduction. As a result, people were afforded more sexual liberties. One of the impacts was an increase in sexually transmitted diseases. As a result, many decided to adapt their sexual behavior or to use other contraceptives.

What were the impacts of the birth control pill? Conservatives made its introduction the beginning of a "moral decline," while Liberals praise its contribution to the emancipation of women. Its introduction filled a need that caused a co-evolution of technology and society. Major new technologies are causes of social change and social change creates new needs for technologies. In short, the establishment of the impacts of new technology requires analysis of the dynamics of technological change in its social context. Because this context is open in space (everything on this planet is somehow related to everything else) and time (every impact might create another higher order impact), Technology Impact Assessment has to set a boundary for its analysis. However, it is important to realize that this boundary is an arbitrary one.

A one-to-one substitution of a technology is exceptional. In general, technological change creates more impacts: it requires a new source of power, it increases efficiency, it creates additional output or requires changes in maintenance. These additional impacts are often overlooked. Even designers of new products do not recognize the impacts of their products and think in terms of substitution: the first cars were designed as "horseless carriages." However, cars brought far more changes than the disappearance of the horse from the scene. The first mobile phone was intended to replace the radiotelephone. The radiotelephone was mainly used by medical doctors, for emergency use. Because of this rather limited market, telephone operators received the licenses to install the first generation mobile phone networks for free. However, governments "learned" how the mobile phone changed the telephone landscape: when the second generation was introduced, licenses were auctioned for unprecedented amounts. Although impacts are hard to predict, claims that a new technology is a one to one substitution of an outdated technology need to be distrusted because history has proven that such claims are often completely inaccurate.

Problems of Technology Impact Assessment

The mapping of "all" impacts of a new technology is problematic as there is no guarantee of completeness and reliability. Yet a political decision based on a Technology Impact Assessment, with all its shortcomings, is preferable to political decisions that are merely based on the claims of designers, funding authorities or companies. The commitments that people involved in innovation develop often prohibits them from judging the pros and cons of that technology in an unbiased way. Disadvantages that come to light might even be obscured.

Another problem showed up: Impact Assessment was only carried out if there were reasons for concern. This meant that there were already investments made and commitments created. In effect, the expected positive impacts were already clearly heralded in the media, which meant that the Technology Assessors got the role of (also) bringing a nasty message, "Yes, there are drawbacks to this technology." That brought technology assessors in a bad position. Companies started complaining that "Technology Assessment is Technology Arrestment" or even "Technology Harassment" (Bell Laboratories' Leon Green and William O. Baker, in Medford, 1973). On the other hand, there were critics that pointed to the difficulties that were met when attempts were made to shape a more socially optimal technology. For example, in the early 1970s the US government introduced the Clean Air Act that aimed at pushing US car makers to produce cleaner cars: tight emission standards for cars were set five years before, in order to force car makers to innovate. This "technology forcing" was not very successful. Instead of investing in innovative technologies, car makers hired lawyers and lobbyists to get rid of the obligation. The intended innovations were reached eventually, but much later than planned (Gerard and Lave, 2005).

Finally, there was also quite strong criticism aimed directly at Technology Assessment. Critics argued that Technology Assessment was a form of repressive tolerance: decision-makers tried in advance to make their plans invulnerable by including the results of Technology Assessment studies. Instead of impact studies, these critics demanded democratization of decision-making on technology. That democratization should give the public a say when the introduction of new technologies was at stake. In the 1980s and 1990s, these rather different forms of criticism led to three new forms of Technology Assessment:

a   Public Debate
b   Constructive Technology Assessment
c   Interactive Backcasting

These new forms of TA are all much more comprehensive than Impact Assessment. That is not to say that the analysis of potential impacts of new technology has become redundant. It is rather that Impact Assessment should be embedded in carefully shaped interaction and learning processes. In this way, the analyses can contribute to a better debate, to learning among participants and improved feedback to decision-makers and technology developers to reduce the gap between a new technology and its social environment. Constructive Technology Assessment and Public Debate will dealt with in the following paragraphs. Backcasting is a separate chapter in this book (Chapter 7).

Public Debate

Technology and Public Debate

Sometimes technologies were developed which initially hardly created any public debate. However, a changing Zeitgeist, and a vastly expanding public interest could lead to quick changes. "Atoms for Peace" striving to develop nuclear electricity, was uncontroversial in the 1950s and 1960s but led to a sharp controversy from the early 1970s. Similar controversies (though less extensive) developed around drinking water fluoridation, genetic modification and screening techniques, various medical technologies, nanotechnology, personal data storage, underground CO_2 storage and various large-scale infrastructure projects like airports, motorways, railway lines, ports, tunnels, etc. (Nelkin, 1979; Mazur, 1981).

The cause of many of the controversies was in fact that citizens interfered in discussions that until then had only involved experts. Expert communities were not used to dealing with citizens. They often attempted to fend citizens arguing that they lacked expertise, or that citizens would only be driven by ideologies. Experts were often accused of being biased and only serving the "establishment" (Nowotny, 1979). However, soon it turned out that expert communities were no monoliths. Some experts started actively supporting citizens groups and many university lecturers and students supported civic groups. In the 1970s controversies arose in which experts and civil society groups played a role. Those controversies had advantages and disadvantages. The main advantage was that the parties engaged in public controversy were forced to tighten their arguments. In fact the contestants made Impact Assessments to support their position. However, these were far from neutral, but were generally made from a specific perspective (Rip, 1986).

Orchestrated Public Debate and Citizens Panels

Public debates on new technologies, or large-scale implementation of technologies, are generally occurring spontaneously. The responsible authorities are in general not very happy becoming caught in these debates. However, timely societal debates regarding expert issues is much better than "no debate"; the worst scenario of decision-making is that a serious debate arises after all decisions have been taken and considerable investments have been made: it might imply that the investment will be lost. A timely debate might prevent that. For example, in several places, energy companies obtained licenses for shale gas exploration without any political debate. After debates emerged on "fracking" decision-makers faced serious dilemmas between compensating the license holders and disappointing their own constituents. The controversy over biofuels (food/fuel) implied that a company in Rotterdam (the Netherlands) could close down its brand new bio fuel refinery before ever being used.

An early warning can therefore be very useful: not just to prevent a large hazard, but as a trigger for discussion regarding new issues. A famous example is the paper by biochemists in 1974 that warned of the dangers of escaping genetically modified organisms (Berg et al., 1974). This paper created much discussion but ultimately not a sharp controversy. The same applied to the very early warning of Drexler (1986) for the risk of self-replicating nano-machines that could devour the whole world. This warning led to much concern, but gradually ebbed away. In 2004 it was concluded that there was no risk of a "runaway self-replicating machine" (Phoenix and Drexler, 2004). Scientists are sometimes reluctant to initiate a public debate as it as seems betraying their colleagues.

Hence there are good reasons to stimulate public debate before the massive introduction of novel technologies. There are a number of new methods that have been developed to involve citizens in expert issues. In Denmark, an approach has been developed called "Citizens Panel." The core of this approach was the creation of a representative panel of citizens. A 15–30 person panel was assigned the task to draw up a policy recommendation regarding a controversial expertise related issue. The panel was provided with all resources that it needed. For example, the panel could invite experts and commission specific analyses. The final recommendations of the panel were to be the result of a final debate session. It was the intention to make this debate a media event. In this way, wider discussions regarding the issue would be triggered. Hence, the cooperation of the media was important. Policy-makers had to treat the citizens panels seriously to contribute to the clout of the panel. In various countries (Denmark, Japan) citizens panels were successful in stimulating public debate regarding expert issues (Joss and Durant, 1995). In other cases, the evaluation of citizens panels showed more mixed results considering societal and political impact (Guston, 1999; te Molder and Gutteling, 2003; Boussaguet and Dehousse, 2008).

Citizens panels are a good method to create dialogue regarding issues which are strongly linked to norms and values. For example new medical technologies often create such issues. These technologies are often related to ideas about "perfection" and "imperfection" of human life, the "value" vis-à-vis "quality" of life, or to ideas about the "divine"/"natural" of life vis-à-vis medical interference in life and death.

Public debates regarding societal issues that have less of an intimate personal appeal, and are less determined by innovation, such as large-scale infrastructure development for example, could use more large-scale approaches that allow citizens and NGOs to discuss all options before any decision is made. However, also in such debates, there is an issue of expertise. How to create a useful dialogue based on rich insight with non-experts? Scenarios are an option to present a range of viable alternative courses of action. Also films and festivals are used to inform and initiate discussion on novel technologies with potentially far-reaching effects. By these means, larger audiences can be reached while still maintaining the option of discussion.

Whenever new generic technologies emerge, or key decisions are to be made, the absence of controversy should not be interpreted as consensus. In those situations, it is important to initiate public debates. The main challenge for such a public debate is linking expertise and values regarding issues that sometimes even did not exist before. Various issues have been scrutinized in such organized public debates: brain science, biotechnology and nutrition, airport expansion, genetic manipulation of animals.

In setting up a citizens panel it is important to have a wide variety of opinions. The panel does not necessarily have to be fully representative for the constituency, as long as the main viewpoints are represented. It should be well facilitated but basically determine its own route to come to a final statement regarding the issue.

Constructive Technology Assessment

CTA Workshops

Technologies are only functioning well within certain societal arrangements: they need manufacturing, maintenance, a sales organization, education of personnel, users that can handle the technology, legislation regarding safety/pollution of technology, taxation, etc. For new technologies, all these arrangements are not in place, they should be created. Mismatches between development of new technologies and the required societal arrangements can easily occur. Constructive Technology Assessment (CTA) aims at lowering the societal costs of technological renewal by managing the mutual adjustment of a new technology to societal arrangements.

Especially in a time when society is requiring a higher speed of innovation and innovations that reduce pollution and resource consumption, reducing the societal costs of innovation is important. The desire for a greater speed of innovation often leads to the message that critics should swallow their criticisms. That is no solution, on the contrary, it entails the danger that dissatisfaction will surface in a much later stage, without any possibility of adjusting the technology. This might lead to sharper controversies and higher costs.

New technology is often modified and adjusted after its introduction. This improvement is based on customer experience and learning in manufacturing. By this learning, producers can better accommodate societal demands, in performance, costs and environmental burden. This refinement process often determines the ultimate success of a technology. CTA aims at improving this learning process by offering options for societal interaction in an earlier stage. The sooner such interactions take place, the more scope there is for learning (Rip et al., 1995). CTA is constructive in two ways:

- it aims at making Technology Assessment "constructive," i.e., more aimed at positive results by not aiming at an external assessment of technology, but by establishing interaction and learning;
- it focuses on the construction phase of technology.

For many actors in the innovation process, CTA procedures only seem to delay innovation and make it more expensive. Criticism toward new technologies is easily dismissed as "conservatism" or as motivated by self-interest. However, if signals of societal discontent are ignored, they might easily lead to a complete failure of a new technology.

Technology designers are driven by expectations regarding what could be achieved. They often have various implicit and explicit expectations about the context in which their technology will function (van Lente, 1993). Technology designers assume certain user roles and user interests that might turn out not to be self-evident for the users. For example, audio equipment designers developed all kinds of filters to create the perfect sound. However, many users were confused by the number of buttons on their equipment, and never used the options that the engineers created. After clear consumer signals, the audio industry discovered that "ease of use" is often a more relevant feature of audio equipment than the perfect sound that engineers were focused on. Better interaction with audio consumers might have led to earlier adaptations. But it is not always a question of better listening to the consumer. Innovation processes take place in rather complex situations.

A manufacturer of micro-electronic equipment was developing Body Area Networks (BAN, a wireless network of wearable computing devices) for monitoring vital body functions. The technology was crucial for high risk patients, but the company aimed at developing the larger market for patients with an increased risk. Heart disease patients supported them as the technology allowed patients a "normal" life. The cooperation of health insurance companies and general practitioners (GPs) was crucial to monitor the patients, and provide warnings to patients. However, GPs were really negative: accepting and hosting patient data implied accepting the responsibility for analysis, proper storage and giving access to the data, a tremendous task for which they would not have the capacity. And will the devices create perhaps too much trust among patients that prevents them from taking normal checks? Could patients check their own data? Could the data be used for suing GPs in case they missed something? Health insurance companies offered to host the patient data, but patients as well as GPs expected them to commercially exploit the data.

In such complex situations, institutional change is required before the new technology can be introduced. As a result, the introduction of new technology is often delayed or might even fail altogether.

The problem in these situations is that various stakeholders have a limited view of the implications of the new technology, and of each other's perception of these implications: patients see a life-saving technology that cannot be used, GPs a risk and a threat to their professional judgment, and health insurance companies see a costs saving device with potentially even wider applications. In such situations, it is important to organize learning processes between the various parties to obtain a better understanding of the mutual perspectives and the factors and actors that determine the outcome of the entire process. It is important that stakeholders can recognize future arrangements that can deal with each other's fears. Hence, scenarios (see Chapter 4) might play an important role in Constructive Technology Assessment, to assess the future as perceived by other actors.

CTA(-scenario) workshops require a very good preparation. Through clarifying the real life dilemmas that play a key role for the various actors, the analyst can penetrate into the world of the stakeholders. High-quality input is required to obtain rich learning experiences in a workshop.

Niche Experiments

In order to promote interaction between technology development and the intended social context of the technology, there are often options to organize limited real life experiments. Especially unintended use and abuse of a technology might show up in these experiments, which might lead to redesign. Moreover, minor flaws might be repaired. However, sometimes also institutional change could be required. For example what traffic regulations should be adapted before allowing automated guided vehicles to intermingle with ordinary traffic? Naturally this first requires closed experiments, but later on also more real-life settings. In general, a somewhat protected part of reality is a good setting for such kind of learning experiments. For example for experiments with electric vehicles, charging points are needed, and the cooperation of garages is desirable. Sometimes it is desirable to keep competing technologies out of the experiment, which makes islands ideal places for traffic experiments. Finally, some regulations should be lifted for experiments and subsidies might be required. One needs a protective part of reality, a niche, for this kind of learning.

Generally, the aim of a niche experiment is a rapid sequence of technological modifications and improvements, as well as institutional adaptations that enable the improved technology to escape the niche and enter competition with incumbent rivals. So far that goal has not always been achieved. The CFC-free refrigerator has been a successful example: the members of Greenpeace functioned as a niche for development and introduction of a refrigerator without ozone depleting refrigerants. The success of this refrigerator among Greenpeace members made the white goods industry accept this design, despite a slightly higher risk associated with the flammability of the refrigerant (Mulder, 2011).

A single niche experiment is usually not enough for a radical innovation. One might plan for several subsequent niche experiments in a focused strategy. This requires careful planning of experiments and feedback loops, and is known as Strategic Niche Management (Kemp et al., 1998).

CTA is a means to facilitate social learning that is necessary for technological innovation. Such a process that is aiming at innovation in its early stages could be deemed to be at odds with the protection of proprietary information. However, CTA is not aiming at the technical ingenuity that constitutes proprietary knowledge. Moreover, the interactions that it aims for, do not have to take place in public. Media pressure might be a barrier to mutual learning, as in public debates actors are obliged represent the viewpoints of their constituents. However, business competition and protecting strategic information might be an important barrier to engage in CTA processes.

Technology Assessment, How?

The emergence of Technology Assessment marks the changes in thinking about technology and society over the past decades. From a science driven technological optimism in the 1950s, and a negative attitude toward technology in the 1970s, a more pragmatic attitude arose based on the assumption that deliberate efforts are required to embed new technologies in society. These efforts can utilize analysis tools such as impact assessments as well as other tools discussed in this book such as scenarios, trend analysis, etc. However, embedding technology in society cannot be a mere desk exercise. Interactive learning processes take real interaction.

The approaches that have been discerned in the third section of this chapter can be distinguished by the type of problem that creates the point of departure:

- In (interactive) Backcasting (Chapter 7) a future societal need/challenge is the starting point to generate pathways toward a solution.
- In Constructive Technology Assessment, both as workshop and as experiment, new (often science-based) technology is the starting point. Such technologies often lead to social promises (new applications, improving efficiency) that legitimize continued investment in research but also fears of new risks. Workshops are more appropriate for technologies in the lab phase while niche experiments are more appropriate in later phases (Van Den Ende et al., 1998).
- In (stimulated) Public Debates, a (perceived) threat to a societal value by the introduction of new technology, is the starting point. This may involve new risks, new forms of inequality or the deterioration of religious norms.

How to Set Up a Technology Assessment Project?

An organization that considers setting up a Technology Assessment project should first consider the type of challenge that it faces:

1 guiding technology to specific societal goals;
2 societal embedding (science-based) technology;

3   (re-)developing consensus regarding values that are challenged by science/technology.

The first challenge is further dealt with in the backcasting chapter (Chapter 7). The second challenge is dealt with by a CTA project while the third challenge leads to some form of public debate.

Public and private organizations have different responsibilities in this regard. Companies can engage in CTA, but in general they have to engage at sectoral or societal level. Sectoral organizations might be more appropriate. Company or sector interest in the outcome of the process could deteriorate credibility. In such cases, an appropriate government agency or an independent consultant might be a more appropriate organizer.

Companies should be very reluctant to organize public debates regarding values. However, they might set up a panel representing various viewpoints in society to get a better understanding of the issues at stake. For example food companies sometimes created panels in regard to genetically modified ingredients in food.

A further point to consider before engaging in a Technology Assessment project is the level of controversy regarding the problem. Without any controversy, TA would be a boring exercise. However, with too much controversy, a constructive dialogue becomes impossible (cf. Mulder, 2012). In general, in case of too much controversy, the issue is often postponed.

Experts are important for every form of TA. It is important that their expertise is tapped and made available for lay people. Only in this way, a high quality debate is possible. But who is an expert? As a successful technological innovation project requires many factors to be in place, there are many "experts." The user is an expert in "the use" of a product, like the service engineer, etc.

There are no privileged actors in TA projects as success means to establish a new arrangements of technology, actors and institutions that is accepted by all.

Technology Assessment, Upcoming Challenges

Technology Assessment gradually evolved from impact assessment to "managing technology in society." This trend has not come to an end. A number of important developments can be observed that might affect the TA process in the coming decades:

- Emancipation: inequality in education declines as countries develop. An increased level of education implies that citizens will increasingly demand a role in decision-making on issues that were left to experts before.
- Complexity and systems integration: technologies are becoming increasingly complex. Products are far less stand-alone operated, but part of systems that include a wider range of technologies. Systems are again linked to other large systems. This increases vulnerability. Moreover, change becomes increasingly difficult as change will affect the links between systems.
- Increased speed of innovation: although change becomes harder, more new ideas will emerge by an unprecedented number of researchers and technology

designers. Larger parts of an innovation budget will therefore be devoted to the implementation of change.

- Globalization of technology development: technology is shaped by the social environment in which it is created. For a successful global diffusion of technology, which is often an economic necessity, a fit with the user context is crucial. Technological design will be the motor of material globalization.
- Global challenges: the world reaches the limits of its own finite resources. Unbridled (material) growth becomes impossible. Mission-oriented technology development will be more important (Mulder, 2005).

References

Bauer, M. (1997). *Resistance to new technology: nuclear power, information technology and biotechnology*. Cambridge: Cambridge University Press.

Berg, P., D. Baltimore, H.W. Boyer, S.N. Cohen, R.W. Davis, D.S. Hogness, D. Nathans, R. Roblin, J.D. Watson and S. Weissman (1974). Potential biohazards of recombinant DNA molecules. *Science*, Vol. 185, No. 4148, p. 303.

Boussaguet, L. and R. Dehousse (2008). Lay people's Europe: a critical assessment of the first EU citizens' conferences. European Governance Paper No. C-08-02, July 21.

Busse, M. (1978). *Arbeit ohne Arbeiter*. Frankfurt am Main: Suhrkamp.

Carson, R. (1962). *Silent spring*. London: Hamish Hamilton.

Castells, M. (1997). *The information age: economy, society and culture. Vol. 2, the power of identity*. Oxford: Blackwell.

Cetron, M.J. and L. Connor (1972). A method for planning and assessing technology against relevant national goals in developing countries. In J. Cetron and B.B. Marvin (eds.), *The methodology of technology assessment*. New York: Gordon & Breach Science Publishers.

Collingridge, D. (1980). *The social control of technology*. London: Pinter.

Drexler, K.E. (1986). *Engines of creation: the coming era of nanotechnology*. Garden City, NY: Anchor.

Ellul, J., J. Wilkinson and R.K. Merton (1964). *The technological society*. New York: Vintage Books.

Flink, J.J. (1990). *The automobile age*. Cambridge, MA: MIT Press.

Gerard, D. and L.B. Lave (2005). Implementing technology-forcing policies: the 1970 Clean Air Act Amendments and the introduction of advanced automotive emissions controls in the United States. *Technological Forecasting and Social Change*, Vol. 72, No. 7, pp. 761–778.

Guston, D.H. (1999). Evaluating the first US consensus conference: the impact of the citizens' panel on telecommunications and the future of democracy. *Science, Technology and Human Values*, Vol. 24, No. 4, pp. 451–482.

Hicks, J. (2011). Pipe dreams: America's fluoride controversy. *Chemical Heritage Magazine*, Vol. 29, No. 2. Retrieved from www.chemheritage.org/discover/media/magazine/articles/29-2-pipe-dreams-americas-fluoride-controversy.aspx.

Joss, S. and J. Durant (1995). *Public participation in science: the role of consensus conferences in Europe*. London: Science Museum.

Kemp, R., J. Schot and R. Hoogma (1998). Regime shifts to sustainability through processes of niche formation: the approach of strategic niche management. *Technology Analysis and Strategic Management*, Vol. 10, No. 2, pp. 175–198.

Mazur, A. (1981). *The dynamics of technical controversy*. Washington, DC: Communications Press.

Medford, D. (1973). Environmental harassment or technology assessment? Amsterdam: Elsevier.

Mulder, K. (2001). Niederlande. In N. Malanowski, C.P. Kruck and A. Zweck (eds.), *Technology Assessment und Wirtschaft, eine Länderübersicht*. Frankfurt/New York: Campus Verlag.

Mulder, K. (2011). Chlorofluorocarbons: drivers of their emergence and substitution. In K. Mulder, D. Ferrer and J. van Lente (eds.), *What is sustainable technology? Perceptions, paradoxes and possibilities*. Sheffield, UK: Greenleaf.

Mulder, K. (2012). The dynamics of public opinion on nuclear power: interpreting an experiment in the Netherlands. *Technological Forecasting and Social Change*, Vol. 79, No. 8, pp. 1513–1524.

Mulder, K.F. (1996). Maatschappelijke aanvaarding van Duurzame Technologie, een inventarisatie van culturele weerstanden, Delft, Interdepartementaal programma Duurzame Technologie Ontwikkeling, werkdocument CST2.

Mulder, K.F. (2005). Managing the dynamics of technology in modern day society. In R.M. Verburg, J.R. Ortt and W.M. Dicke (eds.), *Managing technology and innovation: an introduction*. London: Routledge.

Nelkin, D. (1979). *Controversy: politics of technical decisions*. Beverly Hills, CA: Sage Publications.

Nowotny, H. (1979). *Kernenergie: Gefahr oder Notwendigkeit: Anatomie eines Konflikts*. Frankfurt am Main: Suhrkamp.

Office of Technology Assessment (May 1993). *Policy analysis at OTA: a staff assessment*. Washington, DC: OTA.

Phoenix, C. and E. Drexler (2004). Safe exponential manufacturing. *Nanotechnology*, Vol. 15, No. 8, p. 869.

Rip, A. (1986). Controversies as informal technology assessment. *Science Communication*, Vol. 8, No. 2, pp. 349–371.

Rip, A., T.J. Misa and J. Schot (1995). *Managing technology in society*. London, New York: Pinter.

Smits, R. (1990). State of the art of technology assessment in Europe: a report to the 2nd European Congress on Technology Assessment: people and technology, ways and practices of technology management, Milan, 14–16 November 1990. Commission of the European Communities.

Smits, R. and J. Leyten (1988). Key issues in the institutionalization of technology assessment: development of technology assessment in five European countries and the USA. *Futures*, Vol. 20, No. 1, pp. 19–36.

te Molder, H. and J. Gutteling (2003). The issue of food genomics: about reluctant citizens and united experts. In R. van Est, L. Hanssen, O. Crapels and J. Vermolen (eds.), *Genes for your food – food for your genes: societal issues and dilemmas in food genomics*. The Hague: Rathenau Institute.

Van Den Ende, J., K. Mulder, M. Knot, E. Moors and P. Vergragt (1998). Traditional and modern technology assessment: toward a toolkit. *Technological Forecasting and Social Change*, Vol. 58, Nos. 1–2, pp. 5–21.

van Lente, H. (1993). *Promising technology: the dynamics of expectations in technological developments*. Enschede, the Netherlands: Universiteit Twente.

7 Backcasting

Jaco Quist

Introduction

Whereas the predictive approach and the exploratory approach to foresight are applied most widely, this chapter focuses on the normative approach to foresight and futures studies. This kind of foresight includes normative forecasting (Jantsch, 1967), roadmapping (see Chapter 8) and transition management (Rotmans et al., 2001; Grin et al., 2010; Loorbach, 2010), as well as design (oriented) scenarios (e.g., Silvester et al., 2013) and several types of policy scenarios. However, this chapter focuses on backcasting, which has become a widely applied normative futures approach since the 1970s, and expands on earlier work, in particular on Quist (2012, 2013).

Backcasting literally means looking back from the future. It has been defined as "generating a desirable future, and then looking backwards from that future to the present in order to strategize and to plan how it could be achieved" (Vergragt and Quist, 2011, p. 747). It may, but not always does, include the implementation and generation of follow-up activities contributing to bringing about the desirable sustainable futures. Backcasting is a normative approach to foresight that uses desirable or so-called alternative futures, instead of likely or possible futures (Quist 2007, 2013). Backcasting is very different from regular forecasting, which looks to the future from the present and is not normative. Backcasting is also different from exploratory scenario approaches, which generally aim at mapping uncertainty and complexity. Whereas forecasting is used to generate likely futures, also referred to as Business-As-Usual (BAU) scenarios, exploratory scenario approaches – like the context scenario methods developed by Shell or the model-based scenarios generated by IPCC – are used to generate plausible or possible futures, also referred to as exploratory scenarios. For a discussion on different types of futures (studies) and the related types of scenarios, see, for instance, Linstone (1999), Vergragt and Quist (2011), Börjeson et al. (2006). Due to its normative nature, backcasting is very well suited for sustainability-related challenges, because (i) sustainability is also a normative concept, and (ii) sustainability also involves long-term goals and changes.

Backcasting is particularly useful in addressing complex problems, when there is a need for major change, when dominant trends are part of the problem, when there are side-effects or externalities that cannot be satisfactorily solved in markets

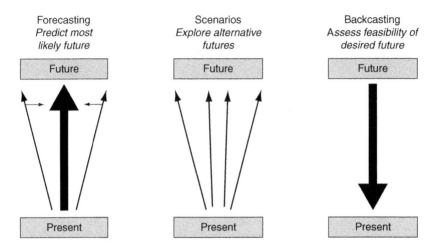

Figure 7.1 Three types of futures studies focusing on (i) likely futures using forecasting, (ii) possible futures, using exploratory scenario approaches, and (iii) desirable futures, using backcasting or other normative foresight approaches.

and when long time horizons allow for future alternatives that need time to develop (Drehborg, 1996). These kinds of problems have also been referred to as "wicked" or "unstructured" problems, which obviously apply to most problems surrounding sustainability. Höjer and Mattson (2000) have pointed to the relevance of conducting forecasts and trend extrapolations to determine whether backcasting is needed. Finally, Giddens (2009, pp. 98–100) has proposed using backcasting as a sustainable alternative to traditional planning, and as a tool for moving toward alternative futures when dealing with climate change.

Short History and Recent Developments

Backcasting was proposed in the 1970s in energy studies (e.g., Lovins, 1977; Robinson, 1990) and later also applied to sustainable planning (e.g., Robinson 1990) and to sustainable organizations (Holmberg, 1998). Since the early 1990s, it has developed into a participatory approach, taking off in the Netherlands (Weaver et al., 2000; Quist and Vergragt, 2006), Canada (Robinson, 2003) and Sweden (Holmberg, 1998; Dreborg, 1996; Carlsson-Kanyama et al., 2007).

Other examples of participatory backcasting can be found in various European collaborative research projects (e.g., Kok et al., 2006, 2011), while related participatory vision development and assessment projects can be found in various countries (e.g., Eames and Egmose, 2011; Sondeijker, 2009). Although most participatory backcasting studies involve (expert) stakeholders, citizens, consumers or end-users have increasingly been involved. For instance, the "Strategies towards the Sustainable Household" (SusHouse) project involved societal stakeholders like consumer associations and environmental organizations in visioning and backcasting workshops, as well as consumers and citizens in focus groups (Quist et al., 2001; Green and Vergragt, 2002; Quist, 2007). In addition, citizens were involved in vision development and backcasting workshops in sustainable urban planning (Carlsson-Kanyama et al., 2007), and in developing and evaluating local and regional energy futures in Canada (Robinson, 2003; Robinson et al., 2011). Strong citizen involvement was also part of local vision development (Kok et al., 2006) and defining sustainability research agendas in the UK (Eames and Egmose, 2011). Interesting recent participatory backcasting studies involving citizens or consumers include the SPREAD project (Mont et al., 2014; Neuvonen et al., 2014), the Consensus project in Ireland (e.g., Doyle and Davies, 2013; Davies, 2014) and some local climate change studies in Sweden (Milestad et al., 2014; Carlson-Kanyama et al., 2013). Furthermore, backcasting and transition management have been combined in the community arena methodology in the "Individuals in Context" project (Wittmayer et al., 2014), while transition management has also been applied at the local level (Nevens et al., 2014) and with teenagers (Iacovidou and Wehrmeyer, 2014).

Variety in Backcasting

More detailed overviews of the development and types of backcasting can be found elsewhere (Quist and Vergragt, 2006; Quist, 2007; Wangel, 2011). These reviews show a considerable variety in backcasting approaches and in the way they are turned into methodologies. Variety can be found in how stakeholder participation is organized, the kind of methods being applied within backcasting frameworks, the topics and the scale involved (e.g., local, regional, national), different types of systems (e.g., consumption systems, industrial systems, supply chains, geographical systems) and whether the focus is on impact (e.g., Quist et al., 2011) or diversity (Van de Kerkhof et al., 2003). There is also variety in the terminology being used. Several authors only refer to backcasting as a backward-looking step or analysis, using different terms for the overall approach. For instance, Van de Kerhof et al. (2003) call their approach Participatory Integrated Assessment, while Rotmans et al. (2001) include backcasting as part of transition management. There is also variety in the combination of backcasting with other approaches, like exploratory scenarios (Kok et al., 2011), Agent Based Modelling (Van Berkel and Verburg, 2012), adaptive management (Van der Voorn et al., 2012) or with a Delphi study (Zimmermann et al., 2012). The Delphi method is discussed in Chapter 4.

There are several types of backcasting (Wangel, 2011, see also Höjer et al., 2011):

i   target-oriented backcasting, which focuses on developing and analyzing target-fulfilling images, in which the target is usually expressed in quantitative terms;

ii pathway-oriented backcasting, in which setting strict goals is considered less important; the focus is on how change can take place and on measures that support the changes, like policies, taxes or behavioral changes;

iii   action-oriented backcasting, in which the main objective is to develop an action agenda, strategy or plan; the focus is on who could bring about the changes and realize buy-in and commitment among stakeholders and

iv   participation-oriented backcasting, in which backcasting is especially used as a creative workshop tool.

It is important to realize that different types can be combined within a single backcasting study. In fact, the variety is even greater, as the term backcasting is used to refer to an overall approach (e.g., Quist et al., 2011; Quist and Vergragt, 2006; Robinson, 1990; Wangel, 2011) as well as to a specific backwards-looking step or tool within a given methodology (e.g., Rotmans et al., 2001; Van de Kerkhof et al., 2003). As mentioned in the introduction, backcasting, in all its varieties, can be seen as part of a family of foresight approaches that share the development of normative or desirable future images, which also includes transition management and regular roadmapping (for the latter, see Chapter 8).

The extent to which impact and spin-off of backcasting occurs varies as well. For instance, a study on the impact of several backcasting experiments in the Netherlands (Quist, 2007; Quist et al., 2011) showed that participatory backcasting may, but does not automatically, lead to substantial follow-up and spin-off at the level of niches in the research, business, government and public domains (Quist, 2007; Quist et al., 2011).

Criticisms

Backcasting has also been criticized for generally neglecting aspects of governance, agency and implementation in visions and pathways (e.g., Wangel 2011). Also, it does not build on system innovation theory or transition theory, unlike transition management, and generally does not include economic conditions and aspects (Vergragt and Quist, 2011). In backcasting studies, the focus is often on changing existing socio-technical systems, while paying limited or no attention to cultural or economic changes that could support the envisioned changes.

Methodological Framework for Backcasting

Backcasting (Quist and Vergragt, 2006; Quist, 2007) can thus be seen as normative, long-term oriented, system-oriented and sometimes participatory in nature, and as adopting a broad view on sustainability (see Figure 7.2). Based on the shift toward participatory backcasting and the increasing focus on realizing implementation, follow-up and spin-off in the direction of sustainable development, backcasting can be seen as consisting of four key elements:

* *Participation*, involving stakeholders in a meaningful process of learning and vision generation.
* *Learning*: stakeholders learning from each other and from developing visions that are aimed in particular at so-called higher order learning through reflection on one's own assumptions and worldviews.

- *Developing visions* that are images of alternative, desirable, sustainable futures, but that also have the potential to become vehicles for dialogue and learning, as well as shared social constructs (visions) that can provide guidance (what to do) and orientation (where to go).
- *Using a range of tools and methods*, such as participatory tools, design tools, analytical tools, and organizational tools within the framework of an overall backcasting approach in order to realize a multi-disciplinary and trans-disciplinary study.

In a participatory backcasting study, stakeholders meet and are involved in developing, assessing, discussing and adjusting future visions. Ideally, the backcasting study functions as a protected experimental space in which ideas can be articulated and discussed, while ignoring the interests and rules of the outside world. This all stimulates both first- and higher-order learning among the stakeholders involved (Quist, 2007; Van de Kerkhof et al., 2003; Brown et al., 2003; Quist and Tukker, 2013). First-order learning reflects new insights into the options regarding a given problem within a given context, while higher-order learning has to do with new insights at a higher level with regard to problem definitions, standards, values, goals and convictions of actors, and on ways to solve the problem (Quist, 2007). On the one hand, learning may lead to increased awareness of and support for these sustainable futures and the actions that are needed to realize them and, on the other hand, it may lead to an increased understanding of how these futures are connected to strategic opportunities for stakeholders. Stakeholders seizing opportunities in a future vision can then initiate activities or begin working together to initiate joint actions and activities, for instance research, business applications, policy development, and user pilots. This process also leads to diffusion of the visions, which can become guiding images to the actors involved (Quist, 2007; Quist et al., 2011).

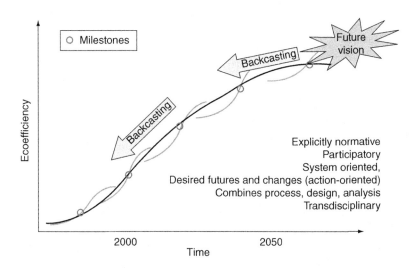

Figure 7.2 Backcasting: key concept and characteristics.

To deal with the variety in backcasting, four different backcasting approaches have been analyzed and compared (Quist, 2007, pp. 24–30). Building on Robinson (1990), the Natural Step backcasting methodology (Holmberg, 1998), the backcasting approach applied at the Dutch STD program (Weaver et al., 2000) and the backcasting methodology applied in the international Sustainable Households project (Quist et al., 2001; Green and Vergragt, 2002), a more comprehensive methodological framework for participatory backcasting has been developed (Quist, 2007), which is shown in Figure 7.3.

The framework consists of five steps and the outline of a toolkit containing four groups of methods and tools. The five steps are as follows:

STEP 1 Strategic problem orientation
STEP 2 Developing future visions
STEP 3 Backcasting analysis
STEP 4 Elaborating future alternatives and defining follow-up agenda
STEP 5 Embedding results and agenda, and stimulating follow-up

The backcasting approach reflected by the framework is not only inter-disciplinary (by combining and integrating tools, methods and results from different disciplines), but also trans-disciplinary, in the sense that it involves stakeholders, stakeholder knowledge and stakeholder values. It must be noted that, although the approach appears to be linear, it definitely is not. Iteration cycles are likely to occur, while there is also a mutual influence between the consecutive steps. In addition, the first step includes defining and bounding the system, and defining the time horizon, the number of visions to be developed, and developing the trans-disciplinary or multi-disciplinary research design.

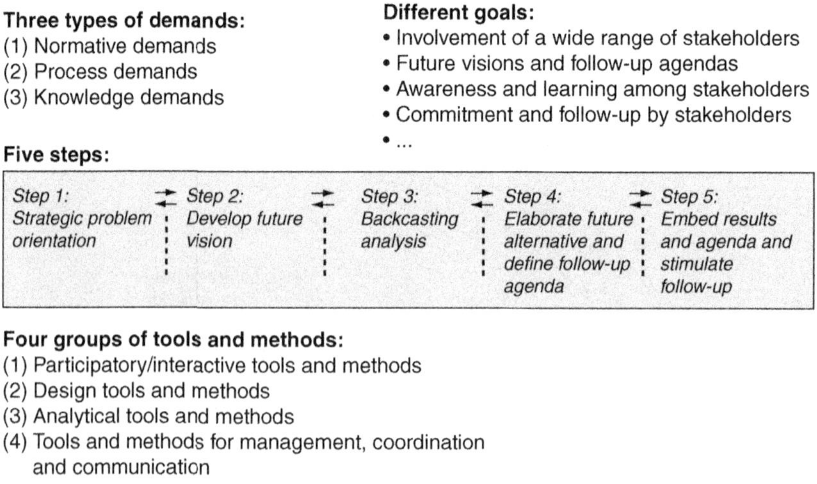

Three types of demands:
(1) Normative demands
(2) Process demands
(3) Knowledge demands

Different goals:
• Involvement of a wide range of stakeholders
• Future visions and follow-up agendas
• Awareness and learning among stakeholders
• Commitment and follow-up by stakeholders
• ...

Five steps:

Step 1: Strategic problem orientation	Step 2: Develop future vision	Step 3: Backcasting analysis	Step 4: Elaborate future alternative and define follow-up agenda	Step 5: Embed results and agenda and stimulate follow-up

Four groups of tools and methods:
(1) Participatory/interactive tools and methods
(2) Design tools and methods
(3) Analytical tools and methods
(4) Tools and methods for management, coordination and communication

Figure 7.3 A methodological framework for participatory backcasting (source: Quist, 2007, p. 232).

Furthermore, four groups of tools and methods are distinguished. In each step of participatory backcasting, methods and tools from each group can be applied. The four groups of tools and methods that make up a toolbox for backcasting are (Quist and Vergragt, 2006):

- *Participatory tools and methods.* This group includes all the tools and methods that are useful for involving stakeholders, and generating and guiding interaction and dialogue among stakeholders. It includes interviews, workshop tools, creativity tools, focus groups, other group discussion tools and tools supporting stakeholders during backcasting and participatory envisioning.
- *Design tools and methods.* This group consists of tools and methods for scenario construction, as well as for the elaboration and detailing of future systems, and for the design of the stakeholder involvement process. For instance, a vision can be developed through brainstorming, followed by clustering, through morphological methods, in which core dimensions are defined and altered, and by setting targets.
- *Analytical tools and methods.* This group of tools and methods is meant for assessing scenarios and designs, and includes consumer acceptance methods, environmental assessments, sustainability analysis and economic analyses. It also includes methods for the evaluation of stakeholder learning, network analysis and stakeholder analysis.
- *Tools and methods for management, coordination and communication.* This group consists of methods and tools that are relevant to managing the project and the stakeholder involvement process. These tools include the methods that can be used to shape and maintain stakeholder networks, communication and coordination, and are sometimes also referred to as organizational tools.

The framework also distinguishes three types of requirements or criteria: (i) normative requirements, (ii) process requirements and (iii) knowledge requirements. *Normative requirements* reflect the goal-related requirements for the future vision, as well as how sustainability is defined in the case in question, and how sustainability is turned into principles or criteria that future visions should meet. *Process requirements* are requirements related to stakeholder involvement and their level of influence in the way issues, problems and potential solutions are framed and resolved in the backcasting study. *Knowledge requirements* can be set to distinguish between the intended scientific and contextual knowledge and how these are valued against each other. Generally speaking, stakeholder knowledge and interdisciplinary knowledge does not fully meet regular disciplinary academic standards, but it is crucial for both process and content. Most requirements need to be specified at the start of a backcasting study. This can be done by the organizers, but it may also be the outcome of early stakeholder involvement. It is also possible that the requirements are partly defined by the organizers and are partly based on stakeholder discussions. Due to their trans-disciplinary nature, participatory backcasting studies can be seen as processes of co-production of knowledge, in which the stakeholders involved not only articulate desires, ideas and expectations on sustainable futures, but also actively contribute to generating and integrating knowledge by bringing their (contextual) expertise and knowledge to the backcasting study.

In addition, backcasting studies can have various goals, which can be process-related, content-related variables or knowledge-related. The difference between goals and requirements is that goals refer to the achievements at the end of the study, while requirements refer to conditions and criteria, either for the future vision or for the backcasting process. In general, multiple goals are set in participatory backcasting, although they are not necessarily all equally important.

Example: Sustainable Household Nutrition[1]

The EU-funded SusHouse (Strategies towards the Sustainable Household) project involved the development and evaluation of strategies for transitions toward sustainable households. The starting point was that a combination of technological, cultural and structural changes is necessary to achieve a Factor 20 environmental gain in the next 50 years through system innovations, taking both consumption and its interconnection with production, through products and product usage, into account. Another starting point was that sustainability in household consumption was approached from key activities conducted in the household, which relate both to consumption and to lifestyles.

One of the case studies was Sustainable Household Nutrition (SHN) in the Netherlands, which focused on the food system from a household and consumer perspective. The SHN experiment was also referred to as Shopping, Cooking and Eating (SCE), and involved a broad range of stakeholders from research, business, government and societal groups, which also met in two one-day workshops. The results of this case are presented below, following the five steps of the backcasting framework presented earlier. The case was conducted by a project researcher in collaboration with several colleagues involved in the local research team.

STEP 1 "Strategic Problem Orientation" consisted of analyzing the current household food consumption system in the Netherlands, including a stakeholder analysis, a system analysis and the identification of major trends and sustainability issues. An overview of the system, distinguishing four levels, is shown in Table 7.1. The stakeholder analysis included stakeholders on the demand and supply sides, research bodies, government and public interest groups. The research involved both a desk study and interviews with major stakeholders. The interviews were also intended to generate support and involvement for the workshops.

In STEP 2 "Develop Future Visions" selected stakeholders were invited for a stakeholder creativity workshop to identify sustainable ways of future function fulfillment. The workshop yielded clusters of ideas for future sustainable household food consumption, as well as some initial backcasting results, which were further elaborated by the project researcher after the workshop. Visions consisted

Table 7.1 The four-level food production and consumption system as defined for SCE

Level 1: The "core" function Shopping, Cooking, Eating
The core covers all activities of the household directly associated with the purchase, storage, cooking, eating and clearing up of food and drink, including:
- 'home' cooking, storage, clearing up after eating (including washing-up)
- the purchase of take-away food to eat in the street or at home, including the delivery of cooked food and meals
- eating in restaurants and work or office canteens
- production of food in householders' gardens or small-scale plots
- household transport associated with the purchase of food from shops and supermarkets, take-away and transport to restaurants

Level 2: Distribution
All retailing and wholesale of food, including the transport involved

Level 3: Agriculture, Processing and Durables
- production of basic food products (i.e., agriculture, including imports)
- food processing of any kind
- manufacture of kitchen equipment (for storage, food preparation, cooking, eating and clearing up)
- all transport involved, moving foods from farms, etc., to factories and between factories

Level 4: Delivery of inputs into other levels
The manufacturing of inputs at other levels, including agricultural chemicals, fertilizers and packaging

of (i) a core description with a focus on key activities like acquisition, storage, treatment (cooking), use (eating) and disposal; (ii) story boards showing how people lived in a single day in the vision; (iii) a drawing; (iv) proposals that matched the future vision. Box 7.1 summarizes one of the visions, including a preliminary backcasting analysis.

Three future visions were developed based on the results of the first stakeholder creativity workshop:

- In the first vision, entitled "Intelligent Cooking and Storing," environmental improvement was based on high-tech and ICT-based solutions, facilitating a lifestyle that highly resembles existing urban lifestyles in developed countries.
- In the second vision, which was called "Super-Rant," eating out and food shopping were integrated in a neighborhood center, also using eco-efficient technologies.
- The third vision, which was called "Local and Green," was based on the idea of Do-It-Yourself (DIY), in which people grow vegetables themselves, in addition to buying from local and regional food chains as much as possible.

Box 7.1 Intelligent Cooking and Storing Vision and Preliminary Backcasting Analysis (Quist, 2007, p. 136)

Intelligent Cooking and Storing

Intelligent Cooking and Storing (ICS) involves a household that can be characterized as a high-tech, convenient, do-it-yourself and fast way of living. Kitchen and food management is optimized with the help of intelligent technology, which also organizes ordering (electronically) and delivery, with the use of a so-called Intelligent Front Door. Water and energy are re-used wherever possible through cascade usage. Meals are either based on a mixture of sustainable ready-made and pre-prepared components (including vegetarian or novel protein foods replacing meat) or ready-made meals containing a microchip that provides cooking instructions to the microwave oven. Packaging is biodegradable and contains a (plastic) microchip with relevant consumer information about origin, treatment and preparation.

Proposals included (1) Intelligent kitchen; (2) Biodegradable and intelligent packaging; (3) Sustainable ready-made meals and meal components; (4) Food delivery service and intelligent front door; (5) Novel Protein Foods from non-animals sources.

Stakeholder Panorama

In this vision, the key stakeholders are consumers, retailers, food processors, packaging manufacturers, kitchen equipment and appliances producers, and government.

Environmental Profit Stems From:

- sustainably grown ingredients (including new ingredients taking over the function of unsustainable ingredients like novel protein foods);
- system optimization (through an integrated approach to the kitchen and to waste reduction);
- re-use of heat and water and cascade usage in the household;
- waste composting and biodegradable packaging.

Necessary Changes (Preliminary Backcasting Analysis)

- *Technological*: new kitchen technology and appliances (including a huge efficiency increase), new ICT for kitchen systems and production chain management, plastic chips, biodegradable packaging, cascade usage for water and energy, sustainable transportation, distribution and delivery systems.
- *Cultural/behavioral*: sustainability is taken for granted, further shift toward ready-mades and convenience, acceptance of new technologies, shift toward more sustainable substitutes (e.g., meat alternatives instead of meat), shift toward services.
- *Structural/Organizational*: the role of supermarkets will change due to large-scale delivery and a shift toward food management services, kitchen manufacturers deliver complete automated systems that communicate, instead of individual kitchens appliances, close cooperation and joint management throughout the complete production chain plus making information available to consumers; sustainable food production (regional or efficient large-scale production where this can be most environmentally efficient).

The *backcasting analysis* of STEP 3 was conducted in part by the project researcher by elaborating visions based on the creativity workshop results (see also Box 7.1), and in part during a second stakeholder workshop focusing on backcasting and implementation. In the second stakeholder workshop, the participants also evaluated the visions, using a specific evaluation technique that asked for positive aspects, negative aspects and what was missing. The discussion showed that the Intelligent Cooking and Storing vision was seen as the dominant direction, whereas the Super-Rant and Local and Green visions were appreciated because of their community and public values, which may also be essential for a sustainable future, but which would require more support than the dominant development direction of high-tech and individualization.

The backcasting discussions took place in sub-sessions involving each alternative vision, were guided by questions like "What changes are needed for bringing about this vision?" "How can this vision be brought about?" and "Who are needed to realize the changes and activities required?" and yielded suggestions for the follow-up agenda constructed in STEP 4, which is discussed next.

In STEP 4 "Elaborate future alternative and define follow-up agenda," three assessments of the future visions were conducted: (i) an environmental assessment using a systems approach, in combination with indicators; (ii) an economic assessment using a questionnaire to assess each vision in terms of its socio-economic aspects and (iii) a consumer acceptance analysis involving three different consumer focus groups, to evaluate the acceptability of the visions to consumers and to identify adopter profiles. The assessments, which were also used as input in the second stakeholder workshop, showed that the Intelligent Cooking and Storing

Figure 7.4 Drawing of the ICS vision.

vision and the Local and Green vision could reduce the environmental burden considerably. Surprisingly, with regard to the Super-Rant vision, it turned out that, on the basis of the energy requirements of restaurants in the late 1990s, the environmental impact could actually increase significantly. Interestingly, the focus groups liked the Local and Green vision most, especially because of the rural and suburban living, and houses with gardens. It was not possible to select the single most sustainable future vision, but each vision arguably depicted a more sustainable alternative to existing ways of living.

The "Define Follow-up Agenda" part of STEP 4 to a large extent took place during the second stakeholder workshop, through parallel sessions, in which both short-term implementation proposals and policy recommendations for each of the three future visions were developed and reported back in a plenary discussion session. After the workshop, the project researcher further elaborated the agendas and proposals.

STEP 5 "Embedding and Follow-up" started at the second stakeholder workshop. After the workshop, several spin-off meetings and initiatives with smaller groups of stakeholders were organised to develop research and demonstration proposals. This included a workshop focusing on domestic appliances for treating meat alternatives at home, a research proposal on optimizing kitchen appliances and food supply chains from an environmental point of view, and a program proposal for sustainability transitions in the eating-out and food-service sector. The results were a source of inspiration for the development of polices for sustainable consumption at the Ministry of the Environment.

Backcasting Step by Step

This section elaborates upon the five steps defined for backcasting, while a full overview of sub-steps is provided in Table 7.3.

Step 1: Strategic Problem Orientation

This step starts with a definition of normative assumptions, requirements and targets, which can also be done through stakeholder participation, while a (research) team needs to be established as well. Initial activities should include elaborating a backcasting methodology, using the methodological framework discussed in this chapter as a starting point, but tailoring it to the topic in a meaningful way, including how stakeholder involvement will be organized in line with the process requirements that have been set.

This aim of this step is to explore the problem from a systemic viewpoint, possible problem definitions, major sustainability issues, opportunities and possible solutions, as well as identifying and involving relevant stakeholders. In addition, it should be analyzed how the problem is perceived by different stakeholders, how it relates to function fulfillment, how other stakeholders evaluate and judge the different problem formulations based on their own mindset, values and interests, and how the supply chain and the demand side are interdependent and influence each other. It is important to adopt an integral viewpoint, while taking related consumption and production systems into account, and including trends and developments for the entire system. Involving stakeholders through interviews, focus groups or a Delphi study is also important, because they are experts in the field or system under study.

Van de Kerkhof (2004, pp. 26–27) has provided three major arguments for stakeholder involvement in (public) decision-making: (1) increased legitimacy of the decision, because more stakeholders have been involved; (2) increased accountability, because the stakeholders have become co-responsible for the decision and for related activities and action plans; (3) increased richness of the process, due to the input a wider range of viewpoints, interests, information and expertise about the topic under consideration. In this way, stakeholder participation in science and policy-making can contribute positively to dealing with uncertainties and contextualizing knowledge, and also in terms of structuring and defining complex unstructured societal problems. There are different degrees of participation. Table 7.2 distinguishes between High, Moderate and Low degrees of stakeholder participation.

Robinson (1990) has pointed to defining external variables, which are those factors and trends that are assumed to be steady or cannot be influenced from within the system under study.

Based on the discussion presented above, the following sub-steps can be distinguished, for which a range of methods is available (e.g., Enserink et al., 2010, see also stakeholder analysis in Chapter 15):

1A Setting demands/criteria, basic assumptions, process plan, methodology.
1B System analysis.
1C Stakeholder/actor analysis.
1D Trend and problem analysis.

Step 2: Develop Sustainable Future Visions

The results of the Strategic Problem Orientation step are used as a starting point for the construction of desirable future visions or scenarios in which the identified

Table 7.2 Degrees of participation

Degree of participation	In policy-making
High	Stakeholder control Delegated power Partnership
Moderate	Placation Consultation
Low	Information Therapy Manipulation

Sources: Van de Kerkhof (2004), Quist (2007).

sustainability issues and other problems have been solved. Stakeholder participation is important here, so workshops and focus groups are important tools in this step, although various other participatory methods can also be used. A key decision is whether to develop a single vision or multiple visions. Normative requirements for the future visions also need to be defined, if this has not yet been done in STEP 1. In addition, targets can be identified or elaborated.

Furthermore, there are different ways to develop future visions. For instance, creativity methods can be used, such as brainstorming, in combination with clustering, as was done in the Sustainable Households project (e.g., Quist et al., 2001; Quist, 2007). It is also possible to start by setting targets, which was done in the Sustainable Technology Program in the Netherlands (e.g., Weaver et al., 2000) and in many studies in Sweden (e.g., Höjer and Mattson, 2000; Höjer et al., 2011; Wangel, 2011). Changing systematically along different dimensions of the systems under study has also been done, which can be seen as the type of morphological analysis that is more widely applied in design processes. Morphological analysis, in the sense of creating diversity for different dimensions of the system under study, is not always mentioned explicitly, but can be seen in the results of multiple vision backcasting studies (e.g., Giurco et al., 2011; Quist et al., 2001; Höjer et al., 2011). Q-methodology, a method from social sciences that is applied to study diversity in viewpoints, can also be used to generate future perspectives (e.g., Cuppen, 2010) and may yield up to five or six future perspectives.

In a backcasting study, it is possible to develop a single vision or multiple visions. A single vision is more appropriate for developing ownership among stakeholders, whereas multiple visions studies are more appropriate for learning about differences and for stimulating dialogue among stakeholders. This subject is discussed in Quist (2007) and Quist et al. (2011). It is also possible to add first estimates or preliminary assessments for particular aspects, like environmental improvement potential, consumer acceptance, socio-economic aspects, as was done in the Sustainable Household example.

The following sub-steps can be distinguished.

2A   Detail (normative) demands and targets.
2B   Idea articulation and elaboration.
2C   Generation of one or several visions.

Step 3: Backcasting Analysis

Although the overall approach is named after this step, it is actually the step that has been elaborated and described least in the backcasting literature. Sometimes, only forward-oriented pathways are given, without showing the preceding backwards-looking analysis. Elsewhere (Quist, 2007; Quist, 2012), the suggestion has been made to guide the backcasting step with specific guiding questions like "What are the necessary changes needed to bring about this future vision?"

A more elaborated version calls for the use of WHAT–HOW–WHO questions (Quist, 2012, see also Wangel, 2011). *WHAT* questions focus on the changes that are needed to bring about the desirable future vision. This includes not only technological changes, but also cultural and behavioral changes, institutional and economic changes, and changes in the way society is organized. *HOW* questions look at how changes can be realized and provide an overview of the activities and actions that are needed. This question not only involves R&D activities, but also product development, regulation, policies, network formation, strategic alliances, public communication and education (programs). The *WHO* question examines which actors and stakeholders are needed to bring about the changes and to carry out activities that have been identified. Sometimes, new alliances and collaborations are needed, while it is also possible that actors and stakeholders are required that operate outside the system under examination and that were not included in the initial stakeholder analysis.

The aim of a more detailed version of backwards-looking analysis is to identify in-between targets and milestones. If these are set, it becomes possible to describe the narrative for different time periods. However, this is done more often in a forward-looking way by creating a pathway description, which is part of STEP 4. Finally, the backcasting analysis can be extended with an analysis of the drivers and barriers for each future vision.

The following sub-steps can be distinguished, while the key questions are also mentioned.

3A WHAT–HOW–WHO analysis part one: identification of changes,
   WHAT changes (technological, cultural-behavioral, organizational and structural-institutional) are needed to realize the vision?
3B WHAT–HOW–WHO analysis part two: required actions and stakeholders.
   HOW can these changes be realized? *WHO* should do this?
3C Drivers and barriers analysis.

Step 4: Elaboration and Defining Follow-up Activities and Agendas

The visions can be elaborated and assessed in several ways, depending on to a considerable extent the capacity, budget and time available. Assessments, analyses and feasibility studies are important in the first part of this step, while defining follow-up activities and agendas that enable the longer-term implementation and realization are important in the second part, and can be developed into a full pathway description. The following sub-steps can be distinguished:

4A Scenario elaboration (e.g., turning vision into quantified scenario).
4B Scenario sustainability analysis.
4C Generation of follow-agenda and proposals.
4D Develop transition pathway.

Step 5: Embedding of Action Agenda and Stimulating Follow-up

If the goals of a specific backcasting study include bringing about change processes, system innovations or transitions toward sustainability, it is important for the outcomes of the backcasting study to be embedded and taken further by stakeholders or groups of stakeholders. In the case of more complicated system innovations and transitions, contributions are required from government, firms, research organizations and civil society, and each societal group has to make a specific contribution that cannot easily be made by another group. Interestingly, the future vision can act as a guiding image that provides orientation (where to go) and guidance (what to do). In addition, follow-up activities can be stimulated, and process and learning evaluations are recommended as well.

The following sub-steps can be distinguished:

5A Dissemination of results and policy recommendations.
5B Stimulate follow-up activities.
5C Stakeholder learning evaluation.

Conclusions

In this chapter, it has been argued that backcasting is a useful approach in futures and foresight studies. An overview was provided of the current variety in backcasting and a methodological framework was presented that covers most of this variety, as illustrated through a backcasting study on Sustainable Household Nutrition in the Netherlands.

Table 7.3 Overall scheme for backcasting

Step 1: Strategic problem orientation
1A Setting requirements/criteria, basic assumptions, process plan, methodology.
1B System and regime analysis.
1C Stakeholder analysis.
1D Trend and problem analysis.

Step 2: Generating future visions
2A Detailed (normative) standards/criteria and targets.
2B Idea articulation and elaboration.
2C Generation of one or several visions.

Step 3: Backcasting analysis
3A WHAT–HOW–WHO analysis part 1:
     WHAT are the (technological, cultural-behavioral, organizational and structural-institutional) changes?
3B WHAT–HOW–WHO analysis part 2: required actions and stakeholders.
3C Drivers and barriers analysis.

Step 4: Elaboration and follow-up agenda
4A Scenario elaboration (e.g., turning vision into quantified scenario).
4B Scenario sustainability analysis.
4C Generation of follow-agenda and proposals.
4D Develop transition pathway.

Step 5: Embed results and stimulate follow-up
5A Dissemination of results and policy recommendations.
5B Stimulate follow-up activities.
5C Stakeholder learning evaluation.

It has been argued that backcasting is particularly useful in the case of complex societal problems, when there is a need for major change, when dominant trends are part of the problem, when there are side-effects or externalities that cannot be satisfactorily solved in markets, and when long time horizons allow for future alternatives that need several decades to develop. Backcasting is very well equipped to deal with sustainability, as sustainability is a normative concept, and backcasting is a normative approach to foresight that leads to normative scenarios and addresses the question as to what future we would like to have. Although, very often, a problem-oriented perspective is adopted, it is also possible to start a backcasting project from a socio-technical point of view.

This chapter has also provided a methodological framework for backcasting, consisting of five steps, four groups of tools and methods, and three types of requirements. This has been elaborated into a more detailed methodology, identifying sub-steps that can be seen as key activities in a backcasting study.

Acknowledgments

This chapter is based in part on work for the Glamurs project, which has received funding from the European Community's Seventh Framework Program (FP7/2007–2013) under grant agreement No. 613420. It is also based in part on work conducted for the "Next 50 Years" project, which was funded under the Energy Delta Gas Research (EDGAR) program.

Note

1 Taken from Quist and Vergragt (2006), Quist (2007) and Quist et al. (2011).

References

Börjeson, L., M. Höjer, K.H. Dreborg, T. Ekvall and G. Finnveden (2006). Scenario types and techniques: towards a user's guide. *Futures*, Vol. 38, No. 7, pp. 723–739.
Brown, H.S., P. Vergragt, K. Green and L. Berchicci (2003). Learning for sustainability transition through bounded socio-technical experiments in personal mobility. *Technology Analysis and Strategic Management*, Vol. 15, No. 3, pp. 291–315.
Carlsson-Kanyama, A., H. Carlsen and K.-H. Dreborg (2013). Barriers in municipal climate change adaptation: results from case studies using backcasting. *Futures*, Vol. 49, pp. 9–21.
Carlsson-Kanyama, A., K.-H. Dreborg, H.C. Moll and D. Padovan (2007). Participatory backcasting: a tool for involving stakeholders in local sustainability planning. *Futures*, Vol. 40, pp. 34–36.
Cuppen, E. (2010). Putting perspectives into participation: constructive conflict methodology for problem structuring in stakeholder dialogues. PHD thesis, Free University of Amsterdam.
Davies, A.R. (2014). Co-creating sustainable eating futures: technology, ICT and citizen-consumer ambivalence. *Futures*, Vol. 62, pp. 181–193.
Doyle, R. and A.R. Davies (2013). Towards sustainable household consumption: exploring a practice oriented, participatory backcasting approach for sustainable home heating practices in Ireland. *Journal of Cleaner Production*, Vol. 48, pp. 260–271.

Dreborg, K.H. (1996). Essence of backcasting. *Futures*, Vol. 28, No. 9, pp. 813–828.

Eames, M. and J. Egmose (2011). Community foresight for urban sustainability: insights from the Citizens Science for Sustainability (SuScit) project. *Technological Forecasting and Social Change*, Vol. 78, No. 5, pp. 769–784.

Enserink, B., L. Hermans, J. Kwakkel, W. Thissen, J. Koppenjan and P. Bots (2010). *Policy Analysis of Multi-Actor systems*. The Hague: Lemma Publishers.

Giddens, A. (2009). *The politics of climate change*. Cambridge, UK: Polity Press.

Giurco, D., B. Cohen, E. Langham, M. Warnken (2011) Backcasting energy futures using industrial ecology. *Technological Forecasting and Social Change*, Vol. 78, pp. 797–818.

Green, K. and P. Vergragt (2002). Towards sustainable households: a methodology for developing sustainable technological and social innovations. *Futures*, Vol. 34, pp. 381–400.

Grin, J., J. Rotmans and J.W. Schot (2010). *Transitions to sustainable development: Part 1. New directions in the study of long term transformative change*. New York: Routledge Taylor & Francis Group.

Höjer, M. and L.-G. Mattsson (2000). Determinism and backcasting in future studies. *Futures*, Vol. 32, pp. 613–634.

Höjer, M., A. Gullberg and R. Pettersson (2011). Backcasting images of the future city: time and space for sustainable development in Stockholm. *Technological Forecasting and Social Change*, Vol. 78, No. 5, pp. 819–834.

Holmberg, J. (1998). Backcasting: a natural step in operationalising sustainable development.*Greener Management International*, Vol. 23, pp. 30–51.

Iacovidou, E. and W. Wehrmeyer (2014). Making sense of the future: visions and transition pathways of laypeople and professionals from six EU countries. *Global Bioethics*, Vol. 25, No. 4, pp. 211–225.

Jackson, T. (2009). *Prosperity without growth: economics for a finite planet*. Abingdon, UK: Earthscan.

Jantsch, E. (1967). *Technological forecasting in perspective*. Paris: OECD.

Kok, K., M. Patel, D.S. Rothman and G. Quaranta (2006). Multi-scale narratives from an IA perspective: Part II. Participatory local scenario development. *Futures*, Vol. 38, No. 3, pp. 285–311.

Kok, K., van Vliet, M., I. Bärlund, A. Dubel and J. Sendzimir (2011). Combining participative backcasting and exploratory scenario development: experiences from the SCENES project. *Technological Forecasting and Social Change*, Vol. 78, No. 5, pp. 835–851.

Linstone, H.A. (1999). *Decision making of technology executives: using multiple perspectives to improve performance*. Boston, MA/London: Artech House.

Loorbach, D. (2007). *Transition management: new mode of governance for sustainable development*. Utrecht: International Books.

Loorbach, D. (2010). Transition management for sustainable development: a perspective, complexity based governance network. *Governance*, Vol. 23, No. 1, pp. 161–183.

Lovins, A.B. (1977). *Soft energy paths: toward a durable peace*. Cambridge, MA: Friends of the Earth/Ballinger Publishing Company.

Milestad, R., T. Svenfelt and K.H. Dreborg (2014). Developing integrated explorative and normative scenarios: the case of future land use in a climate-neutral Sweden. *Futures*, Vol. 60, pp. 59–71.

Mont, O., A. Neuvonen and S. Lähteenoja (2014). Sustainable lifestyles 2050: stakeholder visions, emerging practices and future research. *Journal of Cleaner Production*, Vol. 63, pp. 24–32.

Neuvonen, A., T. Kaskinen, J. Leppänen, S. Lähteenoja, R. Mokka and M. Ritola (2014). Low-carbon futures and sustainable lifestyles: a backcasting scenario approach. *Futures*, Vol. 58, pp. 66–76.

Nevens, F., N. Frantzeskaki, L. Gorissen and D. Loorbach (2013). Urban transition labs: co-creating transformative action for sustainable cities. *Journal of Cleaner Production*, Vol. 50, pp. 111–122.

Quist, J. (2007). *Backcasting for a sustainable future: the impact after ten years*. Delft, the Netherlands: Eburon Publishers.

Quist, J. (2012). Backcasting. In P. van der Duin (ed.), *Toekomstonderzoek voor Organisaties: handboek methoden en technieken*. Assen: Van Gorcum (in Dutch).

Quist, J. (2013). Backcasting and scenarios for sustainable technology development. In K.M. Lee and J. Kauffinan (eds.), *Handbook of sustainable engineering*. Amsterdam: Springer.

Quist, J. and A. Tukker (2013). Knowledge collaboration and learning for sustainable innovation and consumption: overview and introduction to the special issue. *Journal of Cleaner Production*, Vol. 48, pp. 167–175.

Quist, J. and P. Vergragt (2006). Past and future of backcasting: the shift to stakeholder participation and a proposal for a methodological framework. *Futures*, Vol. 38, No. 9, pp. 1027–1045.

Quist, J., M. Knot, W. Young, K. Green and P. Vergragt (2001). Strategies towards sustainable households using stakeholder workshops and scenarios. *International Journal of Sustainable Development*, Vol. 4, No. 1, pp. 75–89.

Quist, J., W. Thissen and P.J. Vergragt (2011). The impact and spin-off of participatory backcasting: from vision to niche. *Technological Forecasting and Social Change*, Vol. 78, No. 5, pp. 883–897.

Robinson, J. (1990). Futures under glass: a recipe for people who hate to predict. *Futures*, Vol. 22, pp. 820–843.

Robinson, J. (2003). Future subjunctive: backcasting as social learning. *Futures*, Vol. 35, pp. 839–856.

Robinson, J., S. Burch, S. Talwar, M. O'Shea and M. Walsh (2011). Envisioning sustainability: recent progress in the use of participatory backcasting approaches for sustainability research. *Technological Forecasting and Social Change*, Vol. 78, No. 5, pp. 756–768.

Rotmans, J., R. Kemp and M. van Asselt (2001). More evolution than revolution: transition management in public policy. *Foresight*, Vol. 3, No. 1, pp. 15–31.

Silvester, S., S.K. Beella, A. van Timmeren, P. Bauer, J. Quist and S. van Dijk (2013). Exploring design scenarios for large-scale implementation of electric vehicles: the Amsterdam Airport Schiphol case. *Journal of Cleaner Production*, Vol. 48, pp. 211–219.

Sondeijker, S. (2009). Imagining sustainability: methodological building blocks for transition scenarios. PhD Thesis, Erasmus University Rotterdam.

Van Berkel, D.B. and P.H. Verburg (2012). Combining exploratory scenarios and participatory backcasting: using an agent-based model in participatory policy design for a multi-functional landscape. *Landscape Ecology*, Vol. 27, No. 5, pp. 641–658.

Van de Kerkhof, M. (2004). *Debating climate change: a study of stakeholder participation in an integrated assessment of long-term climate policy in the Netherlands*. Amsterdam: Lemma Publishers.

Van de Kerkhof, M., M. Hisschemoller and M. Spanjersberg (2003). Shaping diversity in participatory foresight studies: experiences with interactive backcasting on long-term climate policy in the Netherlands. *Greener Management International*, Vol. 37, pp. 85–99.

Van der Voorn, T., C. Pahl-Wostl and J. Quist (2012). Combining backcasting and adaptive management for climate adaptation in coastal regions: a methodology and a South African case study. *Futures*, Vol. 44, No. 4, pp. 346–364.

Vergragt, P.J. and J. Quist (2011). Backcasting for sustainability: introduction to the special issue. *Technological Forecasting and Social Change*, Vol. 78, No. 5, pp. 747–755.

Wangel, J. (2011). Exploring social structures and agency in backcasting studies for sustainable development. *Technological Forecasting and Social Change*, Vol. 78, No. 5, pp. 872–882.

Weaver, P., L. Jansen, G. Van Grootveld, E. van Spiegel and P. Vergragt (2000). *Sustainable technology development*. Sheffield, UK: Greenleaf Publishers.

Wittmayer, J., N. Schäpke, F. van Steenbergen and I. Omann (2014). Making sense of sustainability transitions locally: how action research contributes to addressing societal challenges. *Critical Policy Studies*, Vol. 8, pp. 465–485.

Zimmermann, M., I.L. Darkow and H.A. Von der Gracht (2012). Integrating Delphi and participatory backcasting in pursuit of trustworthiness: the case of electric mobility in Germany. *Technological Forecasting and Social Change*, Vol. 79, No. 9, pp. 1605–1621.

8 Roadmapping

Ben Römgens

Introduction

A roadmap describes a possible future position of an organization or industry, and alternative pathways to reach this position. However, roadmapping is also a process, which is at least as important as the roadmap reports, because it creates commitment for the actions required to realize the roadmap. Typical for the roadmap process is the demand (need) driven approach, in which the various stakeholders and experts identify and select alternative technical and non-technical options. A roadmap project has a clear objective and results in SMART targets (Specific, Measurable, Acceptable, Result focused and Time-bound). The pathways suggested to realize the objectives should be based on a sound and transparent analysis and are clearly visualized. Finally, a roadmap should include a plan to monitor and adjust the roadmap (see, for example, US Department of Energy, 2000; Phaal et al., 2001a; Römgens and Kruizinga, 2009; McDowall, 2012; UNFCC TEC, 2013).

Motorola developed the roadmap methodology as a strategic explorative foresight method in the 1970s. The explorative character is shown, for example, in the development of specific pathways for different scenarios (Lizaso and Reger, 2004). Since the start of the 1980s, companies in the high-tech industry have used the method to develop strategic, tactical and operational plans for next-generation technologies and products, and to realize a better (quicker) product development. The roadmap is an important support tool for communication between the different parties involved in reaching this future position.

Since the 1990s, roadmaps have also been used frequently by companies in non-tech sectors, sector/trade organizations, countries and cities. Companies develop roadmaps primarily to improve product development and speed up the time-to-market of new products. Nations and cities develop roadmaps with regard to sustainability (the green city), social participation, poverty reduction, energy transition, the future healthcare system and for economic and social revitalization.

The roadmap can be summarized in two visualizations: the multiple layer diagram and the action program. The action program shows the actions needed to meet future requirements, while the multiple layer diagram shows the relationships between external trends and product requirements, production requirements, and technical and non-technical measures needed to meet the requirements. Trends are translated into the requirements that customers have regarding future products. Subsequently, it is shown how this affects the production process. Finally, the necessary measures and resources, such as knowledge and assets, are included. An example of a diagram is shown in Figure 8.1.

The structure of an action program is displayed in Figure 8.2, where the actions are placed in time zones and structured according to their priority: high, medium or low, and the relationships between the actions are displayed as well. Actions are labeled as having a high priority if their contribution to the overall goal/targets is high and/or the results of the action in question are prerequisites for a (group of) actions. It is clear that these prerequisites are often executed at an early stage.

In this chapter, we describe the various objectives and applications of roadmapping, followed by a description of the results and activities regarding the different stages of the roadmapping process. Each stage is illustrated with an example. We conclude this chapter with an overview of the applied literature and suggestions for further reading.

Origin and State of the Art of Roadmapping

Roadmaps as a method to develop product technology and emerging technology was developed in the 1970s by Motorola. The first technology roadmap was published in 1987 by Motorola (Phaal et al., 2010). In the 1980s, roadmaps were mainly used by high-tech companies to improve product development.

The first industry roadmap was published in 1991: the international roadmap for semiconductors. In the same period, Industry Canada, the US Department of Energy (DoE) and the Japanese MATI initiated an elaborate set of industry roadmaps in their countries. In this period, the US DoE initiated over ten industry roadmaps and also coordinated the development of technology roadmaps for, among other things, "ground water" and "robotics and intelligent machines." In the late 1990s, international NGOs started also to develop roadmaps.

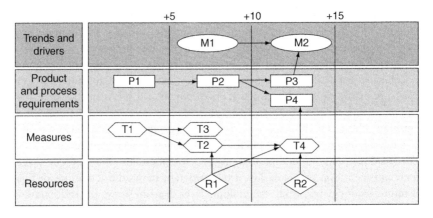

Figure 8.1 The roadmap as multiple layer diagram.

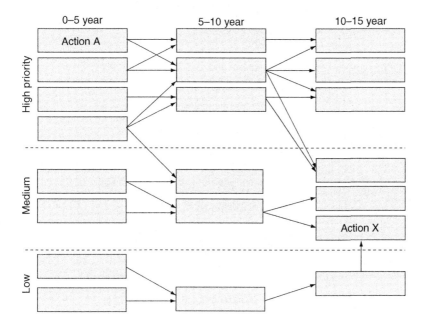

Figure 8.2 The roadmap as action program.

Since the turn of the millennium, the method was developed further. In 2001, the Centre for Technology Management published an interactive roadmapping method called T-plan. With this interactive variant, a group of people executes the entire process during four workshops of (only) half a day or an entire day (Phaal et al., 2001b). Based on this methodology, DNV GL used a slightly modified T-plan approach for industry, organization and issue roadmaps. See Figure 8.3 for the modified T-plan approach.

After the growth in industry and issue roadmaps around the millennium, interest in roadmaps appeared to be declining. However, since the 2008 economic crisis, there has been a big revival. The growing complexity and interconnectivity of issues, industries and networks has generated a growing interest in roadmapping-type methods to mobilize stakeholders in order to analyze and deal with complex problems. The action-oriented part of the roadmap was also a unique selling point in the competition with other foresight methodologies, like scenario planning (see Chapter 4) and technology assessment (see Chapter 6).

The growing popularity of roadmapping can also be seen in recent research of the United Nations (UN). In 2013, the UN identified over 100 roadmaps on renewable energy and other energy-related issues in the new millennium. Almost 50 percent of the roadmaps were delivered after 2010 (UNFCC TEC, 2013). The DoE focuses on roadmaps for energy efficiency and clean cities. The clean city program of the US DoE advances the nation's economic, environmental and energy-related security by supporting local actions designed to cut the use of petroleum in transportation. The program started in 1994 to save 2.5 billion gallons of

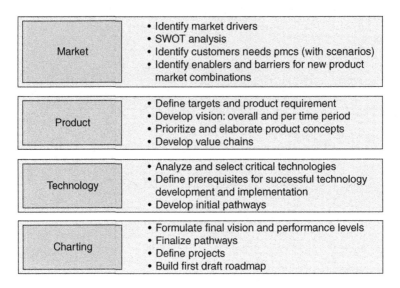

Market	• Identify market drivers • SWOT analysis • Identify customers needs pmcs (with scenarios) • Identify enablers and barriers for new product market combinations
Product	• Define targets and product requirement • Develop vision: overall and per time period • Prioritize and elaborate product concepts • Develop value chains
Technology	• Analyze and select critical technologies • Define prerequisites for successful technology development and implementation • Develop initial pathways
Charting	• Formulate final vision and performance levels • Finalize pathways • Define projects • Build first draft roadmap

Figure 8.3 T-plan approach for industry, organization and issue roadmaps.

petroleum a year by 2020. In 2014, nearly 100 Clean Cities coalitions were active in communities across the country (see www.cleancities.energy.gov). Between 2010 and 2012, the International Energy Agency (IEA) developed over 20 global low-carbon energy technology roadmaps, with the overall aim of advancing global development and uptake of key technologies, and realize a 50 percent reduction in energy-related CO_2 emissions by 2050 (see www.iea.org/roadmaps/).

Over the last decade, several authors have suggested using scenarios to create better roadmaps (Lizaso and Reger, 2004; Römgens and Kruizinga, 2009; Saritas and Aylen, 2010). Scenarios provide insight into the social, political and economic drivers of technical developments. Scenarios are also used to explore future markets and specify product requirements. A good example of this is the roadmap "Moving America away from oil" (Arlington Institute, 2003). Finally, scenarios can help to select and test the robustness of options and develop pathways and calculate impact. Options are robust if it is expected that they can be developed and deployed successfully in a majority of the scenarios. During pathway development, the roadmap team combines options to at least one suitable pathway per scenario. An excellent example of the use of scenarios for pathway development can be found in Industrial Decarbonisation Roadmaps to 2050 of the UK Department of Energy and Climate Change (Parsons Brinckerhoff, DNV GL, 2015).

By now, roadmapping seems to have become a commonly recognized and generally accepted foresight technique for government and companies in the profit and not-for-profit sectors. However, recent analysis shows that it is also becoming a buzzword for an action or project plan. A growing share of recent roadmaps lacks clear targets, actions, alternative pathways and/or visualization (see below, under 'Principles', for further details).

The main challenges in developing and implementing a roadmap are:

- the long and (work-)intensive process;
- the transition from development to deployment;
- analyzing large amounts of data and transforming them into an attractive and understandable visualization.

The relatively long and (work-)intensive process. Smaller enterprises lack the resources (time, money and knowledge) needed to develop and implement a roadmap. In industries where partners are not used to working together, individual partners will not participate unless they have a better insight into the potential outcomes. Even then, a substantial set of roadmaps focuses on pre-competitive research, joint lobby activities and joint marketing to improve the image of an industry.

The transition from development to deployment. Especially for national, industry and issue roadmaps, the major challenge is to mobilize a critical mass of individual players and consortia to carry out follow-up projects. Analysis from, among others, McDowall (2012) shows that a transition toward implementation is more likely if the roadmap is:

- credible: based on sound analysis;
- desirable: meeting the goals of the stakeholders;
- usable: defining effective actions (perspectives) for individual and groups of users;
- adaptable, embedded in a structure with periodic reviews and updates.

Although meeting the first three criteria is only possible if relevant stakeholders (opinion leaders) are involved in the roadmap development process, some countries and companies prefer to develop the roadmap with a small expert team.

Analyzing large amounts of data and transforming them into attractive and understandable visualizations. There is a growing understanding that areas like infographics, serious games, simulations and roadmapping software will contribute to the success of future roadmaps.

In the last decade, there has indeed been a growing group of simple planning software tools adjusted for roadmapping. Most of these tools provide simple graphics of the action program. Software that facilitates the collection, analysis and visualizations of trends, requirements and options is still very rare. These features are available, for example, in Aha product planning software and Planisware software. Aha roadmapping software also includes modules to involve stakeholders in the generation and assessment of ideas.

Board games and computer-based serious games can be used to allow different groups of stakeholders to explore and define common goals and interest, and to determine joint actions and policies in roadmaps where large, system-wide innovations are needed. Developments in Computer-Aided Design (CAD) and Geographic Information Systems (GIS) for creating 3D models of infrastructures, buildings and cities, the availability of (more and more operational) and easy-to-use game development tools, such as Unity 3D and UDK, make game development feasible and cost-effective for a large group of professionals.

The Roadmap Method

Principles

The roadmap method is founded on the following principles:

- integrated analysis of a system;
- need- or market-driven;
- clear targets;
- visualize results in a graphic display (preferably on one A4-sized surface);
- involve all stakeholder groups for optimal results;
- think out of the box and outline alternative pathways;
- clear action perspectives for (groups of) stakeholders;
- understand that the roadmap is a living document.

The central principle of the method is the *integrated analysis of a system*. It is only when the entire system, that is to say, all the relationships between the various components, is complete, that the right measures can be taken. In a roadmap, the entire trajectory from tomato seed to the soup in the consumer's bowl is taken into account. And, of course, with the revival of the circular economy, an increasing number of industry roadmaps show how to close the loop and include a view to reduce, reuse, reform, and recycle or refuse material. The analysis can be consolidated in, for example, a causal or system map. Good examples of a system analysis are included in the Moving America away from Oil roadmap (Arlington Institute, 2003).

Need- or market-driven. A good roadmap is need-driven, not solution-driven. Starting from a market need leads to a broader set of appropriate solutions (options). Roadmapping provides a way to identify, evaluate and select valuable alternatives that can be used to satisfy the need in question (Garcia and Bray, 1997). The market analysis also makes it possible to prioritize the importance of product features and hence the contribution of the technologies involved (Phaal et al., 2001a). Good examples of need driven roadmaps are the Canadian Electric power roadmap from Industry Canada (Industry Canada, 2000), the technology roadmap for the Canadian textile industry (CTI Group, 2008) and A Roadmap US Robotics (Robotics in the United States, 2013).

Clear targets. Clear, preferably quantified, targets and (product and process) requirement are needed to create clear collective momentum, and to select the necessary options and develop the right pathways. Good examples are the road-maps of the European Commission and the IEA on new energy technologies. The analysis by of the UN (UNFCCC, 2013) of more than 100 energy-related roadmaps showed that only 60 percent of the roadmaps include clear targets.

Visualize results, preferably including a one-pager, to give a total overview. The one-pager is an essential tool for communication. The visualization should provide a clear overview of the most important trends, product and process requirements, and options, including the interdependencies. Analysis by the UN (UNFCCC, 2013) reveals that only 45 percent of the roadmaps include a visual presentation of the results. Most visualizations relate to action planning. Visualizations that provide insight into the relations between trends, targets and requirements are very rare. This is consistent with our experience involving industry roadmaps. Figure 8.1 contains a structured example of such a visualization. Other examples can be found in the technology roadmaps of the IEA and the roadmap for the Dutch waste water sector. The waste water roadmap includes visualizations of future options (products, see Figure 8.14, below), and integrated pictures of the optimal future energy, raw material and water cycle for four different geographic areas (one of which is shown in Figure 8.16, below).

Involve all stakeholder groups for optimal results. For positive results and support, analytical and visionary thinkers from companies, chain and knowledge partner have to participate. Besides market, technology and industry experts, the decision-makers are involved as well. For strategic and long-term roadmaps, the participation of outsiders and free thinkers is essential. They will provide a powerful impulse to out-of-the-box thinking concerning future markets and clients.

Think out of the box and sketch alternative pathways. Typical for roadmap project is the broad consideration and alternative combinations of options. The roadmapping project group considers not only the solutions known to the industry leaders, but also different/new solutions for the next decade(s). The team reflects thoroughly about the opportunities of unexpected combinations and wonders what they can learn from other companies or industries. In the roadmap Moving America away from Oil (Arlington Institute, 2003) the Arlington Institute integrated goals and options on energy efficiency, new fuels and new technologies for three different time periods (see Figure 8.4). In the roadmap 2050, from the European Commission (EC, 2010), three specific pathways are modeled. The pathways differ with respect to the shares of Renewable Energy Sources, Carbon Capture and Storage, and Nuclear. In the decarbonization roadmaps paper and pulp industry from Parsons Brinckerhoff and DNV GL pathways differ with regard to ambition and technology orientation. In the "Business As Usual" (BAU) pathway companies only implement mature, easy to implement solutions with short pay back periods. In the "state of the art" pathway companies also implement technologies like state of the art steam systems which require major investments in money, time and knowledge. In the "industrial clustering" pathway companies also implement measures like heat networks that require close cooperation beween companies. In the "max tech" pathway also new and innovative technologies like bio-based CHP are implemented. See Figure 8.4 for a schematic overview of pathways, technology options and interdependencies/relations.

Clear actions. The need to generate commitment for a clear joint action plan/program is often the reason a roadmap exercise is started. Roadmaps for specific products, technologies and organizations always incorporate a specific action plan. However, according to the UN, more than 50 percent of the roadmaps have no action plan, and less than 10 percent incorporate a plan for monitoring the execution and updating the roadmap (UNFCCC, 2013). It is our experience that defining specific actions is very difficult, especially for national and industry roadmaps. Stakeholders are exhausted but happy that they have reached an agreement

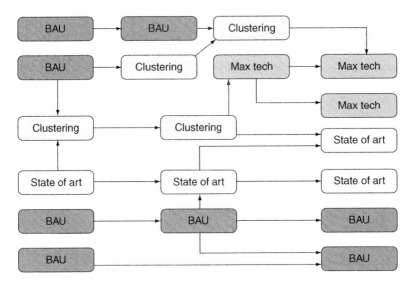

Figure 8.4 Pathways.

on targets and that they have a clear vision. Getting people to agree on the actions seems a step too far. Another reason for a lack of clear action plans in industry roadmaps has to do with the huge differences in the markets, products and production technologies involved. As a result, most actions are only relevant to a sub-set of companies. In addition, most actions are the responsibility of an individual company, which means that developing the action plan is also a follow-up task of an individual company.

The roadmap is a living document. To stimulate a proper implementation of the roadmap, it should be regularly updated on the basis of advancing insight into technology and market developments. The IEA recommends (IEA, 2104) designating a roadmap implementation body early on in the process, to ensure a proper execution. Other lessons from the IEA are:

- Plan a successful roadmap launch to build awareness and create the momentum needed to stimulate action.
- Monitor key energy, environmental and economic indicators to track progress.
- Conduct regular roadmap revision workshops to adapt goals and priorities to changing circumstances.

Objectives of Roadmap Projects

When we look at different roadmaps, we can distinguish the following objectives:

- raising awareness and creating a sense of urgency for change and future opportunities;

- joint knowledge development;
- synchronization of (R&D, marketing, lobby and standardization) activities;
- design and realization of new (generation) products and technologies.

Raising awareness and creating a sense of urgency. A rough roadmap, which can be created with minimal effort by a small group, serves as a proof of concept and as a concrete support tool to create a sense of urgency among the participants, and to raise awareness of the added value of a roadmap exercise and product.

Joint knowledge development. Consortia of companies and research institutes bundle scarce knowledge and resources, in addition to making it possible to formulate realistic (long-term) objectives and strategies for new technologies in a structured manner. Also, the roadmap supports the exploration and prioritization of investment opportunities.

Synchronization of activities. Product roadmaps are directed toward synchronizing the activities of various teams and organizations. This involves the alignment of content as well as planning. Efficiency improvement, cost reduction (for companies and clients) and competitive advantage via a quick time-to-market are the most important results.

The design and realization of new (generation) products and technologies is the most specific application of the roadmap method. Combinations of companies consistently work on the development and launching of new products and technologies. Take, for example, the development of DVD, CD and Blu-Ray standards, or the development of the Senseo coffee machine.

Types of Roadmaps

There are various types of roadmaps, including roadmaps for technologies, products, organizations, chains (industries) and issues. Developing the various types of roadmaps is a similar process, although the time horizon and focus in the individual process stages may vary considerably. Table 8.1 shows the orientation, time horizon and type of action program for five types of roadmaps.

Table 8.1 Roadmaps in different shapes and sizes

Roadmap type	Focus	Time horizon	Action program
Product	Tactical, operational	≤2 years Outlier toward 5 years	Business plan Operational plan
Technology	Strategic	≥10 years	Development program
Industry	Strategic		Business plans Development programs
Issue	Strategic	Often 15 to 20 years	Policy agenda
Organization	Strategic, tactical, operational	3 to 5 years sometimes 10 to 20 years	Organization design Business plan

Source: © 2009 DNV GL.

A product roadmap defines requirements, as well as an operational development and production plan, for a new or improved product. For consumer products, the time horizon is less than two years. A product roadmap is updated each quarter. The added value is in involving and connecting various (internal) suppliers and customers during the development, production planning and market introduction phases. An example of a product roadmap is presented in Figure 8.5.

Technology roadmaps cover the development and deployment of new or improved technologies. Roadmaps for new production technologies usually have a strategic orientation and a time horizon spanning multiple decades. Technology roadmaps are issued by individual organizations and by government and consortia, with the latter focusing on a joint research and development agenda. Good examples are the roadmaps developed by the IEA concerning plug-in hybrid transportation, wind energy, solar photo voltage (Figure 8.6), nuclear power, bio-based fuels and smart grids, which are designed to realize a 50 percent reduction of energy-related CO_2 emissions.

Industry roadmaps contain a vision and action plan for a sustainable and competitive future of the industry in question. These roadmaps are often initiated by governments, for example in the US, Canada, Australia and Japan. The roadmaps are developed in cooperation with companies and research institutes. Examples of this type of roadmaps are, among others, the US DoE (2000) and the Canadian government (see www.ic.gc.ca/trm). Other (more recent) examples are the Roadmap for US Robotics 2013 edition, the Plastics and Polymer Composites for Automotive Markets roadmap, the Material Handling and Logistics US Roadmap and the Additive Manufacturing Technology Roadmap for Australia.

Issue roadmaps, which are developed mainly by governments and NGOs, focus on issues like energy, water and resource scarcity, poverty and climate change. They have a strategic political orientation, providing a policy agenda

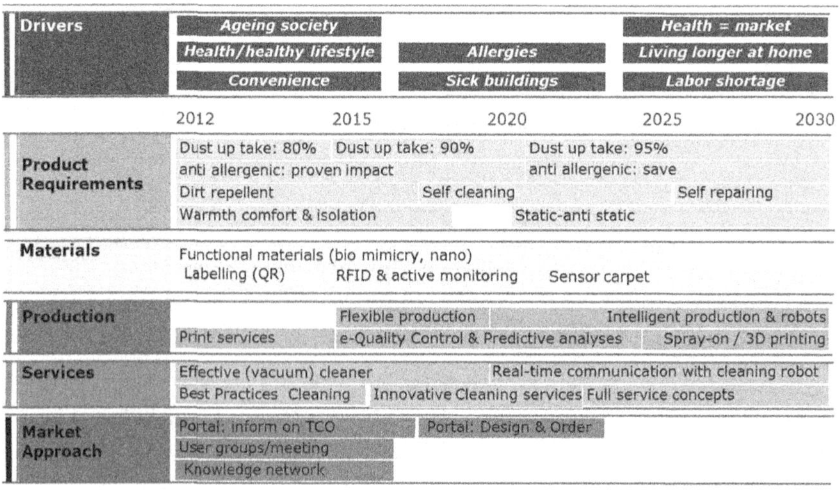

Figure 8.5 Product roadmap, Carpet.

and/or an action program. A well-known roadmap for sustainability is the 2050 vision of the World Business Council for Sustainable Development (WBCSD). The vision and the potential pathways toward a sustainable world are developed by 29 members, mostly multinationals, in cooperation with hundreds of representatives of companies, government and social organizations. Another example is the roadmap of the European Climate Foundation, which shows how Europe,

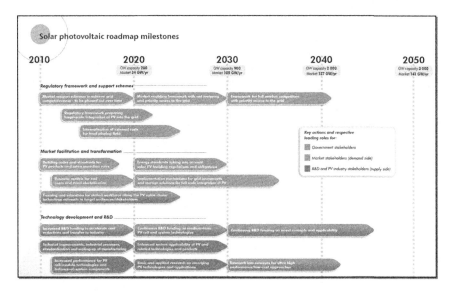

Figure 8.6 Technology roadmap, photo voltage.

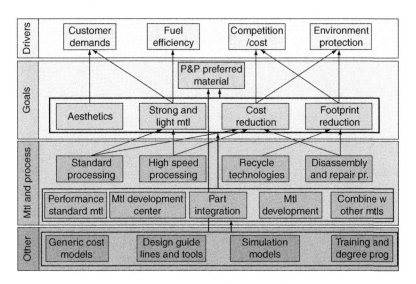

Figure 8.7 Industry roadmap, plastic and polymer composites for automotive markets (source: adapted from American Chemistry Council, 2014).

with the use of existing technologies, can realize a transition toward a sustainable energy supply, without compromising the availability of security (of energy) or economic prosperity. Cities develop roadmaps on issues like climate change, mobility, energy transition and economic and social revitalization. A good example is the Seattle climate action plan (all ingredients of a roadmap are included). More examples can be foud under the US clean city program. In the US DoE's Clean Cities program 100 Clean Cities coalitions bring together stakeholders to deploy alternative and renewable fuels, idle-reduction measures, fuel economy improvements and emerging transportation technologies.

Roadmaps for organizations usually aim at a momentum and a joint direction for the next planning period. Organizations develop roadmaps for any strategic change: entering a new market, preparing a merger, developing a master plan for renewing the IT infrastructure and removing the legacy IT, or preparing for new regulations. For organizations in the manufacturing industry, the results are often similar to those of product and technology roadmaps. Organizations in other industries formulate the roadmap often as a gap analysis which shows the coherent action program needed to achieve the formulated future state.

Roadmapping Step by Step

This section contains a brief description of the steps included in a roadmap project. The most important results and the coherence between the various steps are shown in Figure 8.8.

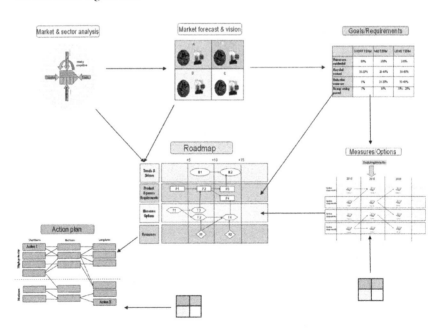

Figure 8.8 The roadmap process step by step.

Define Roadmap Project

In this phase, stakeholders are interviewed to identify the need, added value and scope of the roadmap project. An industry scan, market and technology analysis, and forecasts yield possible issues, ambitions and networks. A strategy is developed to mobilize stakeholders and to prevent the roadmap from becoming a one-time desk-bound activity. Finally, in a workshop, stakeholders develop a first high-level roadmap and discuss the ambitions, approach and concerns of the project.

A roadmap project is carried out by a project team and a (virtual) team or network per focus area. Team members from inside and outside the organization contribute via workshops, interviews and/or Delphi rounds (Chapter 4).

Industry and issue roadmaps often have a separate team for performance requirements, to ensure the transparent and consistent calculations of potential performance improvements. Climate change and energy roadmaps often performing a Life Cycle Asessement (LCA). This is a method used to determine the environmental burdens associated with a product, process or activity, by identifying and quantifying the energy and materials used and waste released. Performing an LCA in an transparent and consistent way requires a profound knowledge of the LCA method, materials and material databases in the entire industry. For industry and issue roadmaps, we also form a separate validation team.

CASE

A car manufacturer wants to improve its competitive position in the market and considers developing a roadmap. The organization has to decide whether to expand the roadmap to integral mobility or focus on the future of the automotive industry. For the latter option, the development and the implementation is less complex. It can even be further simplified if the car manufacturer limits the scope to the engine and moving parts of the car, instead of including the customer perspective as well. After a consultation with suppliers, dealers and government institutions, the car manufacturer decides to develop a roadmap for car transport, including the infrastructure and interface with other means of transport, to ensure that the solutions will meet market requirements.

Analyze the Market and Sector

This phase describes and analyzes (potentially per market segment) the developments over recent years in terms of market scope, customer segments and product portfolios. The most important characteristics, strengths and weaknesses of the sector, product portfolio and working processes are also described, and the competitive forces are analyzed. The analysis gives a singular starting point for the following roadmap phases.

The market and sector analysis consists of literature reviews, interviews and workshops. Outsiders and external experts are invited to challenge the immediate stakeholders. The core of the workshop is a deepening of the SWOT (strengths, weaknesses, opportunities and threats) and competitive forces analysis. In the final phase of the workshop, the participants determine theme-specific research questions. The project team processes the results of the workshops, after which the workshop participants and relevant stakeholders are invited to identify and remove inconsistencies and add missing information.

Explore Future Markets

The primary goal of this step is to envisage specific future markets and customer needs. To stimulate a broad view on future markets a multi-disciplinary group of stakeholders, futurologists and out-of-the-box thinkers is mobilized. This group analyzes trends and scenarios, and develops customer profiles and future product concepts. The results of this step are summarized in collages, drawings and story boards. The central activity is a well-prepared workshop for each market.

Customer profiles can be determined with the persona technique, which gives customers an identity. A persona includes a personal profile (age, sex, education and job), a lifestyle and living environment (goals, skills, attitudes, hobbies and holidays) and a role (tasks, responsibilities and day at work).

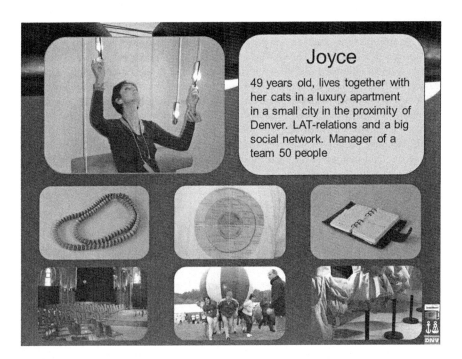

Figure 8.9 Visualization of a customer profile.

CASE: Current and Future Market of the Seattle Climate Action Plan

The analysis of this industry includes the yarn production, SWOT of the production processes and industry, and an analysis of competitive forces. The latter includes, for example, the strategies, strengths and weaknesses of substitutes like the manufacturers of hard floor coverings. The result is an analysis of 15 important issues. During a meeting, the managers of the carpet manufacturers determine the relevance of the issues and the focus of the continuation of the process, resulting in seven focus areas for the roadmap:

- Market issues: home, office and health facility of the future.
- Production issues: bio-based materials and demand-driven production.
- Value chain issues: high-quality reuse and value chain innovation.

The exploration of the future market starts with a literature review and interviews with key stakeholders, to determine the future trends and issues in the three target markets of the carpet industry: healthcare, office and home. On the basis of the research, the project teams develop four customer profiles for each target market. The profiles are discussed in a workshop with market representatives, trend watchers and the general, marketing and operational management of the carpet manufacturers. The profiles are used to gain a better understanding of the specific situation and potential requirements of future customers. For the healthcare facility, we identified the requirements of care takers and patients around the themes of living, sleeping, caring and eating. Insights are translated into product requirements and concepts. In the second part of the workshop, the participants identify the most important conditions for a successful introduction of the selected concepts. They also indicate which steps are necessary to realize these concepts.

Based on the results of this future market insight and the subsequent technology assessment and forecast, final goals and requirements are defined by the project team and discussed in an expert meeting with technical specialist and marketing managers. See Figure 8.12, below, for an example.

Develop a Vision

In this step, stakeholders create a clear and shared vision of the desired future. The central question to be answered by the vision is: which opportunities and challenges do we want to work on? The vision includes a specific and inspiring

Figure 8.10 New carpet concepts.

view of the future markets, products and services, and process characteristics. Developing a vision is a joint activity by multiple stakeholders. During a workshop, the participants revisit the scenarios and customer profiles. They identify and discuss inspiring concepts, elements and images. The results are summarized in a table (see Table 8.2). The roadmap team processes the workshop outcomes in a few iterations to a draft version of the vision and to a few pages of illustrated text, consulting relevant decision-makers for approval.

Define Goals and Performance Requirements

The goal of this step is to define a clear set of requirements that customers and other stakeholders will have with regard to future product and process components. The requirements can be identified from the bottom up or from the top down, and should include "given" policy and legal requirements, which are allocated to the different time zones of the roadmap. The requirement levels should be challenging but feasible. Feasibility is tested in the remaining phases of the roadmap process. The status changes gradually from a rough ambition to a clear objective. The identification and focusing of performance requirements is a more or less continuous process, that is often already part of the initial question/goal of the project. Well-known examples are roadmaps on energy efficiency and climate change, where CO_2 reduction targets of 30 to 100 percent are part of the initial assignment. It is also an essential element when specifying customer requirements.

Specify Options

This step starts with a broad identification of alternative options to realize the (critical) performance requirements. The project team, stakeholders, external experts and future planners identify and analyze current and future technical and non-technical options. Non-technical options include regulations and policies, processes and procedures, and knowledge and competencies. This step results in option lists, fact sheets, option assessment schemes and a recipe book.

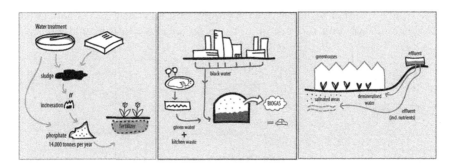

Figure 8.11 Example, recipe book waste water roadmap.

Table 8.2 Summary of vision waste water as production facility of raw materials

	Now–2015	2015–2020	2020–2030
Goals	–	Recover and reuse 60% phosphorus	Recover and reuse 90% phosphorus Recover and reuse 30% other organic materials
Characteristics	3–5 production units for phosphorus	Large-scale fermenting plant One algae biomass pilot plant One cellulose pilot plant One bio plastic pilot plant One multi stakeholders project	Combined processing of food waste, manure and waste water processing Supplying 3 major players Local reuse in newly built neighborhoods
Critical success factors	Clear requirements Open market Medium to high prices for raw materials No/limited legal export barriers Safety public health	Pay back period technologies of 7 to 10 years Image of the products with producers and consumers Choice of technological pathways	Competition for alternative use (as energy source) Mature technologies for syngas production

The recipe book, which is an essential part of an industry or issue roadmap, covers the options, plus a short text on applicability for several sorts of companies in the industry, and a coherent set of options that a specific organization may deploy to realize the defined requirements/goals.

Fact sheets include:

- A definition, explanation of an option.
- Current characteristics, strong and weak points.
- The expected developments and potential applications of the option.
- Critical success factors of the development and application of an option.
- Impact on the requirements.

Option assessment schemes include:

- The current maturity level.
- Current adoption rate.
- Development potential. This assesses the likelihood of a successful development of an option. Rogers's innovation diffusion model and criteria, e.g., amount of publications, research projects, patent application, usability (areas of application), size and financial health of equipment manufacturers, can be used to assess the development potential.
- Future adoption potential. To assess the possibility of the successful deployment of an option, we recommend defining the specific competences that are needed to implement an option and determining how easy it is to integrate an option into a production line. Lack of space can often be a major obstacle.
- Impact on requirements and/or specific characteristics of a technology group.

In addition, Life Cycle Analysis (LCA) has gained popularity as an aid to realize an integrated assessment of performances and sustainability of technologies, processes and value chains.

Table 8.3 Requirements: carpet industry

Requirements	2012–2015	2015–2020	2020–2030
Effective dust uptake	80%	90%	95%
Anti-allergen/asthma	Demonstrated	Better	Save
Cleaning (convenience)	Demonstrated	Better	Excellent
Energy reduction cleaning	25%	50%	75%
Flexibility production and delivery	All sizes	On demand	Customization
Bio based	2–5%	20%	20–50%
Design for recycling	5%	50%	100%
Retour non-residential	80%	100%	100%
Recycled content	10–20%	20–40%	50–80%
Reduction water use	–	10–20%	30–40%
Energy saving per m^2 production	5%	10%	10%–20%
Energy saving in chain	5–10%	10–20%	20–30%

CASE: 50 Percent Energy-Efficiency Improvement in the Dutch Meat Industry

As part of the roadmap, 20 representatives from the industry identified seven focus areas in two workshops. In one workshop, representatives from the industry, research institutes and equipment suppliers identified 40 technological options for preservation. A quick intuitive assessment of the potential resulted in 12 high potential innovative technologies, for which expert produced fact sheets and assessment schemes. The results were discussed in a second workshop by the same stakeholder group. The results regarding adoption rates and timings were adjusted considerably based on input from the industry and the equipment suppliers.

Table 8.4 Technology assessment scheme: meat preservation

	Shelf life	Waste	Energy V	Energy Σ	Cost	Development potential	Adoption potential
Short term (2012–2015)							
MAP packaging (30% CO_2, 70% O_2)	n.a.	5%	2.0–2.2	4–6	12 cents	+	++
MAP packaging (30% CO_2, 70% N_2)	17–18	3%	2.0–2.2	3–4	8–12	++++	+++
Vacuum packaging	21–28	2%	0.9–1.0	1.5–2	12 cents	++	++
Easy to open, reseal packages	n.a.	n.a.	n.a.	n.a.	+1 cent	+++++	+++++
High care production environment	+5–7	3%	++	+++	?	+	+++++
Reduced production space	n.a.	n.a.	75%	n.a.	+	+	+
Mid-term (2015–2020)							
Smart packages with dynamic expiration dates	+	+++	n.a.	+++	– –	+++++	++++
Reusable packaging (MAP and PET)	n.a.	5%	1.0–1.1	2–3	13 cents	+++++	++++
RF-pasteurization	28–42	0/+	0/+	0/+	10 cents	++++	++
High pressure sterilization	350	0/+	+/++	0/++	>10 cents	++++	+
Long term (2020–2030)							
Sustainable bio-degradable packages	n.a.	n.a.	1.0	1	14 cents	++	+++
Mono material shell for MAP	n.a.	5%	++	2–3	12 cents	++	+
Robotica	n.a.	0/+	–	n.a.	– –	+++++	+

Identifying options is an iterative analytical research-oriented task, with several more creative side steps, designed to identify new options. In a combination of creative brainstorms, storytelling and analytical dialogue, stakeholders identify and analyze the best options for each requirement. Workshop results are elaborated further into a draft option list. To assess the need and likelihood of a successful development and implementation of an option, the team can use scenarios to conduct a robustness test (see also Chapter 2) or perform a sensitivity analysis to assess the sensitivity of an option to specific economic, social or political developments. Surveys and/or Delphi rounds are carried out to determine a final list of options, while experts finalize fact sheets for the critical options. A seminar is organized to transfer, check and deepen the results. Based on the results alternative pathways are developed.

Develop Action Program

The project team defines an overall plan and an integrated action plan for each focus area. The action plan includes research programs, partnerships and fusions, as well as plans for process optimization, product development and implementation. The different plans are analyzed to identify joint actions. Stakeholders are interviewed and consulted to identify their contribution (in kind and/or financial) to implementing the plans.

Develop Roadmap Report

The results of the different steps are updated and integrated into the roadmap report. To create an overview, visualizations are created for the entire roadmap and for the various projects, with an explanation added to the visualizations.

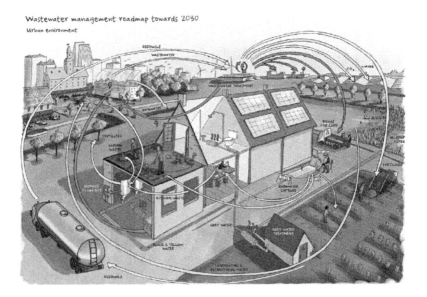

Figure 8.12 Visualization roadmap waste water in an urban environment.

Summary

Table 8.5 summarizes the activities and results of the steps.

Table 8.5 Overview of roadmap process: activities and results

	Activities	Results
Define project	• Interview key stakeholders • Scan existing industry, market and technologies reports • Id entify existing networks • Define project plan • Check plan with key stakeholders • Communicate plans to stakeholders	• Project plan • Clear scoop • Clear objective and indicative goal • Team members • Workshop participants • List with available reports
Analyze market and sector	• Analyze existing sector, market and technologies reports • Interview market analyst and stakeholders • Perform SWOT analysis • Stakeholder analysis • Create report	• SWOT analysis • Stakeholder analysis
Explore (future) markets	• Analyze market forecasts, trend, technology and scenario studies • Develop scenarios and customer profiles • Interview customers and experts • Identify new product–market combinations • Define requirements for future products • Create report	• Trend analysis and forecast • Sector scenarios • Customers profiles (personas)
Create vision	• Develop future vision with key players • Validate vision	• Inspiring vision • Support of key stakeholders

continued

Table 8.5 Continued

	Activities	Results
Define requirements	• Analyze policy frameworks • Define requirements • Define requirement levels • Validate levels	• Requirements per product and/or process • Support of key stakeholders
Select and analyze options	• Create long list of alternative options per requirement • Identify critical options • Develop fact sheets and assessment table for critical options • Validate feasibility, support for options with specialists and key stakeholders	• Option list • Fact sheets critical options • SWOT analysis options • Technology hype cycle • Technology readiness levels • Option assessment schemes • Recipe book • Pathways
Roadmap	• Integrate results • Validate feasibility • Create visualization	• Integrated report • Visualizations
Action plan	• Develop action plan for each focus area • Integrate actions in logical clusters • Validate plan • Create visualizations	• Validated plan • Short description of the projects (1/2 A4)

Source: © 2008–2011 Ben Röngens.

Further Reading

Garcia, M.L. and Bray, O.H. Fundamentals of Technology Roadmapping (1997).
This is where the victory of technology roadmapping started. Famous and well-written document on the why, what and how of technology roadmapping.

Phaal, R., Farrukh, C. and Probert, D. Technology Roadmapping: Linking Technology Resources to Business Objectives (2001).
An excellent article with a short introduction on the roadmapping process, the structure of eight different kinds of roadmaps, illustrated and explained. They also include a clear example of the various types of roadmaps. The article discusses roadmapping for product planning, service and capability planning, strategic planning, long-range planning, knowledge-asset planning, program planning, process planning and integration planning.

Phaal, R., Farrukh, C. and Probert, D. *T-Plan the fast start to technology road mapping, planning your route to success* (2001).
Manual for a quick roadmap project. Originally developed for product development, but we have also used it frequently for strategic, industry and technology roadmaps. The various steps involved in this approach are explained and illustrated with examples. Short workshop agendas are included, as well as a (CD-ROM) with EXCELL-matrices that can be used in workshops, surveys and reports.

Canadian Industry. Technology roadmapping website. A website with more than 20 technology roadmaps for several Canadian industries, most of which were developed in the second half of the 1990s. The site also has a page with valuable documents on the roadmap process and the role of government, as well as evaluations of some roadmap projects. See www.ic.gc.ca/eic/site/trm-crt.nsf/eng/Home.

International Energy Agency (IEA). Road map site. Between 2010 and 2012, the IEA developed over 20 global low-carbon energy technology roadmaps, the overall aim being to advance the global development and uptake of key technologies, to realize a 50 percent reduction in energy-related CO_2 emissions by 2050 (see www.iea.org/roadmaps/).

References

General

Garcia, M.L. and O.H. Bray (1997). *Fundamentals of technology roadmapping*. Sandia National Laboratories.
Industry Canada (2000). *Evaluating technology roadmaps: a framework for monitoring and measuring results*. Ottawa, ON: Government of Canada Publications.
International Energy Agency/OECD (2014). Energy technology roadmaps: a guide to development and implementation. Paris: OECD.

Lizaso, F. and G. Reger (2004). Scenario-based road mapping, a conceptual view. Paper presented at the EU-US seminar *New technology foresight, forecasting and assessement methods.* Seville.

McDowall, W. (2012). Technology roadmaps for transition management: the case for hydrogen energy. *Technological Forecasting and Social Change,* Vol. 79, No. 3, pp. 530–542.

Phaal, R., C. Farrukh and D. Probert (2001a). *Technology roadmapping: linking technology resources to business objectives.* Cambridge: University of Cambridge.

Phaal, R., C. Farrukh and D. Probert (2001b). *T-Plan the fast start to technology road mapping, planning your route to success.* Cambridge: University of Cambridge.

Phaal, R., C. Farrukh and D. Probert (2010). *Road mapping for strategy and innovation: aligning technology and markets in a dynamic world.* Cambridge: University of Cambridge.

Pruit, J. and J. Grudin (2003). Personas: practice and theory. Paper presented on the 2003 Conference on Designing for User Experiences (DUX'03). ACM Press.

Römgens, B. and E. Kruizinga (2008). *Industry road mapping step by step part 1–3.* Dutch document.

Saritas, O. and J. Aylen (2010). Using scenarios for road mapping: the case of clean production. *Technological Forecasting and Social Change,* Vol. 77, No. 7, pp. 1061–1075.

UNFCC Technical Executive Committee (2013). Background paper on technology road maps.

US Department of Energy (2000). Applying science and technology roadmapping in environmental management.

Roadmap Examples

American Chemistry Council (2014). Plastics and polymer composites technology road map for automotive markets. Washington.

American Society of Transportation and Logistics et al. (2014). Material handling and logistics US roadmap. Chicago.

Arlington Institute (2003). A strategy: moving America away from oil. Berkeley Springs.

CTI Group (2008). Technology roadmap for the Canadian textile industry. Indianapolis.

European Commission (2010). A roadmap for moving to a competitive low carbon economy in 2050. Brussels.

Foster, J. and others (GGLO) (2013). Seattle climate action plan. Seattle.

Industry Canada (2000). Canadian electric power road map. Ottawa.

International Energy Agency (IEA) (2014). Technology roadmap solar photovoltaic energy. www.iea.org/publications/freepublications/publication/technology-roadmap-solar-photovoltaic-energy--2014-edition.html. Paris.

Parsons Brinckerhoff and DNV GL (2015). Industrial decarbonisation and energy efficiency roadmaps to 2050 paper and pulp. London.

Robotics VO (2013). From internet to robotics, a roadmap for US robotics.

Römgens, B. and P. Koppert (2012). Roadmap Dutch carpet sector 2030. Zeist.

Römgens, B. and E. Kruizinga (2012). Roadmap waste water 2030. Bilthoven.

Römgens, B. and M. van der Vight (2012). Energy efficiency roadmap meat industry. Bilthoven.

Wohlers Associates Incl. (2011). Additive manufacturing technology road map for Australia. Fort Collins.

World Business Council for Sustainable Development (WBCSD) (2010). Vision 2050, the new agenda for business. Geneva.

9   Interviews

Johan den Hartog

Introduction

An interview is a conversation, usually involving two people, in which it is the interviewer's aim to obtain reliable and useful information from a respondent. An interview is different from an ordinary one-on-one conversation in that the interviewer has more or less explicit intentions with the interview. In effect, an interview is a conversation in which the interviewer asks questions and the respondent answers those questions.

Interviews differ in a number of aspects from other forms of conversation. In *ordinary conversations* "over coffee," opinions, ideas, facts and feelings are exchanged without much order or coherence. Although they also involve questions and answers, the initiative moves back and forth between the participants, who usually discuss a whole array of subjects in a random sequence. In addition, neither of the participants is explicitly in control of the conversation. While *ordinary conversations*, generally speaking, do not have a conscious, predetermined objective, the explicit aim of interviews is the transfer of specific information. The fact that the interviewer is in control of the conversation provides a structure that is absent in ordinary conversations.

An interview is also different from an *instruction*. Although in the latter case there is also a transfer of information, there is a difference compared to an interview, based on the question as to who is in charge. In the case of an instruction, it is the person providing the information, the instructor, while, in the case of an *interview*, the person receiving the information is in charge. In the case of interviews, the nature and content of the conversation is mostly influenced and decided on by the interviewer. Anything the interviewer does not mention will not be discussed, any subject the interviewer does not initiate to talk about will be, preferably in a polite manner, ignored. And whereas an instructor has to motivate his audience to be quiet and listen, the interviewer has to motivate the respondent to talk about subjects in which the interviewer is specifically interested.

As a form of conversation, an *interrogation* closely resembles an interview, in that its purpose is for the person with the least information (the detective) who is also in charge of the conversation to acquire information. The difference between an interrogation and an interview can be expressed in one word: power. The use of psychological or (the threat of) physical pressure (for example when the interviewee is suspected of having committed a crime) is not excluded. The detective conducting the interrogation has legally defined pressure instruments at his disposal, which the person conducting an interview has not and, by the way, should not want to have. Generally speaking, people participate in an interview on a voluntary basis.

There is also a difference between an interviewers and *journalists*, whose goal it is to publish the information being obtained, preferably to a large audience. In some cases, that means that the journalist has some additional power over the interviewee. Publication of unfortunate statements and less popular ideas of a well-known person frequently has unwelcome consequences, and politicians depend on the media for their publicity. Here, too, the transfer of information is the main aim, albeit from the interviewee to a large audience, and it also takes on the form of an interview.

To finish this summary of different forms of conversation, we need to add that the difference between a questionnaire and an interview is only a gradual one. The difference is above all related to the structure. A questionnaire is an interview, the structure of which has been determined in detail in advance. The interviewer puts the same questions to all the interviewees, in the same order and using exactly the same words. In many cases, there is a large number of interviewees. Often, the possible answers have also been determined in advance:

"In the last months, have you ever considered looking for another job, or working for another company?" (Please indicate the answer that applies to you)

- no, never
- no, virtually never
- yes, on occasion
- yes, often
- yes, quite often

In a free, less structured, interview, the interviewer might have asked: "I would now like to discuss your attitude towards your job. Do you ever think of leaving this company and looking for another job?"

In all likelihood, the answer to this question will not be just "yes, often," or "no, never." The respondent will elaborate, for instance by telling at which companies he has already applied for a job and what motivates him to leave his current job.

The Interview

An interviewer manages the interview (1) through the structure of the interview, (2) through the nature of the questions he asks and (3) by consciously using some communication techniques that are used much less often in an ordinary conversation.

The Structure

The interviewer prepares the interview by determining the order of the subjects he wants to make sure to address during the interview. The subjects are ordered based on their importance and included in a list of questions, which can be used as an agenda for the interview.

During the interview, transitions are made from one subject to the next through summaries, which serve multiple purposes:

- They allow the interviewer to make sure he understands and interprets the answers provided by the respondent correctly.
- When done correctly, summaries assure the respondent that his information has come across clearly and accurately. In other words, the interviewer understands him. This means that there is room for trust to grow between interviewer and respondent, which may persuade the latter to be more open and more willing to share information and opinions.
- As mentioned earlier: summaries are a natural way to move from one subject to the next.

Types of Questions

Generally speaking, interview questions can, technically speaking, be divided into two categories: open questions and closed questions. The difference between these two types of questions is gradual in nature. Depending on purpose and moment, the interviewer can decide to use more open or more closed questions. An open question, asked politely, is aimed at persuading and stimulating the respondent to talk. The more open the question being asked, the more room the respondent has to answer the question, which means that, although the interviewer is in charge of the question and has determined (in advance) which questions to ask, it is often the respondent who, through the answers he provides, steers the interview in a certain direction. If that is the case, the interview may move in a direction that is less relevant as far as the interviewer is concerned. By asking follow-up questions, the interviewer can move the interview back to the list of questions he has prepared in advance. Generally speaking, these follow-up questions are less open in nature. Because of the mutual influence that interviewer and respondent have on the course of the interview, the personal interview is also called a half-open and/or half-structured interview. This kind of interview requires highly developed improvizational skills on the part of the interviewer and a proactive attitude. The power of the personal interview lies in the possibility of gaining a deeper insight into the opinions and thoughts of the respondent with regard to certain statements and factual information. In many cases, this type of interview will cause the respondent to take a closer look at his own opinions, and in doing so to make possibly interesting discoveries, and maybe even allows him to express opinions for the first time.

In their most extreme form, *closed questions* limit the options of an respondent to a bare minimum. This is their strength as well as their limitation. It is strength,

172 J. den Hartog

because closed questions allow the interviewer total control (often, the interviewee's options are limited to answering Yes or No), and it is a limitation, because Yes or No answers reveal very little about the underlying opinions and motivations of a respondent. An interview that consists mainly of Yes or No questions can easily be replaced by a written questionnaire with pre-structured answers that will save time and money. Closed questions are a good way to keep an respondent on subject, to steer the interview back on course or to slow the respondent down, which can prove to be necessary when one interviews people who take part in an interview voluntarily, who are experts in certain subjects and who use the interview to showcase their expertise.

Other Communication Techniques

"Face to face" communication between people uses three channels: verbal, paralinguistic and non-verbal. In the verbal channel, a speaker expresses all the information to the recipient in spoken language and words.

The paralinguistic channel is used to send all the information that is expressed in sounds that are not language, for example volume, tone, exclamations, laughter, crying, acquiescent humming. The non-verbal channel is used to send all the visual information.

Based on the assumption that the communication process starts as soon as the two participants in the interview see each other, and that non-communication is not an option in that kind of situation, it makes sense to include all three channels in assessing the quality of the interview. In everyday conversation, most people tend to focus primarily on the verbal aspect. That is not surprising, because the verbal channel contains the content of the message being sent back and forth. However, to understand verbal aspects completely, taking the other two communication channels into account is indispensable. In fact, we usually respond as much, if not more, to the message being transmitted via the non-verbal channels. If someone expresses something different with words from the accompanying non-verbal signs, we tend to believe what we see, sooner than what we hear. If someone who is clearly overwhelmed by grief tells us they just won the lottery, that person will find it hard to appear credible.

We are often unaware of our non-verbal communication. With an effort to consciously use his body language and voice, an interviewer can increase the quality of the interview. For starters, it means that he needs to be aware of what happens in the other communication channels, in other words what he and the respondent are expressing through those channels. In the paralinguistic and non-verbal channels, the respondent expresses how he perceives his relationship with the interviewer as well as how he perceives the relationship as it is expressed by the interviewer. If the interviewer, through clumsy non-verbal behavior, gives the respondent the impression that he is dealing with a novice, that may mean that the interview will take a less desirable course as far as the interviewer is concerned. To respondents, it may be important for the interviewer to make a professional, reliable and experienced impression.

The meaning of the words that are being used is expressed primarily through the verbal channel. All other relevant information, for instance about how the participants perceive their relationship, is expressed through the other channels.

In literature about communication skills (for example Hargie, 1997), it is often argued that most communication consists of non-verbal elements. About 7 percent of communication is expressed verbally, 38 percent through voice, tone, volume, speed, intonation and 55 percent through facial expressions and body language (Mehrabian, 1972, quoted in: Hargie, 1997). To which we should add that the environment in which the interview takes place also plays a certain role in the relative success of the interview. In a noisy hallway or a badly shielded corner of a cafeteria, it may be difficult to obtain important information through an interview.

Concluding

The selection of respondents often only takes place after a preliminary exploration of the area of research in question, of which the interview is a part: which potential respondents are located in key positions in the research domain and who may reasonably be expected to have developed a vision regarding the research questions. In order to be able to make more generally applicable statements about certain developments, it makes sense to interview multiple respondents, in addition to using other research methods like, for instance, literature studies following socio-economic and cultural trends, as well as following areas of research and technology that are relevant to the research in question.

A good interview has a good flow and, at face value, often resembles an ordinary conversation, in which questions and answers, brief remarks and somewhat longer considerations are exchanged in a natural sequence. What is special is that the interviewer is in charge of the conversation and carefully carries out his agenda, while focusing on the respondent's story. A respondent who is approached with respect and care will be happy to tell his or her story. A good interviewer prepares carefully and knows with whom he needs to speak about what. He learns the trade through practice: he becomes a better interviewer by taking a critical look at his experience. Above, we have outlined the measuring stick against which he can measure that experience.

Finally, some future-related questions that can be asked during an interview, a number of which have been identified by the McKinsey consulting agency:

- The oracle: if you were to meet people who actually know about the future, what would you ask them?
- A good world: suppose everything was to go as desired, what would the world look like?
- An unpleasant result: assuming things did not develop well, what would that mean?
- Organizational culture: how must the organizational culture change to realize the desired change?
- Learning from the past: what can we learn from past mistakes and successes?

- Future questions: which critical questions and issues will be relevant in a few years?
- Which successes do you want to celebrate ten years from now?
- If there were one trend you could influence, which would it be?
- The obituary: how do you want to be remembered as a manager?

Acknowledgments

This chapter is based in part on a handbook that was originally written by Dr. L. ten Horn and Dr. M. Wiethoff, who both worked at the former Labor and Organizational Psychology Section at Delft University of Technology.

With many thanks to Ruud Maltha, English teacher, for his help with improving this translation

Literature

Hargie, O. (ed.) (1997). *The handbook of communication skills*. London: Routledge.
Sarantakis, S. (2005). *Social research*, Aldershot, UK: Palgrave Macmillan. Chapter 12, regarding interview techniques, is interesting and illuminating. It is a big plus that Sarantakis discusses both face-to-face and telephone interviews.
Wiertzema, K. and P. Jansen (2005). *Basisprincipes van Communicatie (Basic principles of communication)*. Amsterdam: Pearson, Edition Benelux.

10 Workshops

Henk-Jan van Alphen

What is a Workshop?

The term "workshop" is so widely used nowadays, that its real meaning is somewhat obscured. Many events are named "workshop" while they are mostly key note presentations with some interaction or a seminar. Or in cases where the main goal is to acquire a certain skill, such as training or masterclass. To delineate the term workshop, we assign to it the following connotations:

In a workshop:

- a group,
- works,
- on an assignment,
- outside the daily routine.

Additionally, a moderator usually guides the group process, participants are experts or stakeholders in the subject and there is a limited time frame. Together, these elements make a workshop distinctly different from a meeting, seminar, training or masterclass which usually address only one or two of these elements.

Why Organize a Workshop?

Focus on One Topic

A workshop allows participants to focus on one single topic, for instance the future of their organization. Isolation from the outside world (no smartphones!) and a limited time frame allow for a high intensity that allows people to dive deep into the topic and use different points of view.

People Work with More Enthusiasm and Energy

The common goal, the limited time frame and working in a team, without the usual hierarchy, allow participants to access their reserve capacity. In a well-organized workshop, people are more enthusiastic and more energized than in most other working conditions. It is thus important to allow people to recuperate after a full (or multiple) day workshop.

Synergy

"1 + 1 = 3" or "the whole is greater than the sum of its parts" are management clichés that apply equally well to workshops. Combining the knowledge of different experts often leads to new insights, that would not have been acquired in isolation. The combination of different kinds of knowledge and different viewpoints enhances creativity (see also Chapters 13 and 14 on creativity). Workshops yield better results than separate interviews with the participants.

Workshops Create Support

Ideas, innovations and insights which are developed in workshops are the products of a group process. Usually the group as a whole is supportive of the results of the workshop. In an expert workshop, that creates legitimacy. In a workshop with stakeholders, it creates support. This is of particular use when developing future scenarios.

Side-Effects

In a well-organized workshop, participants learn to work together, have an open mind for other opinions and learn to communicate effectively. Most participants are able to push their limits, both intellectually as well as in terms of performance. Workshops provide a context for encounters that prove to be valuable for the future.

What are the Success Factors?

Visualize Constantly

In a workshop participants rapidly express their ideas, questions and opinions. As the workshop progresses and the participants become enthusiastic, the intensity usually increases. There is a risk that good ideas get lost in the process. Therefore, it is important to capture visually what is being said by the participants. Either on flip charts, brown paper, pin boards or just post-its on a wall. The shape does not matter: you can use single words, drawings or symbols. Of course, you can also use the acceleration method (see Chapter 12 on the acceleration method).

Keep Participants Active

Essential to a successful workshop is the active participation of all participants. They can't be allowed to withdraw from the process or have a passive attitude. The moderator needs to ensure that everyone is actively involved in the process; for example, by asking questions or working in small groups. Long presentations or discussions in large groups are not suitable for a workshop.

Positive Atmosphere

The atmosphere in a workshop is affected by many factors. The most important is a positive attitude of the participants toward each other. It is the job of the moderator to make sure discussion is constructive and that people feel safe enough to come up with bold ideas. Much of the atmosphere is determined by the preparation: the tone of the invitation, the reception of the participants, composition of the group, the location and even lunch menu.

Flexible Schedule

Although a workshop should be well prepared to be successful, the time schedule should never be too tight. Group processes are always unpredictable and your time schedule may prove to be too tight. A good moderator feels if a certain format works or not and is able to make on the fly adjustments.

How to Organize a Successful Workshop

The Goal of the Workshop

To be demonstrably successful, a workshop must have a clearly defined goal of which the attainment can be determined afterwards. This can be a substantive goal, such as inventing new products or analyzing trends, or a process-oriented goal, such as thinking about the future together or the developing of a common vision.

Composition of the Group

The success of a workshop depends largely on the people involved. Obviously, it is important that all participants have an understanding of, interest in, or are involved in the topic of the workshop. This motivates them to participate and determines the quality of their contribution.

It is also important that the participants do not conflict with each other too much or feel hampered by each other. For instance, the presence of a CEO can inhibit the creativity of its employees, unless it is explicitly stated that the workshop is separate from daily practice. Participants with diverse interests also pose a risk, unless of course the purpose of the workshop is to bring them closer together.

The number of participants should be limited to around 20. With such a number it is important to disperse regularly in groups of three to five people. This increases productivity.

Finally, it is interesting to bring together different people. So men and women, alphas and betas, creative and logical thinkers, people of different cultures. By combining different perspectives, chances are that there are surprising insights for all participants. That is essential for most forms of foresight.

Agenda and Timing

It is tempting to take up too much time for a workshop. Workshops with a long duration have the disadvantage that people get tired which usually means a drop in both atmosphere and productivity. Generally, two half-day workshops are more successful than one full-day workshop.

A good agenda is important to keep people active. Ensure that plenary discussions are alternated with work in groups and keep a strict time limit for group assignments. In addition, it is important to have regular breaks, in which people can go out and take a walk.

Location, Location, Location

The location for a workshop is very crucial for its success, but is often underestimated. In a poorly ventilated back room without windows in the main building of the organization itself, without access to sufficient food and drinks, it is almost impossible to have a successful workshop. In a bright room with large windows in a natural environment with friendly service and coffee, tea, water and fruit it is almost impossible *not* to have a successful workshop.

Ideally, the location is supportive of the objective and the success factors of the workshop. So if you want your team to come up with new ideas and stretch their imagination, then don't organize a workshop in their regular meeting room. If you want people to engage in a free and open discussion, make sure that no two rows of tables stand between them. And if you want people to think creatively, make a lot of distractions in the environment, with colors, objects and a nice view.

Moderation

The moderator of the workshop is responsible for the course of the workshop and the achievement of the set of goals. In almost all cases it is advisable to ask someone "outside" to moderate a workshop. That means someone who does not work daily with the participants, is not an expert in the subject at hand and has no interest in a particular outcome.

A good moderator monitors the progress by asking questions, summarizing discussions, avoiding unnecessary repetition and stimulating participants to use their knowledge and creativity. In addition, the moderator also monitors the group process. He must provide a positive and open atmosphere in which people are able to speak freely and suggest bold ideas. That also means that he or she must have a keen eye for resistance, undermining behavior or disinterest and must act to neutralize that as quickly as possible.

A moderator has to operate at multiple levels and take on multiple roles: discussion leader, devil's advocate, critical questioner, coach, timekeeper and host.

Materials

As indicated earlier, it is important continuously to visualize discussions. This avoids the group going around in circles and helps people to build on each other's ideas. There are many ways to do this, but few are as effective as the combination of brown paper and self-adhesive stickers. Brown paper is large and can be used to cover large surfaces. The self-adhesive stickers make it possible to cluster and to structure the different ideas. Moreover, it is a very accessible instrument: anyone can pick up a pen and use it. This is much less the case with electronic devices such as laptops or smart boards, which also run the risk of people checking their e-mail.

Workshops and Foresight

Foresight that is intended for policy and strategy development is not a matter of desk research. If foresight should lead to a policy or organizational change, it is important that the results of the research are broadly supported. The best way to create support is to engage people at an early stage of the foresight. For instance by letting them participate in workshops.

Normative beliefs, incomplete information and uncertainty play a relatively large role in foresight. It is not unusual that there are several future scenarios, that each have their supporters and opponents. In foresight it is important to bring different perspectives together. This sharpens the differences between the future scenarios, as well as the assumptions upon which they are based. In the context of a workshop, it is possible to do this in a controlled and structured manner.

Foresight is often used as a tool for strategy and policy development. The results of the foresight can be used for a strategic discussion in the form of a workshop. Decision-makers and stakeholders can discuss the implications of the foresight for their vision, mission, strategy or policy in a structured manner.

Conclusion

A workshop is, if well prepared, one of the most powerful and efficient tools in foresight. A good workshop allows people to deliver great results in a short time. In addition, the combination of different views often leads to new and surprising ideas. Although a workshop benefits from a positive atmosphere and a flexible program, it must be thoroughly prepared and closely controlled to be successful.

References

Kwakman, F. and A. Postema (1996). *Het team als probleemoplosser.* Amsterdam: Kluwer.
Lipp, U. and H. Will (1996). *Das Große Workshop-Buch.* Weinheim/Basel: Beltz.

11 The Future Recycled

Meta-analysis for Foresight

Patrick van der Duin and Susan van 't Klooster

Introduction

Carrying out good foresight is often a time-consuming process. In this chapter, we want to show how it is possible to use existing foresight studies in a smart way to develop "new" foresight studies (for instance in the form of scenarios) that have a high quality (for instance, consistent scenarios, validated statements, surprising results) but require less time and money. In other words, not a second best solution, but a viable alternative. This approach can be seen as *recycling* existing foresight.

Although books about foresight pay no attention to it, many foresight professionals are familiar with the recycling of existing research (see Van Asselt et al., 2010). A common way to reuse existing foresight is to adopt existing scenarios. For example, in the Netherlands, for a joint scenario study called "Welfare and Living Environment" (Janssen et al., 2006) by the Bureau for Economic Policy Analysis (CPB), the Environment and Nature Agency (MNP) and the Institute for Spatial Research (RPB), the scenario framework of the CPB report "Four Futures of Europe" (de Mooij and Tang, 2003) was used. And the WLO report was in turn reused in other futures studies about subjects like land use, climate adaptation, shipping and in various regional studies.

In addition to reusing existing foresight, it can also be further developed in "new" foresight. This is necessary when existing studies do not completely match the specific question about the future. Although it is possible to set up entirely new futures studies, reusing existing studies by analyzing and combining them is a good alternative.

The possible advantages of reusing existing futures studies are:

- Efficiency: it is not necessary to conduct a new study, which can save a lot of time, money and other resources that can be used to determine the consequences and recommendations of futures studies.
- Recognizability: the futures studies that are used are recognizable for users and policy-makers. It is possible to refer to the original studies before making decisions, allowing users and policy-makers to prepare themselves for the use of the study. It is also good for the buy-in of the study to refer to high-quality existing studies.

• Synthesis: bringing together various futures studies so they can be compared and connected.

Both forms of recycling (applying existing studies and analyzing and combining existing studies) require the use of the principles of meta-analysis. Meta-analysis is often used in science, for instance in medical science, where it is used to make a general statement about various studies into, for example, the effect of a certain kind of food on people's health. By comparing different studies on the same subjects, an attempt is made to arrive at a unified verdict. In foresight, a meta-analysis can be used to produce a new and meaningful synthesis of the insights provided by earlier studies.

Depending on the nature of the studies being compared and the research question or issue, a meta-analysis can be quantitative and/or qualitative in nature.

Below, we propose seven steps for recycling foresight, an important element of which is looking at relevant futures studies that are relevant.

1   *Determining the goal of the futures study.*
    Goals can be placed on a continuum from narrow to broad. A narrow goal is, for example, mapping the "mental models" regarding a given subject, while a broad goal is, for example, mapping possible trends and developments. The breadth of the meta-analysis affects the quantity and diversity of the studies that are included in the analysis. The broader the goal, the higher the number of studies to be included, and vice versa. Do we want to develop knowledge about the future of the Internet, about which trends are relevant in the area of biotechnology, or about future scenarios about Islam? After that, the search for futures studies begins.

2   *The search for futures studies.*
    When looking for and collecting futures studies, the following five steps can be observed:

    • Determining the *keywords* on the basis of the research question or issue: every study has an origin, introduction and research problem, and often certain core concepts are mentioned in their descriptions. These core concepts are the keywords on the basis of which it is possible to look for various sources.
    • Determining the time frame: how far back in time does one want to look for relevant futures studies?
    • Selecting the sources: which databases will one use? Examples of scientific databases are ScienceDirect, GoogleScholar and LexisNexis.
    • Using references:

        • "Snowballing" (backward citation): to which existing publication does the publication one has found refers?
        • Forward citation: which later publications refer to the publication one has found?

- Asking experts: which publications are recommended by experts? After all, the database does not necessarily contain all the relevant publications and expert opinions can serve as a validation to determine whether one has missed any publications that are relevant.

3 *Selecting the publications.*

The longlist of publications from step 2 can indeed be very long, perhaps too long. To make sure that the longlist is manageable (and becomes more of a shortlist), the most relevant publications can be selected by focusing on:

- studies that deal explicitly with the applied method of futures exploration;
- most recent publications;
- most frequently cited publications;
- least frequently cited publications.

The choice between these four criteria depends on the question that is being asked. If one is looking for futures studies with "deviating" or surprising outcomes, the "least frequently cited" criterion becomes more relevant, while if one is looking for more mainstream studies, the "most frequently cited" criterion is the more sensible one. We do feel, however, that the methods being used should at all times take precedence, because it is an indication of the professional quality of the publication. To that end, it needs to be clear how the futures studies came about, what method was used, what the results were and how statements about the future are founded. The crystal ball must not be a black box!

4 *Structuring the shortlist.*

Next, the shortlist must be further structured. This can be done by dividing the list of publications, for example on the basis of:

- type of foresight method: for example, scenario method, roadmapping, Delphi, backcasting, trend analysis;
- the domain in question, for instance, IT, demography, economy, or within the IT domain: mobile Internet, open software, social media;
- the type of use: for the development of, for instance, innovation policy, strategy or vision.

5 *Studying and coding the selected futures studies.*

In this step, the collected futures studies are studied and analyzed, with the aim of identifying differences and similarities between the various studies. This is done by *coding* the studies in question on the basis of keywords, either manually or by using special software, like Atlas, or special *textmining* software. During the coding, there is also a *snowball* effect. At the start, there is a limited number of keywords, but that number will increase along the way, ultimately reaching an optimum. There have to be enough keywords to describe properly the diversity of the studies, but if the list of keywords becomes too long, their ability to provide a meaningful distinction is diluted. In the case of a meta-analysis focused on foresight, the keywords are also foresight-related, for example driving forces, geographical reach, time horizon, strategy, vision.

6   *Characterizing, clustering and analyzing the futures studies.*
In this step, the content-related keywords are used to characterize the various visions for the future in the selected futures studies. It is important to make sure that the keywords do not turn into pre-defined categories, because in that case, new aspects from the studies in question fail to get noticed sufficiently.

It is possible to translate the keywords into *key sentences*, to turn the analysis into a running text. The core visions can then be further founded in a qualitative or quantitative manner.

When a large number of futures studies are included in the analysis, the risk of overlap in future/visions increases. It may be necessary to cluster future visions with comparable characteristics, like their underlying assumptions, dynamics and conclusions.

When such a clustering has been made, it is also important to look at the future visions that fall outside the clustering (Van Asselt et al. (2005) refer to these as "lone scenarios," the "D" presented in Figure 11.1).

Box 11.1 Scenario Families

Van Asselt et al. (2005) refer to such a new clustering of future visions (in particular scenarios) with the term "scenario families." Within a scenario family, there is a shared core vision, but the different future visions also have their own specific characteristics. Each scenario family is given its own "family name," which reflects the core vision of each family. In other words, a scenario family consists of future visions that are the focus of many futures studies.

---

7   *Feedback to research goal.*
In this last step, one has to determine how and to what extent the results of the meta-analysis match the research goal and the research question of the original study. The following questions can be posed:

•   What are the "white spots?" In other words: what subjects have not been sufficiently addressed yet?

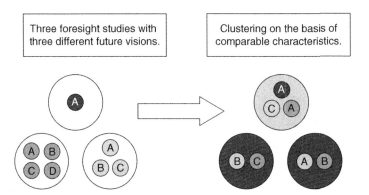

Figure 11.1 Clustering of future visions.

- What do we now know and what knowledge is still missing?
- What stands out? What striking observations can be made? What meets or does not meet our expectations?

Finally, it is also about the question whether or not a *new* study is needed after all. If not, the meta-analysis provided enough answers to the research question. If a new study is needed, there is a well-founded motivation to set up a new futures study.

As far as the longer term is concerned, the process outlined above can be applied as an ongoing activity, building a knowledge database with studies in the process. The benefit of this form of recycling is that it makes it easier to tailor-make the future visions and scenarios, to make sure they match the new area of study and focuses more on the needs of the customer.

References

de Mooij, R. and Tang, P. (2003). Four Futures of Europe. CPB Netherlands Bureau for Economic Policy Analysis, the Hague.

Janssen, L.H.J.M., Okker, V.R. and Schuur, J. (2006). Welfare and Living Environment. A scenario study for the Netherlands in 2040. CPB, MNP and RPB, The Hague.

Van Asselt, M.B.A., J.W. van der Pas and R. de Wilde (2005). *The future starts today: inventory futures studies: research report*. Maastricht University, the Netherlands (in Dutch).

Van Asselt, M.B.A., S.A. van 't Klooster, P.W.F. van Notten and L.A. Smits (2010). *Foresight in action: scenarios for public policy*. London: Earthscan.

12 The Acceleration Method

Bram Castelein

Introduction

In this chapter it will be explained what the acceleration method is, what the crucial success factors by application are and what this method in particular can mean for foresight.

The Acceleration Method

The base characteristic of the acceleration method is a facilitated group process that is supported by specific software. The result of this is that groups will arrive at new concepts and/or decisions in a way that is faster and more effective in comparison to more traditional collaboration forms, for example a meeting. This software is referred to under different names such as: group support system, collaborative system, group decision room, acceleration room. In this contribution the name Group Support System (GSS) will be used, because this designation fits best the base characteristic as described above. In a short lead-time, the use of this software makes it possible to gather a large amount of ideas and also to edit them. The participants in the session enter their ideas on their own laptops and, after tapping the enter button, their input appears on their own screen but also on the screens of the other participants and usually also on a large screen centrally positioned in the room.

The import of ideas into GSS is simple. Usually, people first enter their own ideas and only start to read the input of others just when they have finished their own input. Reading other ideas encourages and delivers a second wave of new ideas; variation in work forms can start up a third wave. This sequence eliminates for a part groupthink, bringing also unconventional, unorthodox ideas into the picture. This process is somewhat paradoxical: everyone talks as it were through each other, but understands each other anyway and inspires each other. One reads each other's input without knowing whose input it is. This anonymity characterizes the acceleration method and encourages participants to generate ideas freely: an idea is indeed assessed on content and not on the person who sent the idea. A pleasant side-effect of this is that people who are reluctant to provide input in a traditional setting, are now experiencing little or no barrier to entering their ideas and do not hesitate to comment on these ideas in a discussion in plenary. Incidentally, the software optionally provides the ability to provide ideas automatically with a tag that corresponds to the one who sent the idea.

The short lead-time in collecting a lot of input, in other words diverging, is one side of the coin. The other side is that the software also offers the functionality to bring fast focus, in other words converging. A session is strictly speaking an iterative series of divergence and convergence: this is also referred to as "making rhombuses." Convergence can start for example by organizing items in a set of categories, the so-called "buckets." Then the items can be prioritized by, for example, marking promising ideas, dividing an amount of points over the collected ideas, dragging ideas in a certain order with the most interesting idea on the top of the list, or positioning ideas along a scale "agree or disagree," or some other criteria.

The prioritized results can be seen directly in text, tabular and/or graphics. A characterizing advantage of the acceleration method is that the input provided by the participants during the session, as well as the performed statistical analyses and generated tables and graphics, are immediately available after the session in, for instance, a Word editable document with chapters and a table of contents in a pre-defined lay-out. This is an important advantage in comparison to, for instance, working with the metaplan method, because the sticky notes need to be "manually digitalized" by the facilitator after the session is finished.

GSS is marketed by different suppliers. In terms of functionality these packages exhibit large similarities. One can use it to brainstorm, prioritize, evaluate, categorize and comment. There are differences in accessibility, user experience and level of detail. Below is a list of some of these software packages:

- ThinkTank (www.groupsystems.com);
- Spilter (www.spilter.nl);
- Crealogic (www.crealogic.eu);
- TeamSupport (www.teamsupport.net);
- MeetingSphere (www.meetingsphere.com).

Thus the acceleration method is a facilitated group process that is supported by software called GSS. The deployment of GSS is an accelerator that effectively contributes to the gathering of a large amount of input in a short lead-time and provides the ability to process this input immediately.

The Role of the Facilitator and Other Success Factors

An important role, probably the most important one when using the acceleration method, is the role of the facilitator. This role starts by identifying the desired result during the discussion the facilitator has with the client prior to the session. This requires the facilitator to listen well, to ask and ask again and, when necessary, get the question behind the question on the table. Based on this information the facilitator designs the session and facilitates its implementation and any follow up.

The composition of the group that is invited to the session is also a key success factor. When issues are at stake such as the development of new concepts, it is wise to invite experts, but also laymen who can look at the subject with fresh eyes, unencumbered by preconceived ideas; thus contributing to the thoughts of the experts. Another example: when during a session decisions have to be taken, it will be agreed upfront with the client if he will make the decision on his own, or based on group consensus. This consideration has its effect on the composition of the group of participants. In the implementation of the session it could occur that the role of facilitator is run by two persons: one who facilitates the group process and one who serves the software GSS, also known as the "driver." The point of attention being that this means an additional coordination link.

Another key success factor is the balanced use of GSS. In the application of the acceleration method, the exchange of ideas and the accompanying discussion can happen entirely electronically, but it is recommended that the participants be offered the opportunity to discuss the "harvest" in plenary. The group therefore remains active, sharp and fully involved. Also the combination with other techniques, such as creative techniques and the use of energizers, contributes to this. What occurs during a session, is that differences in seniority and job function often no longer matter: walls fall away very easily. Evidence shows people have fun acting this way: this fun factor is very important. An interesting practical example is the case where a group entered around 100 ideas in a short time. The facilitator then asked the participants to identify eight categories required to group these ideas. In dialogue with the group the facilitator created these categories in GSS. He then asked the participants to drag ideas with the mouse to a desired category. Then the hilarity begins: the moment you want to drag an idea into a desired bucket, another one is faster than you and "steals" the idea before you have even touched it. No problem though, because within a few minutes, hundreds of ideas are neatly organized into eight categories and the facilitator can discuss the items per category with the group. This is also called a "bucket walk."

The assumption so far is that it is a physical meeting, in other words people meet at an agreed time at an agreed place. However, for deployment of the acceleration method this is not necessary; the method can be used place- and/or time-independent over the Internet as well. This gives a different dynamic. A question posed to the participants need not be discussed right away. The time to collect ideas can last longer, for example several days. In the meantime the participants have an opportunity to involve and consult other persons. Regarding the role of the facilitator, the emphasis is on managing the input and less on managing the group. The facilitator has more time for analysis and the formulation of targeted follow-up questions to the participants.

The Acceleration Method in Practice

In this section three practical examples illustrate the use of the acceleration method in foresight.

The Acceleration Method and the Delphi Method

The Delphi method is well suited for the deployment of the acceleration method based on a location- and time-independent approach and on anonymity when generating input. The participating experts are invited via email to answer the formulated questions. The facilitator analyzes the data after a certain time interval, summarizes and gives back the results to the participants asking them again to provide input. By means of iterations, consensus can be achieved on a number of developments and conclusions can be formulated.

The Acceleration Method and the Scenario Method

In 2007 the Dutch Ministry of Justice issued a book (Wijck and Wit, 2007) containing scenarios and strategies for 2015. During the development of these scenarios the acceleration method was used in a part of this process. First, people outside Justice were interviewed about the ideas they had on relevant developments in the policy of Justice. These ideas were summarized in a first discussion paper. After discussion in a number of expert meetings, a second discussion paper was prepared and completed with information derived from literature and statistics. In this paper five clusters of relevant social developments were recognized. The acceleration method was introduced in the process at this time. Based on the second discussion paper five meetings were organized. In these meetings the inventoried developments for the mentioned areas of Justice were discussed more intensely and attention was paid to the subsequent implications. With the aid of the acceleration method each session was designed following the next steps:

- Each session started in GSS with a round of commentary in which participants could give a reaction on selected developments. They could give their reaction in open text without formal requirements.
- After a discussion in plenary based on this input the participants were asked to drag the developments in GSS in order of policy relevance; the most relevant on top. In GSS the development in first place earned five points, second place four points etc. Then each score was multiplied by the number of participants who gave this score. This activity has produced a clear table and a graph containing the order established by the group.
- Next, the participants were asked to address the implications that could happen when the development would continue until 2015 on the relevant policy. The same question was asked if the development would not take place, but there would occur just a setback. The participants were given the picture that one could imagine the headlines in the newspapers in 2015, or the parliamentary questions that could be asked. In addition to these questions the participants were asked to give their accompanying arguments in GSS on the comment sheet attached to each implication. In GSS it is interesting that one can also supplement arguments on the comments page of implications that are entered by other participants.
- Next the participants were asked to mark in GSS implications they found important for Justice to be taken into account seriously. The facilitator has used a rule of thumb that the maximum number of checkmarks is about 25 percent of the total number of items entered. The graph with the results in GSS was then discussed in plenary.

- The session was concluded in GSS with an inventory of developments that have not been addressed but may possibly be able to play a role.

Based on upfront formulated criteria, two core uncertainties were selected from the results of these meetings. This pair was used as axes of a quadrant on which four scenarios are elaborated (Botterhuis et al., 2010). These scenarios have served as a tool for Justice to assist in the development of strategic tasks.

The Acceleration Method and Risk Analysis

A risk analysis is a process of identification, assessment and control of risks. A risk analysis is carried out to identify all possible risks that may affect a desired result. When the risks are identified an assessment is done to highlight what the greatest risks are and what measures can be taken to control these risks. The acceleration method can be used in foresight as a supporting technique in the form of a risk analysis. This process is as follows:

- *Process step identification*: the participants enter in the GSS the risks they see in some formulated future expectations; each expectation is represented in GSS as a "bucket." The identified risks are then discussed in plenary, are formulated more sharply and duplicate entries are merged. When items are entered exactly the same, GSS offers the functionality to merge the duplicate entries automatically.
- *Process step assessment*: based on the criteria of "chance" and "impact" the participants assess the risks on a previous specified scale. GSS then multiplies probability and impact and ranks the risks from high to low. The data are presented in tabular and graph forms.
- *Process step control*: based on the assessment, eventually one defines in GSS on the comment sheet attached to each selected risk, the control actions to be taken.

Finally

The acceleration method offers a range of options to custom design group meetings and guide them successfully. Results are achieved effectively and in a short lead-time. Relevant success factors are the role of the facilitator, the composition of the group and the balanced use of GSS.

References

Botterhuis, L., P. van der Duin, P. de Ruijter and P. van Wijck (2010). Monitoring the future: building an early warning system for the Dutch Ministry of Justice. *Futures*, Vol. 42, No. 5, pp. 454–465.

Wijck, P. van, R. de Wit, R. Kroon and R. van der Lee (2007). *Justitie over morgen: Scenario's en strategieën voor 2015*. The Hague: DeltaHage.

13 Creativity in Foresight
Seven Exercises

Saskia Bol

Introduction

In this chapter, we discuss seven creative exercises that you can use in different phases of foresight.

What is Creativity?

Generally speaking, creativity refers to the ability to create something new. When a group or individual creates a new concept or object, or comes up with an original solution to a problem, they show creativity. They are able to come up with something new or original by breaking through existing thought patterns in the brain and following a new thought pattern (Byttebier, 2002, pp. 18–23).

Creativity in Foresight

Creativity helps to identify new signals that indicate possible futures. Creativity makes it easier to form an idea of the future and of alternative futures. Creativity helps shape memorable visions of the future.

Picking up trends and developments is not easy. When people perceive things, they only use 20 percent of the overall information from outside. The remaining 80 percent is produced in the brain (Byttebier, 2002, p. 26). As a result, it is hard to allow (new) outside information in. As Johan Cruijff (former Dutch soccer player and coach) puts it: "You only get it when you see it." Creative exercises help us to reduce the amount of information that is produced by the brain and to increase the use of outside information.

Creating possible visions of the future requires knowledge of the factors that play a role. The future is partly uncertain and often different from expected. New factors and events that can determine the future are difficult to recognize with "standard" thought patterns. Creative exercises help to sketch extreme visions of the future that force us to go outside conventional and dominant thought patterns.

Visualization makes ideas more vivid and engaging. Creative exercises are useful to visualize future visions, and stimulate our imagination.

Exercises

The exercises help to form new ideas regarding trends, developments and future visions. They address different creative skills, as described in the previous chapter.

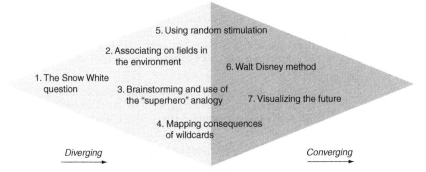

Figure 13.1 The seven exercises in relation to the creative process.

Exercise 1: The Snow White Question

Table 13.1 Creative exercise: the Snow White question

Purpose	Forming new visions of the future.
	The exercise described here is an exercise for the interviewee or respondent. You ask questions to (remarkable) people with a different perspective on the future from yours. This exercise draws you out of your usual thought pattern by putting yourself in a different position and stimulates the creative skill "postponing judgment."
When to use	You can use this exercise in the exploration phase of the research or to strengthen a vision of the future. The question in this exercise can be asked during an interview, during a workshop or during online research.
Futures exploration	Trend analysis, scenarios and Delphi.
What you need	Make sure you are able to record the results of the questions, for instance, in the case of an interview, an audio-recorder.
How does it work?	Introduce the subject of foresight to the person you want to consult. You tell the following story: "Snow white ate a poisoned apple that got stuck in her throat. She dropped down for dead and was laid in a coffin by the seven dwarves, where she remained for five years, until a prince passed by who thought she was so beautiful that he wanted to take her with him. Unfortunately, he dropped the coffin. The poisoned apply flew from Snow white's throat and, after five years, she came back to life" (Nekkers, 2006, pp. 102–103).
	Then you ask the following question: "Imagine the same thing happened to you. What would the future of your organization or company look like?" (Nekkers, 2006, pp. 102–103).
Advice	Do not give examples, let people come up with their own ideas.
Options	You can have the interviewee or respondent answer the question orally, or in the form of a drawing or mood board, which is a collage of images and texts that represents the atmosphere of an idea. This way, the creative skill "making associations" is stimulated.

Figure 13.2 Looking back from the future like Snow White.

Exercise 2: Associating on Fields in the Environment

Table 13.2 Creative exercise: associating on fields in the environment

Purpose	Picking up new trends and developments. By naming important fields in the external contextual environment and coming up with associations around them, you discover unseen trends and developments. Using the creative skill "making associations."
When to use	Use the exercise during the exploration of the environment. You can do the exercise individually, with a group or during online research.
Futures exploration	Trend analysis, scenarios.
What you need	Pen and a large piece of paper, post-its and a computer.
How does it work?	Visualize the contextual environment and the main developments as shown below. Chapter 2 has more information about the contextual environment. During a workshop, ask people to write down specific trends and associations on post-its (individually). Second, have people associate on each other's ideas, add visuals and discuss the results. The exercise will result in a rich overview of the developments in the environment of the organization.
Options	You can add the transactional layer to the model (see Chapter 2).

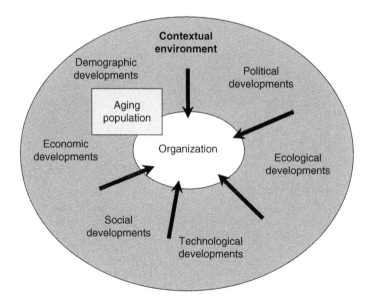

Figure 13.3 Influence of developments in the transactional environment (source: adapted from Nekkers, 2006, p. 60. Copyright 2006 Futureconsult).

Exerise 3: Brainstorming and Use of the "Superhero" Analogy

Table 13.3 Creative exercise: brainstorming and use of the "superhero" analogy

Purpose	Picking up new trends and developments. Creating vision of the future. Sometimes, it is convenient to collect a lot of ideas, with regard to identifying trends and developments, but also with regard to the way you want to present your research results. Instead of coming up with ideas on your own, gather a group of people who can build on each other's ideas. People will use the creative skill "making associations." You start with a brainstorming session in which you come up with as many ideas as possible, after which you continue with more focused exercises. An example of a more focused exercise is the "superhero." By looking at things from a new perspective, that of a superhero, people generate new ideas.
When to use	You can use these exercises always to come up with new ideas.
Futures exploration	All.
What you need	Open light space, pen, post-its and a flip-chart or a large piece of paper to hang on the wall.
How does it work?	Gather a group of about eight people. It can be a random group, but also consist of people who vary in terms of knowledge about the subject or point of view. Use the following rules for the brainstorming session: postpone your judgment (no: "Yes, but…"), built on other people's ideas, use your imagination (Wulfen, 2009, pp. 122–123) and quantity trumps quality. During the brainstorming session, you first ask people to come up with ideas individually, after which the group associates on the basis of each other's ideas. The "superhero" exercise goes as follows: • Choose an important subject from the research question. • Choose a hero who you keep in mind. • Describe the characteristics of this hero. • Describe which answers this hero would give. • Translate the ideas into the answer to the (research) question. (Byttebier, 2002, pp. 117–118, 137)
Advice	Gather a group of enthusiastic people.
Options	• Use, for example, a mind-map program to organize the ideas. • Collect ideas from other people by using co-creation methods. You can use social media and engage online communities to collect ideas. For inspiration, have a look at the BMW Group's Co-Creation Lab (www.bmwgroup-cocreationlab.com).

Exercise 4: Mapping Consequences of Wildcards

Table 13.4 Creative exercise: mapping consequences of wildcards

Purpose	Creating vision of the future.
	You help yourself to imagine other possible futures by thinking about the consequences of possible, high-impact events that are unlikely to happen ("wildcard"). You shift your thoughts from a "likely" future to a "possible" future. You force yourself to imagine something that you think is unlikely. You use all the creative skills.
When to use	At home, during workshops, online research.
	Coming up with alternative futures.
Futures exploration	Scenarios, technology forecasting.
What you need	A list with wildcards, pen and post-its.
How does it work?	• Collect wildcards from books and from the Internet. Examples: global epidemic, time-travel becomes possible, bacteria immune to antibiotics (Petersen, 1999, pp. 60–62). For inspiration, have a look at BBC's future section (www.bbc.com/future).
	• Choose one wildcard and write it down on a post-it. Describe which consequences the wildcard has regarding the future you are investigating. What is the impact of the wildcard? Make a mind-map of the effects of the wildcard. This visual map makes it easy to read back the thoughts (Hampsink and Hagedoorn, 2006, p. 115).
Advice	Use examples of unexpected events with major consequences from the past, like 9/11.
Options	You can rank the consequences: which effect is positive and which effect is negative? Figure 13.4 shows that a positive implication can at first be positive, but that a second implication can be negative, and vice versa.

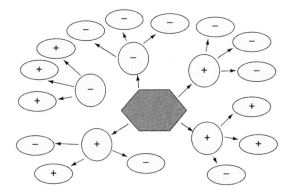

Figure 13.4 Implication tree (source: adapted from Nekkers, 2006, p. 183. Copyright 2006 Futureconsult. Adapted with permission).

Exercise 5: Using Random Stimulation

Table 13.5 Creative exercise: using random stimulation

Purpose	Picking up new trends.
	Creating new visions of the future.
	Shaping vision of the future.
	By confronting yourself with information with which you are not familiar and linking that information back to the issue you are working on, you develop new ideas. You stimulate the creative skill "sharp observation."
When to use	Use the exercise when you are thinking of new ideas and/or when you are stuck.
Futures exploration	All.
What you need	The inclination and time to go out and explore.
How does it work?	Send yourself on a new path and expose yourself to random stimuli, for example:
	• Read a magazine you have never read before. • Listen to a TED Talk about a subject you are unfamiliar with. • Visit a bookstore, museum, exhibition or concert. • Take a walk in unfamiliar environment, and take pictures of people's behavior or other things that fascinate you.
	Make a connection to what you are researching. Write down your new ideas. They don't have to be relevant now, but they can help you later.
Advice	Allow yourself to be influenced by an unknown environment. Let go of the thoughts regarding your research.

Figure 13.5 Examples of places to visit to expose yourself to random stimuli.

Exercise 6: Walt Disney Method

Table 13.6 Creative exercise: Walt Disney method

Purpose	Improve future vision.
	If you cannot come up with new ideas to improve the future vision and you feel something is missing. The Walt Disney exercise forces people to use three ways of thinking (critical, creative and realistic) to improve an idea. It stimulates the creative skills "sharp observation" and "postponing judgment."
When to use	Use the exercise during the development of a future vision or of new concepts.
Futures exploration	Scenarios.
What you need	Pen and paper.
How does it work?	Describe your subject briefly and formulate the problem or question.
	Use your critical thinking style and make a list of requirements, for example that the future vision should highlight changes in mobility and should appeal to the public.
	Use your creative thinking style and dream about new (absurd) ideas.
	Then use the realistic thinking style to translate the aspects of the creative ideas to a realistic idea.
	Repeat the cycle until you are satisfied with the result (Eviont, 2012).
Advice	Do not mix the thinking styles.
Options	You can do this exercise individually or with a group. You can make three spaces and allocate a thinking style to each space (Idea Sandbox, 2012).

Figure 13.6 Cycle of the thinking styles.

Exercise 7: Visualizing the Future

Table 13.7 Creative exercise: visualizing the future

Purpose	Shaping vision of the future.
	Engaging in a dialogue about the foresight you have developed or about intermediate results is easier when you visualize it. You use your own creative skill "imagination," allowing other people to be inspired by what they see.
When to use	You can use the exercise to present trends and developments, scenarios or research results. During a workshop, you can visualize ideas with drawings (as shown in Figure 13.7) and invite a specialist to do this.
Futures exploration	All.
What you need	Depending on the visualization. For instance pencils, markers, visual material, actors.
How does it work?	Translate the text or graphs to a visual story. A vivid vision of the future comes across better than a thick report.
	Examples:
	• Make a storyboard that represents the story in a time line.
	• Make a mood board that expresses the atmosphere of a vision of the future.
	• Write a page in a diary or a vivid story from the future.
	• Write the outline of a play and have it performed by actors.
	• Make a short film from existing images.
	• Make special future rooms/spaces entirely in the feel of the future or make a museum of the future. For inspiration, have a look at the project "Designs for an Overpopulated Planet" (Dunne and Raby, 2009).
	Chapter 17 has information on the different methods.
Advice	Try to create extreme images that inspire others.
Options	Let the people with whom you want to have a dialogue visualize a trend or scenario. They immerse themselves, which gives them greater knowledge of the subject.

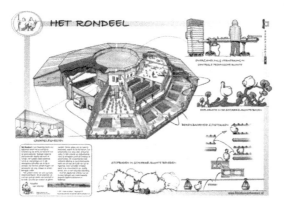

Figure 13.7 Roundel housing system for chickens (www.rondeel.org/uk), visualized by JAM visual thinking (image right 2004 JAM Visual Thinking, www.jamvisualthinking.com).

References

Barber, M.P. (2003, 2004). *Wildcards: signals from a future near you*. Retrieved from www. swinburne.edu.au/corporate/spq/docs/Wild%20Cards.pdf.

British Assessment Bureau (2014, March 26). *A management lesson from Walt Disney*. Retrieved from www.british-assessment.co.uk/articles/a-management-lesson-from-walt-disney.

Byttebier, I. (2002). *Creativiteit Hoe? Zo. Inzicht, inspiratie en toepassingen voor het optimaal benutten van uw eigen creativiteit en die van uw organisatie*. Tielt: Uitgeverij Lannoo.

Creativiteit. Retrieved from http://nl.wikipedia.org/wiki/Creativiteit.

Dunne and Raby (2009). *Designs for an overpopulated planet: foragers*. Retrieved from www. dunneandraby.co.uk/content/projects/510/0.

Eviont (2012, August 23). *Creativiteit nodig? Denk als Disney!* Retrieved from www.eviont. nl/eviont+blogt/creativiteit-nodig-denk-als-disney.

Hampsink, M. and N. Hagedoorn (2006). *Beweging in je brein: zestig werkvormen voor inspirerende trainingen, workshops en presentatie*. The Hague: Sdu Uitgevers.

Idea Sandbox (2012, March 23). *Disney brainstorming method: dreamer, realist, and spoiler*. Retrieved from www.idea-sandbox.com/blog/disney-brainstorming-method-dreamer-realist-and-spoiler/.

Nekkers, J. (2006). *Wijzer in de toekomst: werken met toekomstscenario's*. Amsterdam: Business Contact.

Petersen, J.L. (1999). *Out of the blue: how to anticipate big future surprises*. Lanham, MD: Madison Books.

Roam, D. (2011). *Blah blah blah: what to do when words don't work*. London: Penguin Group.

Rondeel (n.d.). *The system*. Retrieved from www.rondeel.org/uk/the-system/.

Wulfen, G. van (2009). *Nieuwe producten bedenken*. Amsterdam: Pearson Education Benelux.

14 Foresight and Creativity

René Hartman

Introduction

Star Trek and *Star Wars* are fantastic tales about the future, with a certain hint of realism. Showing beautiful images of spaceships and the discovery of new worlds. Products of the brains of scenario writers from Hollywood and "imagineers" like George Lucas. Many science fiction movies have a mix of reality and fantasy. So how do the scenario writers do it? How do they come up with those images of the future?

You see them at every major car show, the magnificent "concept cars." Prototypes of new cars with which manufacturers gives us a peak into their vision about what cars will look like in the future. Sometimes, the prototypes are close to reality, harbingers of car models that will be marketed a year later. But there are also futuristic models that would look out of place in today's streets. For instance the EN-V by General Motors, a two-wheel car for commuters, presented at the 2010 automobile exhibition in Shanghai. Or the Gina concept by BMW, a car with a hi-tech textile body. Are car designers visionaries, do they have a crystal ball?

Figure 14.1 Star Wars pod-racer.

Figure 14.2 GM ENV.

What writing scripts for science fiction movies and designing concept cars have in common is that the imagination is used as an instrument. The application of the imagination is one of the five basic skills of Creative Thinking or Creative Problem Solving. In this chapter, we take a closer look at the power of Creative Thinking.

Creative Thinking

In 1953, in *Applied Imagination*, Alex Osborn for the first time describes the principle of creative thinking (Oxborn, 1966). He came from the world of advertising and was looking for rules to find more and better ideas during meetings. Originally, he called his method "up thinking," later it was called "brainstorming."

In his book *New Think: The Use of Lateral Thinking* (1967), Edward de Bono shows various thinking techniques. Over ten years later, he writes the book *Future Positive*, in which he states: "The quality of our future will depend on the quality of our thinking."

How do we think? How does our brain work? Without being aware of it, we think in patterns. Each time we are faced with new information and process it in our brain, a pathway is created in the form of connections between brain cells. Each time we process similar information, the same pathway is used. And each time, the pathway is deepened just a little bit. That is how habits or routines emerge. They do not require us to think. What was it like again, the first ever driving lesson? You had to think about everything. Starting the engine, shifting

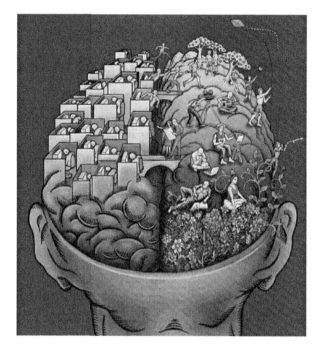

Figure 14.3 The left brain and the right brain.

gear, checking the rearview mirror. After a while, it turned out that numerous complex actions become almost automatic, even allowing us to do or think about other things while we are driving.

There are, of course, situations in which we do not use the pre-paved pathways in our brain, when we cannot or do not want to rely on routines, for example:

- when a problem is not defined unequivocally;
- when the problem is new and there is no knowledge or experience available;
- when information is missing or when there are gaps in the information being presented;
- when you are looking for new, distinguishing solutions.

In these cases, it is obvious not to rely on the existing thinking pattern, but to break through that pattern. Here, we define creative thinking as "the compendium of different attitudes, thinking skills and techniques and thought processes that increase the probability of pattern breaking and the creation of new connections in our brain" (Byttebier, 2007).

Recent management studies, like the biannual study by IBM ("Capitalizing on Complexity," 2010) among 1500 CEOs, also point to the importance of creativity. The CEOs in IBM's study indicate that they expect the complexity in management to increase and that companies are not equipped to deal with this global complexity. They see creativity as the most important leadership skill to discover new opportunities in this complexity.

We all have the skills that are needed for creative thinking, we just forgot them. As early as 1968, George Land and Beth Jarman showed that the creative skills of children decrease significantly between the ages of five and 15. They tested the creativity of 1600 children in the age group three to five years. Five and ten years later, they tested the same children again. While in the first test, 98 percent of the children had the score of "genius," five years later, it was 32 percent and, in the final test, it was only 10 percent. Not much seems to have changed between 1968 and today. Sir Ken Robinson is one of the people referring to this study as "Decline of the Genius."

When we want to think creatively, we will have to "forget" part of what we have been taught. We need to separate ourselves from the logical thinking that makes us head straight for our goal, satisfied with only one solution and stay close to what we know. A creative thinker is prepared to take a detour, wants as many solutions as possible, in order to select the best one, and is always looking for originality. The same values and attitude apply to a foresight professional!

Five Skills

The idea that only some people, like artists, are able to think creatively is completely wrong. It is a skill that you can learn, that you can train. Here, we discuss five basic skills that help us make new connections between our brain cells and stimulate our creativity.

Figure 14.4 Baby genius (source: *Huffington Post*).

1   Sharp observation: we tend to filter incoming information, like the things we perceive. Observations that do not fit a pattern are often ignored. In the case of clear perception, we look for new points of view. What else could you see in a certain trend, in a technical invention? How would a child or older person see this? What other (consumer) information could you get from the newspaper on Saturday or walking the street?

2   Making associations: the smell of coffee that reminds you of Italy, the mail box in the neighborhood that reminds you that you need to send a friend a birthday card. With creative thinking, we use associations as inspiration to solve the problem. For instance, your friend may well have the answer to the question how you can remove that coffee stain from your couch.

3   Coming up with alternatives: research shows us that "quantity breeds quality," which is why we have to look for as many possible different answers to the question, and then pick the best one. Unlike what we are used to, we cannot settle for the first answer, and we can train ourselves to ask constantly: how can this be done differently?

4   Postpone your judgment: by postponing your judgment, you give yourself the chance to explore different sides and possibilities of a question. Often, we need (parts of) naive or absurd thoughts to come to a creative solution to a problem. Later on in the creative process, there is plenty of room for judgment.

5   Using the imagination: in addition to the often verbal intelligence, the imagination is a powerful tool. Einstein once said that his imagination had been more useful than his knowledge. You imagine what something looks like, what it sounds like or how it smells. You place yourself in someone else's position, or in a different place or time. "What would the weather be like in The Hague?" or "Wouldn't it be great if we could...?"

Creative Process

Many versions of the creative process have been described. In essence, what they have in common is that they distinguish two phases:

1   Divergence: the phase of the creative process in which as many answers to a question as possible are thought of, in which the imagination is used, in which methods are applied to remove from the question and in which the judgment about the solutions is postponed. In this phase, it is important to create some distance from the question, to make room for less-than-obvious solutions that may even be crazy or naive. To look for prejudices and to bend them.

2   Convergence: in this phase, the suitable ingredients for the solution are selected; new ingredients are combined and forged into solutions to the problem or issue. Now, people are allowed to judge, albeit in a constructive way. In this phase, there is a real danger of falling back on existing patterns, which is why preventing the "creadox" is very important.

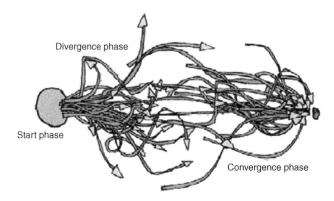

Figure 14.5 Creative process: diverging–converging.

For divergence as well as convergence, many methods are available (also see Chapter 13). Depending on the subject and the level of experience of the group of people involved, climbing or floating techniques can be used. Climbing techniques stay somewhat closer to the problem and are more analytical in nature than floating techniques, which help increase the distance and often result in breakthrough solutions.

Some methods that are often used for divergence are:

- Analogy with nature: you make as many associations as possible with an animal, and use these associations to come up with other new ideas.
- Superhero: you imagine a superhero and their qualities and use those qualities for concrete solutions to the problem.
- Combining: finding solutions in other business or research sectors and transferring these solutions to the area you are working in, known as cross-industry innovation.
- Reframing: which aspects of the context can be changed or can you change the entire context? Challenge yourself to discuss assumptions concerning the future.

An effective method for convergence is the COCD (Centrum voor Ontwikkeling van het Creatief Denken/Center for Development of Creative Thinking) box, which helps people come up with both realistic short-term solutions and ideas that are not (yet) realistic for the long term.

For example, for futures explorations, you can extrapolate existing trends and expectations, as a basis for designing products, services and organizations that will match the needs of "later." This is the so-called climbing technique. You can also map all the images about the future (for instance a bridge that is to be built) and define the assumptions. One assumption could be that every design of the bridge uses pillars. The breakthrough would be to design a bridge without pillars.

You can either use the creative process as an individual or as a group. The group can be homogeneous or heterogeneous, consisting of experts in a specific research field or consisting of, for example, research experts, businessmen and the general public. Design company Ideo in the USA is carrying out global thinking experiments using the Internet. Its subsidiary, Openideo, uses the creative process "to solve big challenges for social good," co-creation with both designers and laymen around the world.

Ultimately, the five basic skills, the creative process and the many techniques for divergent and convergent thinking (see Chapter 13) will help researchers imagine future concepts or different futures. Creativity helps to shape visions of the future and contributes to the significance of foresight.

Method for Future Planning of Companies

A tried and tested method for exploring the future for SMEs is GPS for Enterprises by FlandersDC (see www.flandersdc.be/gps), which was developed by the author and used by more than 5000 SMEs in Belgium and the Netherlands. This co-creation method uses preselected trends, like individualization and aging population. Based on these trends, concrete business ideas are designed for the company in question. Methods like Analogy with Nature and Reframing are used to stimulate the imagination of the participants. After the divergence phase, the ideas are selected via the COCD box, and combined into concrete business concepts. These concepts are elaborated via the Business Model Generation method (see www.businessmod-elgeneration.com). The accompanying Canvas Model is very useful for defining the profit model, keeping in mind the principles of the creative process. Together, GPS with Canvas Model, are integrated in the workshops of Innovationwerkplaats.nl, providing concepts and business models for the future.

Figure 14.6 GPS as a training module.

Figure 14.7 Filling in business model canvas.

References

Bono, E. de (1967). *New think: the use of lateral thinking in the generation of new ideas.* New York: Basic Books.

Bono, E. de (1979). *Future positive.* London: Maurice Temple Smith.

Bruijne, M. de, S. van Iersel and R. Rust (2010). *Lenig denken.* Culemborg: Van Duuren Management.

Bruyne, R. de, G. Aerts, E. Berg, M. de Bruijne, M. de Bruyn, M. Geers, R. Hartman, D. Kooij, M. Stolk and J. van der Weide (eds.) (2013). *Creatieve stromingen.* Rumst: CAW.

Byttebier, I. (2007). *Creativity today.* Amsterdam: BIS Publishers.

Dorst, K. (2015). *Framing innovation.* Cambridge, MA: MIT Press.

IBM (2010). Capitalizing on Complexity. IBM Global Business Services, Somers, USA. Retrieved from public.dhe.ibm.com.

Osborn, A. (1966). *Applied imagination: principles and procedures of creative problem solving.* New York: Charles Scribner's Sons.

Osterwalder, A. (2009). *Business model generation.* Self-publication.

Puccio, G. (2011). *Creative leadership.* Thousand Oaks, CA: Sage Publications.

Vos, K. de (2013). *Brainstormen, 50.000 ideeën per dag.* Amsterdam: Pearson Benelux.

Vullings, R. (2015). *Not invented here.* Amsterdam: BIS Publishers.

15 Stakeholder Analysis

Eefje Cuppen

Introduction

One cannot explore the future without profound insight into the actors who are shaping that future. Stakeholder analysis assists firms, governments, planners, and researchers in developing their strategies, policies and projects. Stakeholders are individuals or groups of individuals who can affect, or are affected by, the issue under consideration in the foresight study. This may concern stakeholders who exist in the present, but also possible future stakeholders. Stakeholder analysis is not a strictly defined method. It is a set of (social science) methods and techniques to investigate, for example, the interests, power, resources and perspectives of stakeholders. The choice of methods for stakeholder analysis depends on the project of which the analysis is part. Stakeholder analysis for foresight should, in any case, be apt to deal with complexity and scientific, strategic and institutional uncertainties (Van Bueren et al., 2003). For example, strategic uncertainty means that different stakeholders have their own strategies, and anticipate strategies of others, which may lead to conflicting strategies. This means that the demarcation of a stakeholder analysis should not be too narrow. Rather, a stakeholder analysis can help to probe the system boundaries. Obviously, the stakeholders of the present are not the stakeholders of the future. Whereas it may for instance be evident who the parties or persons are that may affect or are affected by the implementation of a new policy, this is inherently uncertain in the case of foresight.

This chapter describes stakeholder analysis according to five steps and lists examples of methods and techniques to support each of these steps. The chapter wraps up with practical information on how to conduct a stakeholder analysis.

Steps in a Stakeholder Analysis

A stakeholder analysis consists of five steps:

1   determining the objective of the analysis;
2   demarcating the analysis;
3   stakeholder identification;
4   analysis of stakeholder characteristics;
5   conclusion.

These steps do not necessarily take place in chronological order; rather they are part of an iterative process. It is both possible and useful to go back and forth between these steps. For instance, interviews that are held as part of step 4, analysis of stakeholder characteristics, may provide new information about, for example, marginal stakeholders that were not yet identified in step 3. It may furthermore appear useful after interaction with stakeholders to adapt the objectives of the analysis or project of which the analysis is part. It is therefore important to maintain flexibility throughout the analysis.

Step 1: Objective of the Analysis

Stakeholder analysis can have diverging objectives that may all play a role in foresight. Roughly, these objectives can be grouped in instrumental, normative and substantive objectives (based on Fiorino, 1990). Stakeholder analysis has an instrumental objective, for example, when it is used in project management to take stakeholders into account in the design and implementation of a project to enlarge the chance of a smooth and successful implementation. Normative objectives guide stakeholder analysis, for example, when a project should contribute to sustainable development and thus should not pass risks on to future generations. Involving marginal and future stakeholders may be desirable from a democratic or ethical perspective. Substantive objectives of stakeholder analysis pertain to producing integrated knowledge. The future is uncertain and unstructured. There is a complex interplay of things that determines how the future will look, and only by involving diverse types of knowledge, values, interest etc., of stakeholders can a robust vision (scenario, plan, strategy...) develop.

In general the three objectives will exist at the same time. Within the context of this book we are focusing on stakeholder analysis for foresight. The scope of such an analysis is broad and aimed at opening-up rather than closing-down (Stirling, 2008). In other words, it is aimed at broadening and enriching the scope rather than restricting and excluding. This means that a stakeholder analysis should be able to surprise. This is only possible if there is a certain extent of creativity and out-of-the-box thinking involved in the analysist, both as regards the identification of stakeholders as well as what it is that the analysist wants to know about them. Ideally, it delivers new insights that help the analysis or the stakeholders in developing strategies, actions, projects or policies.

Step 2: Demarcating the Analysis

Depending on the nature of the foresight study, the analysis can take place at several levels (local, regional, national, international). The level of analysis is important to consider, since it determines who should be seen as a stakeholder and how data will be gathered (Varvasovszky and Brugha, 2000). If the analysis takes place on a local level stakeholders can generally be contacted personally and be interviewed individually. When the number of stakeholders is bigger or when stakeholders are more difficult to contact and meet, as in an analysis on an international level, this will be more difficult. In addition to geographical levels, demarcation also takes place on a contents level. For example, the future role of biomass in the energy supply can only be meaningfully explored if also the role of biomass in the chemical and food industry is taken into account. The system boundaries thus determine who is considered a stakeholder and who is not. In general it is advisable to maintain flexibility: growing insight as a result of stakeholder analysis may lead to adaptation of the demarcation of the analysis and thus the need to involve other or new stakeholders.

Step 3: Stakeholder Identification

Because the future is unknown and uncertain, it is not easy to determine who are, or may become, relevant stakeholders. Taking the starting point that stakeholder analysis is about opening-up, it makes sense to focus on diversity. This needs some elaboration. Diversity has three dimensions: variety, disparity and balance (Stirling, 1998). Variety refers to the number of different categories within a population. For instance, a group of students is diverse when it consists of a number of different nationalities. Disparity refers to the extent to which categories are similar or different. A group of Dutch and Indian students is more diverse than a group of Dutch and German students. Balance refers to the size of the categories within the population. A group consisting of ten Dutch students and one Indian student is less diverse than a group of five Dutch and five Indian students.

These three dimensions of diversity can be used for stakeholder identification (Cuppen, 2012). First, it is important to cover the *variety* of stakeholder perspectives, making sure that stakeholders who diverge from the mainstream ideas and networks are included (*disparity*). Then the analysis should be *balanced* in such a way that diverging and marginal perspectives are included on an equal footing. Especially when the analysis is part of a project aiming for systemic change, the involvement of marginal perspectives is crucial. It is those perspectives that can lead to new insights. In the words of Dunn (2001): "Hypotheses that are mentioned more frequently – those on which there is substantial consensus – have less probative value than rarely mentioned hypotheses, because highly probable or predictable hypotheses do not challenge accepted knowledge claims." This means that it can be useful to include people who are not considered primary stakeholders, but who, because of their diverging or remarkable ideas or expertise, may bring in new perspectives. If the variety of perspectives is not balanced, these diverging and marginal perspectives are likely to remain unnoticed or overshadowed by more mainstream actors and perspectives, for example, due to group-think (Janis, 1972).

Mapping diversity requires trying actively to break through existing networks. Within networks people know one another and one another's ideas, which makes it more likely that there will be redundancy rather than disparity (Granovetter, 1973).

Comprehensive introduction to the subject and the stakeholder field is indeed necessary for conducting a stakeholder analysis. Much knowledge will however be gained throughout the stakeholder analysis itself. A preliminary list of stakeholders can be assembled based on general knowledge of the subject of the foresight study, experience and exchange with others. A grouping based on (for the foresight study relevant) categories can be used as a heuristic to cover diversity as much as possible, for instance regime player versus niche player, position in the value chain, opinions on the topic of the future exploration, or affiliation (government, industry, academia, NGO, etc.). Also an internal brainstorm meeting can be held to assemble a preliminary list (HarmoniCOP, 2005). An often used method is snowball sampling. This means that the analyst asks each stakeholder in the first round of interviews to mention someone with a different perspective from him- or herself. In this way the list may be expanded. Also Internet and other media offer different ways to identify stakeholders, both passively, for example, by searching via search engines as well as actively, for example, by distributing a call via social media.

Step 4: Analysis of Stakeholder Characteristics

Depending on the scope of the stakeholder analysis and the foresight study of which it is part, a more or less extensive analysis of stakeholders can be conducted. When the objective and demarcation of the analysis are clear, one can determine what it is that one wants to know about the stakeholder. In backcasting analysis (Chapter 7) for instance it is important to map the expectations and visions of stakeholders. When developing scenarios (Chapter 2), stakeholder analysis can be used to map which stakeholders have the power and resources to influence developments. For foresight studies generally two elements are part of the analysis: (1) analysis of power and interests and (2) articulation of perspectives. These will be subsequently discussed.

Analysis of Power and Interests

Analysis of power and interests helps to understand what the position of stakeholders is in the actor field and how these can or should change in the future. This shows the iterative nature of stakeholder analysis: insight into the positions of stakeholders makes it possible to identify the dominant and marginal networks and stakeholders. This knowledge can then be used to add to the preliminary stakeholder list and thus support stakeholder identification. Data is gathered by means of text analysis (reports, websites, etc.), but may also be collected by means of (semi-structured) interviews and interactive sessions.

A method that can be used in this process is the so-called power-interest matrix (see Table 15.1) (Eden and Ackermann, 1998). On the X-axis of this matrix is power (high to low) and on the Y-axis interests (high to low). In this way stakeholders are categorized in three groups. These groups are labeled "players," "subjects," "crowd" and "context setters" respectively.

Table 15.1 Power-interests matrix

	Low power	*High power*
High interests	"Subjects"	"Players"
Low interests	"Crowd"	"Context setters"

Source: Eden and Ackermann (1998).

A definition of power helps to place stakeholders in this matrix. Power refers to the capacity of stakeholders to mobilize resources to achieve a certain goal (Avelino and Rotmans, 2011). This may concern financial resources, materials, infrastructure, technology, human resources, grassroots support, knowledge, legal authority, and access to networks and individuals. Placing stakeholders in this matrix is not necessarily unambiguous. Within the context of foresight it is important to realize that positions of stakeholders can change over time. The power of "subjects" may for instance increase as coalitions are being built with other parties. In addition, the position of stakeholders cannot always be determined in an "objective" way; different people (in the project team, but also stakeholders themselves) may have different ideas about the positioning of stakeholders. It is these different points of view that are interesting to explore, because these are linked to expectations about actors and their context. Positioning stakeholders in the matrix – especially when this is a joint activity, also with stakeholders – can be a way to unravel power, resources and interests of stakeholders further.

This matrix can serve as a framework for supporting stakeholder identification and further strategy development. For future explorations, it is wise to consider all four groups and not, for example, only the stakeholders with high power and interests. A party that may now be identified as "crowd" may shift position in the future. In addition, due to the complexity of the issue one may overlook certain interests that make stakeholders from the "crowd" actually appear to be "subjects." This is an example of the way in which flexibility can be maintained in the system demarcation.

Articulating Perspectives

The articulation of perspectives pertains to clarifying the ways in which stakeholders view the issues of the foresight study, for instance based on values, visions and expectations of stakeholders. The results of this step play an important role in (re)defining the system boundaries. It was noted above that stakeholder analysis is about "opening-up" and should be able to surprise. This surprise element can only be catered for when the articulation of perspectives is based on a so-called "bottom-up" approach. This means that one does not work with fixed categories or structures for mapping stakeholders and their perspectives, which is the case in, for example, surveys. Rather, the articulation of perspectives relies primarily on qualitative methods. Qualitative methods are indispensable for ensuring that there is a focus on limited aspects of the issue only and that other aspects that may appear relevant in a later stage of data collection and analysis are neglected (Varvasovszky and Brugha, 2000). Interviews (semi-structured) (see Chapter 9) are an appropriate method to map stakeholder perspectives, possibly added by more structured methods such as Q methodology (Brown, 1980). Q methodology combines the open nature of qualitative methods with the structuring nature of quantitative methods. It can be used to map the variety of stakeholder perspectives in such a way that the perspectives are clustered in a (not previously defined) number of meaningful categories (see, for an example of the use of the Q-method for stakeholder analysis, Cuppen et al., 2010). Analysis can also be done in an interactive way, for instance in a focus group or dialogue, possibly supported by software tools such as the acceleration method (see Chapter 12). In that case it is important that the analysis results not only in data collection for the analyst, but also to learning and information exchange amongst stakeholders.

Step 5: Conclusion

In the last step of stakeholder analysis, data and analysis for the previous steps are presented, for example, in a report or presentation, supported by tables and figures. Most of the times the conclusion step will not be the endpoint, but input to further analysis or other methods as described in this book. In this phase, stakeholder analysis can for instance lead to an overview of the most diverging future expectations of stakeholders and analysis of tensions and synergies between these expectations. If a foresight study takes place in a participatory setting – jointly with stakeholders – a choice can be made in this step for stakeholders to invite for further participation in a subsequent trajectory. It may for instance be important for the project to involve stakeholders who have a certain type of power and interests, or who reflect the diversity of perspectives. The stakeholder analysis offers plenty of ground to make such a choice. These are just two examples of the way in which conclusions are achieved in a stakeholder analysis. It is difficult to give a generically valid and detailed description of the conclusion step of stakeholder analysis. The conclusion of stakeholder analysis obviously needs to connect to the method or foresight of which it is part, and thus needs to be adapted and shaped according to this.

Practicalities

This chapter has described stakeholder analysis for foresight in a nutshell. The exact way in which the analysis is conducted depends, apart from the objective of the foresight study, on the available resources and context. The analysis can be done by an individual or a team. To achieve a balanced evaluation of the qualitative data a team approach is preferred (Varvasovszky and Brugha, 2000). A team can consist of "insiders" (people who are directly involved in the issue of the foresight study) as well as "outsiders" (e.g., a consultant). The advantage of a mix of these people is that there is then both knowledge of the culture and context (the insiders) as well as the possibility to take an independent position (the outsiders) (Varvasovszky and Brugha, 2000). Furthermore, the involvement of externals can be welcome if there is not sufficient knowledge, experience and resources to use particular methods (interviews, focus groups, Q methodology). The time needed to conduct a stakeholder analysis varies from a couple of weeks to months, while the latter is more likely in the context of foresight.

214   *E. Cuppen*

References

Avelino, F. and J. Rotmans (2011). A dynamic conceptualization of power for sustainability research. *Journal of Cleaner Production*, Vol. 19, pp. 796–804.

Brown, S.R. (1980). *Political subjectivity: applications of Q methodology in political science.* New Haven, CT, and London: Yale University Press.

Cuppen, E. (2012). Diversity and constructive conflict in stakeholder dialogue: considerations for design and methods. *Policy Sciences*, Vol. 45, pp. 23–46.

Cuppen, E., S. Breukers, M. Hisschemöller and E. Bergsma (2010). Q methodology to select participants for a stakeholder dialogue on energy options from biomass in the Netherlands. *Ecological Economics*, Vol. 69, pp. 579–591.

Dunn, W.N. (2001). Using the method of context validation to mitigate type III error in environmental policy analysis. In M. Hisschemöller, R. Hoppe, W.N. Dunn and J. R. Ravetz (eds.), *Knowledge, power and participation in environmental policy analysis.* New Brunswick and London: Transaction Publishers.

Eden, C. and F. Ackermann (1998). *Making strategy: the journey of strategic management.* London: Sage Publications.

Fiorino, D.J. (1990). Citizen participation and environmental risk: a survey of institutional mechanisms. *Science Technology and Human Values*, Vol. 15, pp. 226–243.

Granovetter, M.S. (1973). The strength of weak ties. *American Journal of Sociology*, Vol. 78, pp. 1360–1380.

HarmoniCOP (2005). *Learning together to manage together: improving participation in water management.* Osnabrück: University of Osnabrück, Institute of Environmental System Research.

Janis, I.L. (1972). *Victims of groupthink: psychological studies of foreign policy decisions and fiascoes.* Boston, MA: Houghton-Mifflin.

Stirling, A. (1998). On the economics and analysis of diversity. *SPRU Electronic Working Paper series, 28.*

Stirling, A. (2008). "Opening up" and "closing down": power, participation, and pluralism in the social appraisal of technology. *Science Technology and Human Values*, Vol. 33, pp. 262–294.

Van Bueren, E.M., E.H. Klijn and J.F.M. Koppenjan (2003). Dealing with wicked problems in networks: analyzing an environmental debate from a network perspective. *Journal of Public Administration Research and Theory*, Vol. 13, pp. 193–212.

Varvasovszky, Z. and R. Brugha (2000). How to do (or not do) ... a stakeholder analysis. *Health Policy and Planning*, Vol. 15, pp. 338–345.

16 Causal Loop Diagramming

Kim van Oorschot

Description of the Method

A causal loop diagram is a diagram that helps to visualize how different variables in a system are interrelated. This interrelation of variables is also known as the feedback structure of systems. Feedback is the core concept of dynamic complex systems. In other words: feedback determines how complex systems behave over time. Understanding the feedback structure of systems and determining the causal loops is part of the system dynamics method. System dynamics was developed by Jay Forrester in the 1950s. System dynamics is a method, a perspective and a set of conceptual tools, to enhance learning in dynamic complex systems. Dynamic complex systems are characterized by interdependence, mutual interaction, information feedback and circular causality (Sterman, 2000). Feedback exists whenever "the environment causes a decision which in turn affects the original environment" (Forrester, 1958, p. 39). As such, feedback means that the system reacts to your solution. The system is not some stable, constant "thing," it is dynamic and it changes over time. If you are always late for a meeting, your solution could be to set your watch five minutes ahead of time. This solution may work for a short while. Then you learn that your watch is not telling you the right time and you start using the extra five minutes for other activities. Soon after this, you will be late again. By changing the time on your watch, you have solved the symptom of always running late, but not the root cause of your problem (e.g., that you have too many things to do, or that you can't prioritize). To understand and really solve the problem you need to look at the feedbacks that operate in the system. You need to understand that your actions or solutions define the situation that you face tomorrow. The new situation may change how you perceive the problem and how you would like to solve it. Furthermore, the new situation may change the behavior of others in the system. The left-hand side of Figure 16.1 presents this feedback perspective (Sterman, 2000).

Problems usually arise when people do not understand the feedbacks operating in the system they are trying to influence. A classic example of this misunderstanding comes from day care centers in Israel (Gneezy and Rustichini, 2000). Parents used to arrive late to collect their children, forcing a teacher to stay after closing time. In a field study in a group of day-care centers, Gneezy and Rustichini introduced a monetary fine for late-coming parents. It was expected that

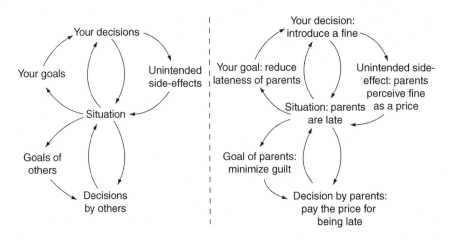

Figure 16.1 Feedback perspective.

this fine would discourage parents from being late. However, the study revealed exactly the opposite. After the fine was introduced the number of late-coming parents increased significantly. To make matters worse, after the fine was removed, no reduction of lateness occurred. The authors explain that before the fine was introduced, parents had to rely on the generosity of the teacher who had to stay late to look after their child. As such, parents had non-financial incentives for being on time, like avoiding feeling guilty about being late and facing the teacher. The fine changed the perception of the parents regarding the environment in which they operated. The fine was perceived as a normal price to pay for day care services. As soon as parents had the option to pay the fine and avoid feeling guilty, they chose that option. On the right-hand side of Figure 16.1 this example is depicted from a feedback perspective.

Causal loop diagrams are a tool for representing the feedbacks in a system. Feedback processes explain *how* decisions can lead to either good control or a dramatic out-of-control situation. Causal loop diagrams are therefore used to improve your understanding of the dynamic behavior (i.e., the behavior over time) of a system. Furthermore, the tool can provide insight in the root cause of the problem and as such in possible solutions to this problem. Examples of how causal loop diagramming was used to gain insight into the root cause of problems and, as such, finding solutions that actually work, can be found in all sorts of sectors and businesses; for example, quality improvement in the automotive industry (Repenning and Sterman, 2002), decision-making processes in an Internet start-up (Perlow et al., 2002), decision-making processes in project management (Van Oorschot et al., 2013), outsourcing in the pharmaceutical industry (Azoulay et al., 2010), and even the obesity problem (Abdel-Hamid, 2010).

A causal loop diagram consists of variables that are connected with each other by arrows. An arrow indicates the causal link between two and only two variables. A causal link can have a *positive* (+) or *negative* (–) polarity. This polarity depicts how the dependent variable (the effect) changes when the independent variable (the cause) changes. A positive link means that when the cause increases (decreases), the effect also increases (decreases). For example: when the temperature rises, ice cream sales increase. A negative link means that when the cause increases (decreases), the effect decreases (increases). For example: when the temperature rises, sales of warm clothes decreases. These links do not say anything about the current behavior of the variables they connect, but they describe what is most likely to happen when there is a change in the cause. The fact that there is a causal link between temperature and ice cream sales is by no means a forecast of tomorrow's weather. As such, causality is not the same as correlation. Correlation between two variables does not reflect the feedbacks in a system. Two variables can have perfect correlation, without one being the cause or the effect of the other.

Two or more variables can be connected with each other in such a way that a *loop* arises. Loops can also have a polarity. *Positive* or reinforcing loops reinforce what is happening to the system. Positive loops bring the system out of its equilibrium. An example of a positive loop is given in Figure 16.2. This figure shows what happens when €1000 are deposited in a bank account on someone's birthday. Every year 2 percent interest is received over the amount. If the money on the account is never used, the amount will increase exponentially over the years. The higher the amount, the more interest is received, which in turn increases the amount even further, etc.

Negative or balancing feedback loops counteract or oppose whatever is happening to the system in an attempt to bring the system back to its equilibrium. Figure 16.3 shows what happens when €1000 are deposited in a bank account on someone's birthday and this person spends 1.5 percent of the remaining amount every year. The more money on the bank account, the higher the amount that is spent, but the lower the amount remaining for next year. This behavior continues until almost no money is left in the account. The system has come to an equilibrium and nothing changes anymore (no expenditures, no increase of the money in the account). This is contrary to the positive loop; this loop will never bring the system into equilibrium.

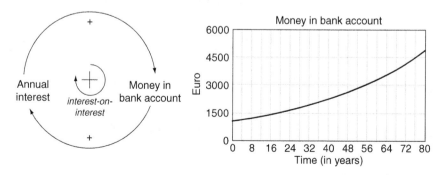

Figure 16.2 Example of the structure and behavior of a positive (reinforcing) loop.

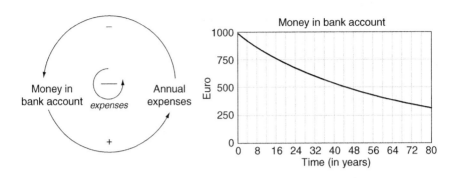

Figure 16.3 Example of the structure and behavior of a negative (balancing) loop.

Complex dynamic systems rarely consist of just one feedback loop. Usually these systems are captured by multiple causal feedback loops. However, all dynamic behavior arises from the interaction of just these two types of causal feedback loops: negative (or self-correcting) and positive (or self-reinforcing) loops.

The most important rules for making a causal loop diagram are:

•   Assign link and loop polarities.
•   Name the loops.
•   Indicate long delays in causal links (i.e., when there is a long time delay between the action and the response, you can depict this in the diagram by either writing down the word *delay* on the link, or by drawing two short lines perpendicular to the link, see also Figure 16.4 for an example).
•   Assign clear names to variables, preferably nouns or noun phrases with a clear sense of direction. Do not use "physical condition" or "sickness," because a condition cannot increase or decrease and when sickness decreases, the implication is somewhat ambiguous: does this means that the person is getting sicker or less sick? In this case it is better to use "health."
•   Make the goals of the system explicit. For example: desired percentage of satisfied customers is 95 percent, desired number of traffic accidents per year is zero, desired percentage of sick leave is 3 percent.

Example of the Method

Problem Description

Every month the owner of a restaurant measures customer satisfaction by asking customers to fill in a short questionnaire after paying the bill. The goal of the owner is to have a satisfaction index of at least eight (on a scale of one to ten). When the scores are below eight, the owner calls in a staff meeting and asks the staff to focus more on the customer, i.e., to say yes to all kinds of special requests concerning the menu, to smile more, to ask them if they like their meal, etc. This extra focus on customers is usually accompanied by a period of hard work. But when the satisfaction scores increase again, the staff can relax a bit. The owner does not understand why it is so difficult to keep the satisfaction scores stable at eight and why these scores keep oscillating between 6 and 9. Also, he does not understand why a high customer satisfaction usually comes with a bad atmosphere in the kitchen. Because the owner is striving for more stability in customer satisfaction, he wants to gain more insight into the root causes of these oscillations in order to prevent them in the future.

Developing the Causal Loop Diagram

A good place to start making a causal loop diagram of this situation is the goal of the owner: the desired customer satisfaction. The difference between the desired and actual customer satisfaction is causing a need to do something: to change the actual customer satisfaction (right-hand side of Figure 16.4). When actual satisfaction is lagging behind the desired satisfaction, the need to improve satisfaction increases. The most obvious solution to do so is to increase the focus on customers. After some delay (because customer satisfaction is only measured on a monthly basis), the owner will discover that actual satisfaction has increased. The first loop is now finished. We call this the *customer satisfaction loop*. It is a balancing loop because it is self-correcting (when satisfaction is low, focus is increased which in turn increases satisfaction).

Now we need to think about possible (unintended) side-effects of the decision to change focus and/or how other people in the system may respond to this action (remember Figure 16.1). By increasing focus and trying to please the customer by fulfilling special menu requests the workload of the staff in the restaurant increases. After some time, the staff will suffer from a continuous high workload: they will have less energy (feeling tired). A tired chef may not feel like changing the recipe or doing something extra to satisfy the customer. So, the

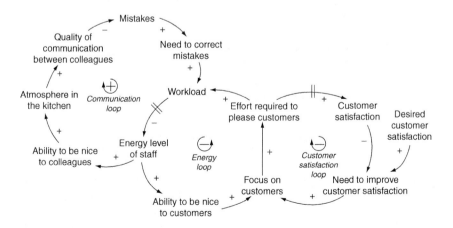

Figure 16.4 Causal loop diagram of the restaurant example.

lower the energy level of the staff, the lower the focus on customers. This side-effect can therefore have a negative outcome on customer satisfaction, while the opposite effect was intended. Now, we have discovered another balancing loop: the *energy loop*. This loop is also balancing, or self-correcting, because low energy levels reduce the focus on the customer which reduces the workload which has a positive effect on energy levels.

The two loops that are now described still do not explain why high customer satisfaction is accompanied by a bad atmosphere in the kitchen. So, we have to dig deeper into this problem. When energy levels are low, staff are not only focusing less on the customer but also on each other. This can lead to all sorts of communication problems that can cause mistakes. For example, the waiter may give the wrong order to the chef. When the customer finds out this mistake, the correct meal has to be prepared, leading to an even higher workload for the chef. We have now found a reinforcing *communication loop*, in which a high workload leads to more mistakes which increases the workload even further. These three loops combined explain how high customer satisfaction can lead to a bad atmosphere in the kitchen (which eventually will have a negative effect on customer satisfaction in the future).

Predicting Future Behavior

Now that we have discovered the feedback structure of the restaurant situation in Figure 16.4, we can use this structure to predict the behavior of the variables in the diagram. The feedback structure depicted in Figure 16.4 gives us foresight. The loops tell us that if the owner keeps pushing staff to focus on the customer, side-effects will eventually occur. These side-effects are counterproductive and will drive the system further away from its goal. Note that this foresight does not tell us exactly when the side-effects will occur and exactly how negative their influence will be. The loops only tell us that negative side-effects will occur and that these effects will make it more difficult to reach our goal.

To determine when which loop is driving the behavior of the system at any point in time, we need to look at (or measure) the behavior over time of individual variables in the loops. The balancing customer satisfaction loop will always try to bring the actual customer satisfaction to the desired level. However, this loop will be hampered by the balancing energy loop. As soon as the owner realizes that the actual customer satisfaction is not moving in the desired direction, this means that the energy loop is becoming more powerful and starts driving the behavior of the system. When customer satisfaction starts behaving in the opposite direction (decreasing), this means that the reinforcing communication loop is taking over control. This causal feedback structure, consisting of three loops, explains why customer satisfaction does not show stable behavior but keeps oscillating from low to high and back to low, etc. The *exact rate* in which satisfaction increases or decreases and the *exact time* at which the loops work against each other is difficult to predict based on the causal loop diagram alone. But an *approximation* of future behavior can be derived. Note that a causal loop diagram is not meant to forecast exactly when customer satisfaction will be equal to 8.3. The diagram is meant to provide insight into how the system will respond when one of the variables in the system starts to change. The feedback structure shown in Figure 16.4 explains why customer satisfaction will only be equal to the desired level every now and then, and why it will not be stable in the long term.

Finding a Solution

A causal loop diagram can also be used to find possible solutions to a problem. Each possible solution can be included in the diagram, including the side-effects of each solution. Based on the feedback structure depicted by the loops, the consequences of each solution (what are the direct effects of the solution, what are the side-effects, what kind of new problems may arise when the solution is chosen) can be analyzed in the long term. The solution with the least severe side-effects is most likely the best solution. In the restaurant example, to keep customer satisfaction at a high level, the owner needs to prevent the energy and communication loop from gaining strength. This could be done by tackling the high workload that comes with the increased focus on the customer. The owner could do this by hiring extra staff in the kitchen, or by preventing mistakes by using an electronic touchscreen ordering system. Or the owner could also try to think of ways to please customers without causing extra work for the kitchen staff (like playing background music, or decorating the table with flowers). As such, a causal loop diagram can support decision-makers in developing foresight.

Understanding the Logic of Future Scenarios

In the example described above, the causal loop diagram is used as a decision support tool. The restaurant owner faces a certain problem and tries to gain insight into the causes and consequences of this problem by analyzing the feedback structure. Understanding the feedback structure improves the quality of decision-making. On a more aggregate level, causal loop diagrams can also be used to gain insight into why certain phenomena in society may or may not exist or happen, in other words, to understand what society could look like in the future and why (the logic behind changes in society). In some societies, it may not make sense for companies (or governments) to invest in high-tech product innovations, simply because economic growth is low and consumers have limited budgets to spend on these new product innovations. In these situations, it could make more sense to focus on process innovations to lower the costs of existing products. This may, in the long term, free up consumer budgets (and hence demand) for more expensive and innovative products. As such, a causal loop diagram helps to understand the logic, or the underlying feedback structure, of certain future scenarios.

References

Abdel-Hamid, T.K. (2010) *Thinking in circles about obesity: applying systems thinking to weight management*. New York: Springer.

Azoulay, P., N.P. Repenning and E.W. Zuckerman (2010). Nasty, brutish, and short: embeddedness failure in the pharmaceutical industry. *Adminstrative Science Quarterly*, Vol. 55, No. 3, pp. 472–507.

Gneezy, U. and A. Rustichini (2000). A fine is a price. *Journal of Legal Studies*, Vol. 29, No. 1, pp. 1–17.

Perlow, L.A., G.A. Okhuysen and N.P. Repenning (2002). The speed trap: exploring the relationship between decision making and temporal context. *Academy of Management Journal*, Vol. 45, No. 5, pp. 931–955.

Repenning, N.P. and J.D. Sterman (2002). Capability traps and self-confirming attribution errors in the dynamics of process improvement. *Administrative Science Quarterly*, Vol. 47, No. 2, pp. 265–295.

Sterman, J.D. (2000). *Business dynamics: systems thinking and modeling for a complex world.* Boston, MA: Irwin McGraw-Hill.

Van Oorschot, K.E., H. Akkermans, K. Sengupta and L.N. Van Wassenhove (2013). Anatomy of a decision trap in complex new product development projects. *Academy of Management Journal*, Vol. 56, No. 1, pp. 285–307.

17 Beyond Visualization

Experiencing the Future

Nik Baerten

We all realize that every choice that we make today influences how the future will unfold. What we often forget, however, is that the images we construct about the future also define our options today. The word image and the associations of visuality and tangibility it evokes may often stand in stark contrast to the mainstream analytical connotation of foresight activities. Nevertheless, the act of rendering the future tangible has increasingly become an important element in the process of exploring the future.

Immersing or engaging people in an as yet non-existent future context, as if it were today, revolves around what one could call the "experience factor," the ensemble of sensorial and narrative triggers that allows one to stimulate people's ability to imagine and empathize. The ways in which a good story is able to draw people in, illustrates how strong empathy triggers them to fill in gaps in the story being told, add detail to the world being described. and make it their own. The image of a cornfield bathing in the sun during summer evokes the image of farmers soon to harvest the corn, which will later be baked into delicious bread and the smell of which will fill the streets surrounding the village's only bakery. At the same time, the sun and golden color of the field recalls the heat of the summer sun burning on one's skin, an overwhelming sense of thirst... It is this chain reaction of imagination that one also tries to trigger within the context of future explorations, for example when analyzing future scenarios. One aims to bring those involved to a point where they will wear the worlds being described as their second skin, even if just for a moment, enabling them to explore the worlds' meaning on the basis of both the rational and emotional reflections evoked by such an experience.

Foresight as a Process

Depending on the phase of the process in which futures are explored, people's imagination can be stimulated in numerous ways using images, objects and stories, nurturing a more profound assessment of the futures at hand.
For example when:

- *Mapping out and analyzing possible future developments*: to inspire by means of images that are representative of these developments, for example, an inspiration card about nanotechnology featuring images of "nanobots" from a science fiction movie.

- *Combining developments into scenarios*: using a storyboard of scenes depicting various developments coming together, for example, a sequence of images in which an energetic 80-year old's walking stick lights up as he walks past a bookshop where the newest book of his favorite novelist has just been put on the shelf.
- *Presenting scenarios to stakeholders*: using a fictional news bulletin from a day in the future, for example, a short video featuring five news items from the public television broadcast in AD 2047.
- *Analyzing scenarios in terms of challenges*: a roleplay in which one team embodies inhabitants of a certain future and another team a group of visitors inquiring about how things work in this new world that they are visiting. Using props and visuals, sensorial experiences may be simulated and narratives recounted.
- *Presenting a future as an envisioned goal*: a video or film depicting a day in the life of a few typical inhabitants of the future world. For example: a film about a day in the life of Mary, a 13-year-old "youngpreneur" from Amsterdam reporting progress to her "kickstarters."
- *Creating concepts for new products or services inspired by a certain image of the future*: make objects as prototypes of products or the physical elements – i.e., touch-points – supporting a service, for example, an information kiosk integrated into a tree providing locals with access to the supply and demands of skills in the local community, or a scale model of a street in LEGO to play out and capture the way in which an electric car-sharing system in the city could work, using stop-motion animation.
- *Test-tunneling strategic concepts through scenarios*: depicting the life of typical users by means of image-based stories, for example, of Jan, a 32-year-old real-estate agent who would experience a different day with different challenges in a world of sustainable living, compared to a day in this high-tech world in which smart houses would constantly adapt to the needs of their comfort-seeking inhabitants.

These are but a handful of examples of ways in which the future can be rendered more tangible and hence provide people with a source of inspiration, stimulate debate and enable a more profound analysis of the meaning of the future(s) under consideration. Moreover, this diversity of modes of experience facilitates the cross-fertilization of ideas and reflections between those who think in terms of words and schemes, and those who find it easier to communicate through images, through tangible interaction or through other ways of "thinking out loud" about the future.

Focus and Choices

Depending on what it is that one wishes to achieve by rendering the future tangible, some approaches are more suitable than others. Examples of factors which may influence one's choice are:

- the *context* framing the foresight activity;
- the *goal* one wishes to achieve by immersing people in the future (e.g., inspiration, discussion and deeper understanding, persuasion);
- the *target group* for the creation and/or presentation of the tangible future;
- the specific *phase* in the foresight process (see above);
- the level of *ownership* one wishes to attain;
- the possible involvement of *experts* in shaping the experience of the future;
- the level of *detail* and *realism* of the form chosen to render the future tangible;
- the *time* and *costs* associated with the tangible futures (their creation and presentation).

Objective

When the aim is merely to inspire people to think through the potential consequences of certain future trends or developments, it generally suffices to employ *singular* (as opposed to *integral*) images of the future, which means using images that focus on one future development at a time, without integrating others that are likely to have an impact on the world at the same time. For instance, one could use so-called *inspiration cards* featuring an image or keywords as triggers for further mental associations, for example, an image of a mix of people working a vegetable garden in a big city labeled "community gardening" as a trigger to think through different modes of food production and/or social cohesion building. More metaphorical images are very suitable to inspire lateral thinking, whereas more concrete images steer the viewer in a specific direction. For example, an image of two queues of people at airport customs, one for EU and one for non-EU citizens, is likely to be interpreted as pointing toward the topics of "migration," whereas an image of grain swinging in the wind is an image that some people will associate with "flexibility," while others will think of "agriculture," "the food chain," "climate," etc.

If the aim is to push for a more *in-depth discussion* of the future as a changing context, more integral images are usually more suitable. Such images portray the future as a dynamic context that is shaped by a complex set of developments mutually influencing one another and hence shaping the world, societies and markets around us. *Collage*-like *image boards* are better suited to show the future in this multi-faceted form.

Also, more interactive activities, such as a guided walk alongside a series of future artefacts or advertising posters of fictitious products, enacted scenes, etc., can leave a strong mark in people's experience of a future. These approaches mix a recognizable present with the surprises of the future, in an attempt to engage people further and stimulate further debate.

It is worth keeping in mind, however, that any experience of the future is but a means in a process and not an aim in itself. It is in this sense that accompanying questions steer and nurture discussions. Questions such as "Imagine that...," "What if..." or "Today we see..., but what if tomorrow..." etc. invite people to translate the images that are being presented into their personal context or that of envisioned stakeholders. The questions steer their immersion and invite them to engage in further, critical assessment of the future world, to flesh it out for themselves and their peers, adding detail while maintaining the consistency of logic of the future world. Ultimately, the effect of the immersion extends beyond the world being rendered tangible through design, triggering new imaginaries, training and growing "imagination muscle." As such, design manifests itself as "a catalyst rather than a source of visions" (Dunne and Raby, 2013, p. 9).

However, if the aim is to convey the future to an audience one wants to invest in realizing the future being depicted, for example, in case of a vision, touching one's audience becomes an aim in itself. In such a setting, it is important for the story to contain enough recognizable detail from the point of view of the audience, for the story to be attractive – or perhaps intelligently seductive – and to anticipate expectable reactions. Because of these constraints, movies or highly visual print works are often used, because, media-wise, they have a low threshold of acceptance, can handle a decent amount of complexity and detail, and are easy to distribute. In any case, the aim is both to establish a link with the present as a starting context and to leave it behind, allowing the audience to cross the bridge from the present to the future in a comfortable way.

From a process point of view, it is better not to add too much (realistic) detail to the images being used, because that could raise expectations too high or evoke criticism, ranging from "unrealistic" to "unwanted," and shut the door to any alternative image of the future. Leaving sufficient gaps in a story, or providing so-called "hooks" for the target audience to hold on to, enabling them to see and describe a role for themselves in the future being portrayed, invites the audience to take part in creating (the image of) the future and enhances their motivation to participate.

Target Group: Explorers vs. Outsiders

After having embarked on a foresight study with a select group of people, one often encounters a moment later on in the process when it is necessary to involve a broader group of people in the analysis. Imagine having to involve the management of an organization or a group of stakeholders in assessing the possible impact and meaning of a particular contextual future scenario, without having involved them in the creation of the scenarios. All of a sudden, one has to convey a wealth of information embedded within the scenario – both explicitly and implicitly – in a short time span, to bring former outsiders up to date.

Fictional newspapers or television news bulletins are a simple yet effective way to create a joint impression of a future world by means of a broad range of distinct characteristics. The challenge lies in bringing the future developments and their possible consequences closer to the target audience so that they can understand, imagine and build empathy. A newspaper headline such as "40% of +65-year-olds scan and print own domestic appliances in neighborhood fablab" will trigger far deeper engagement than, for example, "3D printing gains momentum." The first headline contains more information than the second one and immediately establishes a link to people's lives, enabling them to empathize with the situation in a more straightforward way.

MAN&BIOTOPE

QUARTERLY HYBRID MAGAZINE | MARCH 2023

Transgenic
bred-to-order pigs
top Thanksgiving
sales rankings

PartnerSearch Inc. adopts
StreetScan's SkinResponse
relationship compatibility diagnostics
p37

Diagnostic Dogs
deploys next generation
disease sniffers
at University Hospitals across EU
p14

HealthSync Services
files for Chapter II:
2 million citizens worldwide risk dataloss
p57

Augmented Insects
"Vitamine Search Squad" drones
give AI a whole new meaning
p40

PLUS BACTERIOPHAGE HUNTERS BY JIM REYNOLDS

US $24.99 - CAN $24.99 EU €29.99
another KnowHowWhy® publication

© 2012 Pantopicon

Figure 17.1 Front page from a fictional magazine from the future.

One of the reasons for the success of fictional newspapers and television news bulletins is that their format of information delivery is well known, lowering the threshold for people to interpret the information. In a way, it comes pre-scripted. They address a moment in time by highlighting a variety of events, a patchwork of separate items each describing a different part/aspect of the world, and thus make it possible to convey various distinct events or loosely coupled elements of a future world, packaged as a whole.

Creation by Professionals vs. Co-creation with Lay People

To create a balanced image of the future that takes the relationships between developments and their consequences into account is a tough job, both in analytical and in synthetic, creative terms. Much like in the paintings by Breughel, integral images of future scenarios attempt to capture a world of various narratives in one overall picture. In general, foresight activities aim to explore multiple futures rather than one plausible future. Hence, it is not only the internal consistency within a future world that is important, but also the contrasts between different scenarios, a challenge which translates into the ways in which we try to picture them as well. Believability, consistency and strong storytelling are only a few of the reasons to involve people with expertise and experience in scenario-building and visualization/storytelling when embarking on such a mission.

The *co-creation* of images and stories of the future also has its benefits. In the case of participatory foresight, people from various angles of an organization, as well as external stakeholders, are often brought together in the belief that their different perspectives, which allow them to spot different challenges or changes as well as their potential roles in bringing about positive futures, will enrich the discourse regarding the future.

One could even assert that, with respect to many more complex, imminent future challenges, a participatory approach is not mere fun or fancy, but sheer necessity.

> "Popular engagement in the future is particularly crucial now when so many of the important challenges facing the human species can be influenced – perhaps only solved – by the cooperation and involvement of everyone, not limited to people and organizations that have traditionally held power."
>
> (Tester, 2007)

A sociologist, for example, will paint a different image of a future with weakened social cohesion than an IT-entrepreneur. By involving both in rendering the future tangible, one creates an empathy tool with which to assess the future from each other's perspective and hence enrich each other's understanding of the future, the image of the future itself as well as the discussions it may trigger when presented to a broader audience. Moreover, co-creative imagination exercises make it possible to alternate between receptive-reflective (lean-backward) and more active-creative (lean-forward) moments.

Mood boards or clipping collages are excellent ways to enable lay people to express and discuss their views of the future. Participants are asked to browse for images reflecting their feelings and interpretations of the future world at hand. These can involve specific situations, but also colors, products or spatial configurations that evoke a certain feeling or give shape to (the consequences of) a development. In similar ways, participants can be instructed to fill a future newspaper or magazine. Questions such as "What would *The Times*' front page headlines be, if you were to wake up in this scenario on the morning of January 13th, 2045?" "What about the front page of your academic journal?" can help to kickstart people's imagination.

Figure 17.2 Pair of images used to show the present–future contrast through image manipulation.

Figure 17.3 Neighborhood smart-grid energy system drawn across photograph of existing
situation.

Most inexperienced participants find it hard to start from a blank sheet. To
avoid this, they can also be invited to draw over existing photographs of today's
situations and highlight what is likely to change in the future and how. This
"before-and-after" game emphasizes the contrast between present and future,
nudging people to step (sufficiently far) away from the present as to fuel the
debate.

Last but not least, more interactive forms of rendering the future tangible by
"playing it out" – such as "live action role plays" and all kinds of so-called
"serious games" – offer a wide range of possibilities for large groups of people to
explore and experience the future. There, combined and individual goals stimulate immersion and deep engagement. One is no longer looking "at" a future, but
involved "in" it, taking on a co-creative role in exploring and understanding the
future world through shaping it. This is especially valuable when audiences need
to find their (personal) possible roles in the future or assess responses to future
events and different (inter)action logics.

Levels of Detail: Hi-fi vs. Lo-fi

Although the future is essentially about that which does not yet exist, it often
pays to pretend that it is already here, because that allows people to engage with

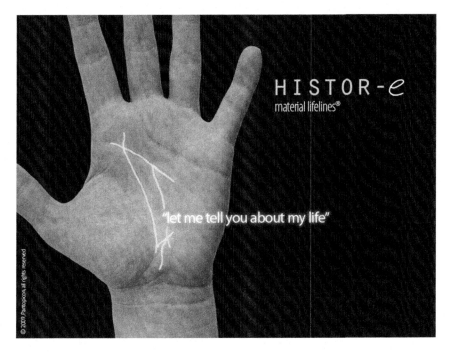

Figure 17.4 Fictional advertisement for a product/service enabling one to question construction materials about their histories, their lifecycle so far.

the future through their senses and physical interactions. This helps elicit valuable information that can inspire anticipatory action. One way to pretend the future already exists is to package it in a format we know how to read today, such as an advertisement for a product or service. Everyone is familiar with advertising campaigns and the codes it uses to communicate with us. Injecting the future into the present by means of a known content vehicle helps people accept things they would otherwise consider impossible. The key experiential value lies less in the representation as such, but more in the interaction and questions it evokes. Trigger questions could be "What do you think this is about?" "Which audience is targeted here and why?" "Which needs does it try to fulfill? Where do they stem from?" "What else could you imagine this world to be about?" "Which developments have led to this product or service?" "Which developments could prevent it from happening?" etc.

Since it tries to attain a certain level of realism and because of its dependency on detail, image manipulation can be considered a *hi-fi*-prototyping approach. A possible drawback, however, is that these prototypes can sometimes become dominant to the point where they tend to narrow down the issue to the illustrated example, preventing target groups from imagining alternatives. As a result, increasing the level of detail can sometimes actually narrow down or reduce the depth of the discussion, when one would actually like to broaden it.

Figure 17.5 Example of a sketch-based scenario-visualization.

So-called lo-fi techniques do not emphasize physical realism, but provide just enough "sketchy" detail to convey the idea and engage people in the intended interaction. They maintain a more open character and provide less of a "finished" or "take-it-or-leave-it" look and feel. Thus, they invite people to construct with/on top of the basis they provide, to shape and reshape, to explore alternatives. An image that lacks detail leaves more room for diversity of interpretation and thus also stimulates discussion.

Although we generally associate the term "sketching" with drawing, it can also be applied to the creation of videos or so-called *future artefacts*, fictional objects or scenes in paper, cardboard, clay, wood and other materials that are easy to manipulate (cf. lo-fi prototyping).

This sketch-like approach is very suitable to be used in the context of a workshop, to allow participants to render explicit the way in which they personally see a future and enter into a dialogue with one another. Often, more than images, physical props invite to interact, to pick up, turn around, explore, show, enact, etc. As they can be placed in front of a group of people, they allow them to explore different interpretations and perspectives together. Sketching and physically creating props tend to leave a more profound imprint in the memory of participants as well, engraving both the created artefacts and the discussions that took place around them.

Figure 17.6 Still shot from lo-fi prototyping activity during a workshop.

Beyond Props

Future artefacts are to be viewed as tools, tangible gateways, modes of transportation that enable people to enter underlying future worlds. However powerful as such, as tools, they fit a broader context in which an *experience* is designed to engage people in exploring the future, and the engagement, in turn, serves a deeper purpose within the overall foresight process. Hence, there is a design challenge that goes beyond the props as such and extends all the way to the design of the context in which they are being used. From setting the stage for people to interact with the objects, to the way of introducing people to them, discussing them, roleplaying their context of use or presentation, etc. All of these factors shape the (quality of the) future experience, the level of engagement and the quality and type of the ensuing discussions and reflections regarding the future and its relation to the present.

This touches upon what one could call a "performative" or "relational" dimension of the design of future experiences. Key to this is the collaborative storytelling relationship that emerges between the designer as stage master of this experience and his/her audience.

For example, in the case of "selling an audience fictional products," the objects themselves do not describe their surrounding world as such, but they do offer cues regarding their place in that world, their use and users, their users' environment, their needs, values, logic, etc., thereby shifting the perspective of the audience to the bigger picture, is triggered by the alienating effect these items have, leading the audience to formulate questions and hypotheses regarding the relationships that shape and are shaped by the objects. One could say that they "function like extended philosophical thought experiments" (Caccavale and Shakespeare, 2014, p. 25).

Through this questioning and experimentation, the alternate reality takes shape in the mind of the beholder, as well as inspiring new details – perhaps even unthought of – in the mind of the designer, who is forced to provide answers and add detail to the future world as the conversation develops. "Why would people use this?" "Why have it as a separate tool and not as an app on a smartphone?" "Where has it been produced?" "Who uses it?" "How did the inventor come up with it?" "Could we also use it as/to...?" etc. While filling in the gaps, a key task of the designer – in this case roleplaying the part of a salesperson – is to safeguard the consistency of the logic of the underlying future world. One can say that the detailing follows from a confrontation between perspectives evolving into an act of co-creation. Thus, the experiencer becomes co-creator of the future alongside the designer of the future experience.

In dealing with the questions and hypotheses of the audience, the designer, or any mediator, is required to take on a role befitting the context in which the future is blended with the present.

Thus, the role of the person shaping the future experience extends beyond the creation of the medium that evokes the future under consideration, entering an interactive dimension that requires him/her to be part of the experience, part of the embodiment of the future. For example, if the fictional products are presented in a shop-setting, by taking on the role of a salesperson, the designer/person presenting the objects enhances the totality of experience. This helps frame and simultaneously deepen the engagement of the audience in exploring the future world behind the props, leading to more profound dialogues, richer future experiences in general and more profound assessments in particular.

A key moment in the dialogue between designer and experiencer is the revelation or realization of the fictional nature of the tangible futures. If successfully managed, this breakdown of the suspension of disbelief, creates a situation in which the experiencer realizes he/she finds him/herself standing with both feet in a future. He/she believed it to have been (part of) a present somewhere, yet realizes that in the co-creation of the future experience, he/she actually crossed a co-constructed bridge connecting present and future. This triggers an active reflection as to what it was that separated present and future in the first place. *Why are these products and services not part of the present reality? What is lacking in the current context for them to exist?*

It is this way of relating future and present, examining the similarities and differences, the gaps in-between and pathways that may lead from one to the other, that are central to anticipatory reasoning in many foresight processes.

In Practice

The methods and tools discussed have been described as methods and tools that are used within the context of a future exploration, a foresight process. Because

Figure 17.7 Booth of fictional startup company Pedras & Sons showcasing its services during the Biennale Interieur Kortrijk 2014 trade fair.

of their attractive form factor, however, project managers sometimes find it hard to resist utilizing these visual and tangible futures beyond their intended context, as process tools. One ought to be careful when doing this, since it is easy for these images to start leading a – decontextualized – life of their own, possibly evoking unexpected negative reactions – for example, when people misinterpret tools for thought as visions or plans. Contrary to cases in which one explicitly wants futures and future-related dialogue to go viral, run-away process tools, risk disrupting the broader process within which the foresight activity takes place.

Furthermore, when seeing the images and artefacts as tools for thought, it is worth keeping them at hand and in sight. Decorating the walls of a workshop-space for example with the futures under exploration helps to immerse and remain immersed in the future context, preventing people from gravitating back toward the present and its familiar logic. Whether merely keeping creative output in sight or creating full-fledged future rooms (a.k.a. scenario rooms) as curiosity cabinets of a scenario, both ends of the spectrum allow people to be physically embedded within a distinct logic, allowing them to physically point toward and grasp images that can help explain their position or perspective regarding the future at hand.

People at the Center

Whichever technique one chooses, it is generally only when one succeeds in translating the possible impact a future might have on a person's everyday life and his/her daily environment, that a true connection can be said to have been made.

Figure 17.8 Two simple storyboards depicting medical concepts inspired by a future scenario.

Questions such as "What does X think, feel, do in this world? What drives her?" "How do developments such as … and … have an impact on her actions?" help examine and detail the image of the future further in an empathic way.

Techniques such as the creation of *personas* make it possible to create archetypes of people through whose perspective we could explore and discover the future world from a different angle. How would, for example, a driven, 23-year-old student-entrepreneur from Antwerp experience a sustainable, community-driven, locally oriented future compared to an 85-year-old lady living in the Tuscan countryside?

Personas are an excellent tool, for instance, to outline a day in the life of someone in the future in a so-called storyboard. Asking "What happened before that? … after that? … in between these two steps?" helps to gradually add more detail to the story.

Finally

Images, objects, physical settings and stories that shed light on the future, as condensed in (fleshed-out sub-scenes of) a scenario can be used to inspire and engage people, to stimulate debate, to add depth to discussions regarding the future and communicate about the future in broader and more efficient ways. A clear distinction needs to be made between futures that are rendered tangible for their own sake on the one hand, and those that serve as a means in a process on the other. In both cases, the tangible elements themselves, as well as the broader experience in which they are brought together in terms of their content, form and process require attention.

In addition to rendering possible futures and their meanings tangible for their inhabitants, the "carriers of meaning" being created can also be used to explore causal relationships, actions and reactions, which means that *seeing* and *acting* are deeply intertwined.

The creative techniques that can be used by professionals and non-professionals alike, within the setting of a workshop or beyond, grow in number and diversity by the day. Each approach uses different means and requires different skills from the participants and facilitators involved.

Experience shows that rendering the future tangible makes it possible to attract a greater number and broader range of people, to explore the future together, the diversity of their know-how and perspectives enriching the discussion, their interaction helping to pave the way for (joint) anticipatory action. By increasing the experience factor and enhancing empathy with the future, people's engagement regarding the topics being discussed also increases. A diverse set of images of what the world may look like decades from now always provides an enriching basis for discussion. As such, these images are never final, but always triggers for new beginnings.

Last but not least, it is worth noting that activities and insights related to rendering the future tangible and deriving value from engagement and empathy still form a relatively young branch within the foresight practice and community. They are very much under development. Through experiments and experiences, knowledge and insight continue to grow, offering interesting avenues for further research and creative experiments.

References

Baerten, N. (2007). Experiencing futures. In: *Proceedings of the COST A22 Conference "From oracles to dialogue: exploring new ways to explore the future."* Athens.

Caccavale, E. and T. Shakespeare (2014). Thinking differently about life: design, biomedicine and "negative capability." In S Yelavich and B. Adams (eds.), *Design as futuremaking*. New York: Bloomsbury.

Candy, S. (2010). *The futures of everyday life: politics and the design of experiential scenarios*. Doctoral dissertation, Department of Political Science, University of Hawaii at Manoa.

Dunne, A. and F. Raby (2013). *Speculative everything: design, fiction and social dreaming*. Cambridge, MA: MIT Press.

Tester, J. (2007). *The case for human–future interaction*. Retrieved from http://future.iftf.org/2007/02/the_case_for_hu.html, Institute for the Future, Palo Alto, CA.

Wired Magazine, *Found*. Retrieved from www.wired.com/wired/issue/found.

Index

Page numbers in *italics* denote tables, those in **bold** denote figures.

CPSIA information can be obtained
at www.ICGtesting.com
Printed in the USA
LVOW13s1559120917

548430LV00012B/1224/P